Tudor England

CONFERENCE ON BRITISH STUDIES
BIBLIOGRAPHICAL HANDBOOKS

Editor: J. JEAN HECHT
Consultant Editor: G. R. ELTON

Tudor England
1485-1603

MORTIMER LEVINE

WEST VIRGINIA UNIVERSITY

CAMBRIDGE

for the Conference on British Studies

AT THE UNIVERSITY PRESS

1968

Published by the Syndics of the Cambridge University Press
Bentley House, P.O. Box 92, 200 Euston Road, London, N.W.1
American Branch: 32 East 57th Street, New York, N.Y.10022

Library of Congress Catalogue Card Number: 68–12060

Standard Book Number: 521 05543 1

Printed in Great Britain
at the University Printing House, Cambridge
(Brooke Crutchley, University Printer)

To the memory of

RACHEL SCHILLER

entirely beloved grandmother

CONTENTS

CONTENTS

PREFACE

Although this handbook is not intended to be comprehensive, its coverage is fairly extensive; both printed sources and secondary studies have been included. Designed to provide a handy guide to works relating to the Tudor period, it should meet the needs of most readers and researchers concerned with that epoch. No attempt has been made to list the various editions of any of the titles included. As a rule, the best edition has been cited, except when it is not readily available or when a satisfactory English translation can be substituted for an edition in a foreign language.

The principal criterion employed in the selection of entries has been potential utility to mature scholars and advanced students. An attempt has been made to include some items concerning every major aspect of life in Tudor times; only literature *per se* has been omitted. When no more than a small sample of works pertaining to a particular aspect could be cited, the existence elsewhere of fuller lists has been noted. Popular and semi-popular works have been omitted, except when the subject is not treated in a scholarly study or when it seems necessary to alert the reader to the true nature of the work.

As a rule, the inclusion of a work may be taken to indicate that it possesses some value. Only those works have been annotated, however, that seem to demand comment, whether positive, negative, or explanatory, and those whose titles are insufficiently revelatory of their contents. Some of the annotations are patently controversial; others are inevitably debatable. All of them are the personal evaluations of the compiler, which in some instances coincide with the opinions of the majority of scholars, in others represent a minority point of view, and in still others may express a solitary opinion.

This handbook is divided into fourteen sections; the last eleven are subdivided into five categories. Neither this nor any alternative division can be perfect. The number of sections has had to be limited to avoid an indefinite multiplication. Therefore, it has been necessary to place some subjects in sections the titles of which do not precisely describe them; for example, law is included in Constitutional and Administrative History, and education and political thought may be found under Intellectual History. Moreover, the lines between sections are not always clear; many works could have been placed in two or more sections. Such repetition, however, would have required either leaving out other items or exceeding a reasonable number of entries. Instead, works have been placed in single sections on the basis of an impression, often by a narrow margin, of where their main value lies. Sometimes the reader is aided in this matter through cross-references. Even the lines between categories within sections are not always distinct, especially those between monographs and biographies where, for the sake of consistency, books have been called biographies whenever possible. In short, the reader cannot always expect to find all the works he is seeking neatly placed in particular sections and categories; occasionally some searching in related sections and categories will be requisite.

If a bibliography is ever to reach a press, the compiler must at some time arbitrarily call a halt. The search for entries for this handbook was terminated on 1 September 1966. Only works of special value that became available after that date have been added. They are identifiable by an *a* after the number.

It remains to make a few personal acknowledgements. I am grateful for the important help in the form of reduced teaching loads and a research grant that I owe to four colleagues at West Virginia University: Drs William T. Doherty, Carl M. Frasure, John F. Golay, and Robert F. Munn. My debt to my late mentor, Dr Conyers Read, should be obvious. His nearly comprehensive bibliography provided a useful starting-point for my search. If some of my annotations are at variance with his, this, I think, can largely be explained in terms of the progress of Tudor studies over the last decade. I am much indebted to the General Editor, Dr J. Jean Hecht. The correspondence between us relating to this pioneer volume of a series has been prodigious. His spot-checking of my entries has saved me from many a fault. My debts to the Consultant Editor, Dr Geoffrey R. Elton, go far beyond invaluable exchanges of letters with this very busy man whose knowledge of the materials of Tudor England is second to none. Debts aside, I assume full responsibility for the contents of this handbook.

MORTIMER LEVINE

Morgantown, West Virginia
January 1967

ABBREVIATIONS

AgHR	*Agricultural History Review*
AHR	*American Historical Review*
AJLH	*American Journal of Legal History*
Arch.	*Archaeologia*
BIHR	*Bulletin of the Institute of Historical Research*
BJRL	*Bulletin of the John Rylands Library*
Camb. Hist. J.	*Cambridge Historical Journal*
CMH	*The Cambridge Modern History*, ed. Lord Acton *et al.*, Cambridge, 1902–26
CQR	*Church Quarterly Review*
Ec. & Soc. Hist.	*Essays in the Economic and Social History of Tudor and Stuart England in honour of R. H. Tawney*, ed. F. J. Fisher, Cambridge, 1961
EcHR	*Economic History Review*
E.E.T.S.	Early English Text Society
EcJ	*Economic Journal*
EHR	*English Historical Review*
Govt. & Soc.	*Elizabethan Government and Society: essays presented to Sir John Neale*, ed. Stanley T. Bindoff, Joel Hurstfield, and Charles H. Williams, 1961
Hist. J.	*Historical Journal*
HLQ	*Huntington Library Quarterly*
Hug. Soc. Proc.	*Proceedings of the Huguenot Society of London*
JBS	*Journal of British Studies*
JEH	*Journal of Ecclesiastical History*
JHI	*Journal of the History of Ideas*
JMH	*Journal of Modern History*
LQR	*Law Quarterly Review*
NCMH	*The New Cambridge Modern History*, ed. George N. Clark *et al.*, Cambridge, 1957–
NQ	*Notes and Queries*
PBA	*Proceedings of the British Academy*
PMLA	*Publications of the Modern Language Association*
PP	*Past and Present*
QJEc	*Quarterly Journal of Economics*
Reappraisals	*Reappraisals in History*, Jack H. Hexter, New York and Evanston, Ill., 1963
Rec. Hist.	*Recusant History*
Ren. to C.-Ref.	*From the Renaissance to the Counter-Reformation: essays in honor of Garrett Mattingly*, ed. Charles H. Carter, New York, 1965
Rev. hist.	*Revue historique*
Rev. d'hist. ecc.	*Revue d'histoire ecclésiastique*
SHR	*Scottish Historical Review*

Stud. Ch. Hist.	*Studies in Church History*, ed. Clifford W. Dugmore, Charles Duggan, and G. J. Cuming, 2 vols., 1964–5
TRHS	*Transactions of the Royal Historical Society*
Tud. Stud.	*Tudor Studies presented to A. F. Pollard*, ed. Robert W. Seton-Watson, 1924
Tud. Tr.	*Tudor Tracts*, ed. A. F. Pollard, 1903
Yorks. Arch. J.	*Yorkshire Archaeological Journal*

EXPLANATORY NOTES

1. When no place of publication is given for a book, its place of publication is London. Where a book appeared in two or more places at the same time, the place or places of publication come from the title page of the volume examined by the compiler.

2. For printed sources where there are no authors' names to be given, editors' names precede titles of works, except in the case of works published by official bodies of the United Kingdom where the opposite order is used.

3. In a few cases the first and middle names of authors and editors appear as initials plus the rest of such names in square brackets, for example, F[rederick] M[aurice] Powicke. This is done to avoid possible confusion where an author or editor's name appears differently on the title pages of different works or where American and British practices differ.

I BIBLIOGRAPHIES

1   *A bibliography of the history of Wales.* 2nd ed., Cardiff, 1962.
2   *Annual bibliography of the history of British art.* 1936–. Begins with publications of 1934.
3   *Annual bulletin of historical literature.* 1912–. Begins with publications of 1911.
4   Beale, Joseph H. (ed.). *A bibliography of early English law books.* Cambridge, Mass., 1962. The standard bibliography of Tudor law books.
5   Callender, Geoffrey A. R. (ed.). *Bibliography of naval history,* part I (Historical Association Leaflets, no. 58). 1924.
6   Carlson, Leland H. 'A Corpus of Elizabethan nonconformist writings', in *Stud. Ch. Hist.*, I, 297–311. A valuable discussion of the material in print.
7   Chaloner, William H. 'Bibliography of recent work on enclosure, the open fields, and related topics', *AgHR,* **2** (1954), 48–52.
8   Chrimes, Stanley B. and I. A. Roots (eds.). *English constitutional history: a select bibliography* (Helps for Students of History, no. 58). 1958.
9   Cockle, Maurice J. D. *A bibliography of English military books up to 1642 and of contemporary books,* ed. H. D. Cockle. 1900. Contains works on the art of war but ignores those on specific battles and campaigns.
10 Franz, Gunther (ed.) *Bücherkunde zur Weltgeschichte vom Untergang des römischen Weltreichs bis zur Gegenwart.* Munich, 1956.
11 Frewer, Louis B. (ed.). *Bibliography of historical writings published in Great Britain and the Empire, 1940–1945.* Oxford, 1947.
12 Gibson, R. W. and J. Max Patrick (eds.). *St Thomas More: a preliminary bibliography of his works and of Moreana to the year 1750.* New Haven, 1961. See also, esp. for later works, Frank and Majie P. Sullivan. *Moreana: materials for the study of Saint Thomas More,* Los Angeles, 1964–, and (52).
13 Gross, Charles (ed.). *A bibliography of British municipal history.* Cambridge, Mass., 1915. Excellent but needs to be brought up to date.
14 Hall, Hubert (ed.). *A select bibliography of the study, sources, and literature of English medieval economic history.* 1914. Of some use for the sixteenth century.
15 Howe, George F. *et al.* (eds.). *The American Historical Association's guide to historical literature.* New York, 1961. Understandably thin on Tudor England. The annotations are usually safe and innocuous.
16 *International bibliography of historical sciences.* Paris, 1926–. Vol. XXXI, published in 1965, covers publications of 1962.
17 Lancaster, Joan C. (ed.). *Bibliography of historical works issued in the United Kingdom. 1946–1956.* 1957.
18 *Local history handlist: a select bibliography and list of sources for the study of local history and antiquities* (Historical Association, special series, II). 1947.
19 Manwaring, George E. (ed.). *A bibliography of British naval history: a bibliographical and historical guide to printed and manuscript sources.* 1930. Printed sources include articles but not books.
20 Matthews, William (ed.). *British diaries: an annotated bibliography of British diaries between 1442 and 1942.* Berkeley, 1950.
21 Maxwell, W. Howard and Leslie P. (eds.). *A legal bibliography of the British commonwealth of nations,* I, *English law to 1800.* 2nd ed., 1955.
22 Milne, A. Taylor (ed.). *Writings on British history. 1937–60,* 8 vols. Covers books and articles published from 1934 to 1945. 6 vols. covering 1901–33 are in preparation. Accurate and close to comprehensive but not annotated.
23 Pollen, John H. (ed.). *Sources for the history of Roman Catholics in England, Ireland, and Scotland from the Reformation period to that of emancipation, 1533 to 1795* (Helps for Students of History, no. 39). 1921.
24 Read, Conyers (ed.). *Bibliography of British history: Tudor period, 1485–1603.* 2nd ed., Oxford, 1959. This most ambitious of Tudor bibliographies is nearly comprehensive to 1 January 1957 and esp. full for printed sources. The longer annotations for many of the major printed sources are quite

informative and useful; the one-word annotations, particularly for secondary works, are hardly helpful.

25 Smith, Lacey B. 'The "taste for Tudors" since 1940', in Elizabeth C. Furber (ed.). *Changing views on British history: essays on historical writing since 1939*. Cambridge, Mass., 1966, pp. 101–18. Discusses writings on Tudor England to Elizabeth's accession. For Elizabeth's reign see (29). Smith's comments are often interesting but sometimes debatable.

26 Tawney, Richard H. 'Studies in bibliography, II, Modern capitalism', *EcHR*, 4 (Oct. 1933), 336–56. Strong on the sixteenth century.

27 Thirsk, Joan. 'The contents and sources of English agrarian history after 1500', *AgHR*, 3 (pt. 2, 1955), 66–78. A fine bibliographical article indicating the progress, problems, and prospects of studies in agrarian history.

28 Walcott, Robert. *The Tudor-Stuart period of English history (1485–1714): a review of changing interpretations* (Service Center for Teachers of History, no. 58). New York, 1964. This model study of its type offers judicious appraisals of recent and some older works.

29 Zagorin, Perez. 'English history, 1558–1640: a bibliographical survey', in Elizabeth C. Furber (ed.). *Changing views on British history: essays on historical writing since 1939*. Cambridge, Mass., 1966, pp. 119–40. Continues (25). Zagorin's comments are generally sound.

II CATALOGUES, GUIDES, AND HANDBOOKS

30 *A catalogue of the manuscripts preserved in the library of the university of Cambridge*. Cambridge, 1861–7, 5 vols. The Cambridge and Bodleian Libraries contain the best manuscript collections for Tudor history outside London.

31 Adair, Edward R. (ed.). *The sources for the history of the council in the sixteenth and seventeenth centuries* (Helps for Students of History, no. 51). 1924. A guide to manuscript and printed material. For an expert discussion of much of this material see (295).

32 Allison, Antony F. and David M. Rogers (eds.). 'A catalogue of Catholic books in English, printed abroad or secretly in England, 1558–1640', *Bibliographical studies*, 3 (Jan.–Apr. 1956), 1–187.

33 Bodleian Library. *Catalogi codicum manuscriptorum*. Oxford, 1845–. Most useful for the Tudor period are the Ashmolean, Rawlinson, and Tanner collections.

34 British Museum. *General catalogue of printed books*. 1965, 261 vols. This photolithographic ed. goes to 1955.

35 —— *The catalogues of the manuscript collections*, 1962. Lists the major collections and their catalogues. The British Museum is second only to the Public Record Office in its manuscript holdings relevant to the Tudor period.

36 Cheney, Christopher R. (ed.). *Handbook of dates for students of English history* (Royal Historical Society guides and handbooks, no. 4). 1948. Basic for such matters as regnal years, saints' days and festivals, and legal chronology.

37 Clark, G. Kitson and Geoffrey R. Elton (eds.). *Guide to the research facilities in history in the universities of Great Britain and Ireland*. 2nd ed., Cambridge, 1965. Indicates the research possibilities of each university.

38 Davenport, Frances G. (ed.). 'Materials for English diplomatic history, 1509–1783', in Historical Manuscripts Commission, *18th Report*, 1917, pp. 357–402. A summary of materials in the British Museum and private collections.

38a Dawson, Giles E. and Laetitia Kennedy-Skipton. *Elizabethan handwriting, 1500–1650: a manual*. New York, 1966. A practical handbook for the secretary hand. More useful than Jenkinson (51) on this.

39 Fisher, Herbert A. L. 'Manuscripts in the Bodleian and college libraries in Oxford bearing on English history from 1485 to 1547', *BIHR*, **1** (1923), 45–8. A companion article to (63), but rather inadequate.

40 Fordham, Herbert G. (ed.). *The road-books and itineraries of Great Britain, 1570–1850*. Cambridge, 1924. A catalogue of particular use for social history.

41 Fowler, Robert C. (ed.). *Episcopal registers of England and Wales* (Helps for Students of History, no. 1). 1918. A brief guide to episcopal records.

42 Gilson, Julius P. (ed.). *A student's guide to the manuscripts of the British Museum* (Helps for Students of History, no. 31). 1920.

43 Giuseppi, Montague S. (ed.). *A guide to the manuscripts preserved in the Public Record Office*. 1923–4, 2 vols. Still worth consulting despite its replacement by (45).

44 Gough, Henry (ed.). *A general index to the publications of the Parker Society* (Parker Society, LV). Cambridge, 1855. A handy key to a principal source of religious history.

45 *Guide to the contents of the Public Record Office*. 1963, 2 vols. The starting-point for research at the Public Record Office. Vol. I gives short descriptions of the legal records there; vol. II does the same for state papers and departmental records.

46 *Guide to the historical publications of the societies of England and Wales* (*BIHR*, supplements I–XIII). 1929–46.

47 Hall, Hubert (ed.). *A repertory of British archives*, pt. I. 1920. Indicates where public records may be found.

48 Hall, Hubert (ed.). *List and index of the publications of the Royal Historical Society, 1871–1924, and of the Camden Society, 1840–1897*. 1925. For a full and up-to-date list see *TRHS*.

49 Historical Manuscripts Commission. *Record repositories in Great Britain*. 1964. A very complete pamphlet, arranged by places and regions.

50 Jayne, Sears (ed.). *Library catalogues of the English Renaissance*. Berkeley, 1956. Inventories of institutional and private libraries.

51 Jenkinson, Hilary. *The later court hands in England: from the fifteenth to the seventeenth century*. Cambridge, 1927. The best introduction to sixteenth-century handwriting.

52 Marc'hadour, Germain. *L'Univers de Thomas More*, Paris, 1963. A valuable guide to chronology and sources relating to More.

53 Mullins, Edward L. C. (ed.). *Texts and calendars: an analytical guide to serial publications* (Royal Historical Society guides and handbooks, no. 7). 1958. An excellent guide to most of the important series. The annotations give a good idea of the contents of vols. but do not attempt to appraise their value.

54 Munby, Alan N. L. *Cambridge college libraries: aids for research students*. 2nd ed., Cambridge, 1962. A helpful introduction to the Cambridge college libraries and their collections.

55 Pollard, Alfred W., Gilbert R. Redgrave *et al.* (eds.). *A short-title catalogue of books printed in England, Scotland, and Ireland, and of English books printed abroad, 1475–1640*. 1926. Indispensable for books and their locations. For checklists and supplements see Read (24), p. 4. A new ed. is under way.

56 Powicke, F[rederick] M[aurice] and E. B. Fryde (eds.). *Handbook of British chronology* (Royal Historical Society guides and handbooks, no. 2). 2nd ed. 1961. Handy lists of rulers, officers of state, bishops, higher nobility, parliaments, and English church councils.

57 *Public Record Office: lists and indexes*, 1892–1936, 55 vols; *Supplementary Series*, 1961–. Detailed lists and indexes of source materials in the Public Record Office.

58 Purvis, John S. *An introduction to ecclesiastical records*. 1953. A useful introduction to research in ecclesiastical administration.

59 *Reports and calendars issued by the Royal Commission on Historical Manuscripts*, 1847–. The great guide to manuscript material in private collections. The material is listed, abstracted, calendared, or transcribed. For the collections containing material on Tudor England see Read (24), pp. 11–18.

See also Mullins (53), pp. 61–90, which is very detailed on the contents of the reports and calendars.

60 *Reports of the Deputy keeper of the public records*. 1840–88. Lists, indexes, calendars, and inventories of materials in the Public Record Office.

61 *Reports of the Royal Commission on Public Records*. 3 vols., in *Parliamentary Papers*, 1912–13, 1914 and 1919. Reports on national and local records.

62 Roberts, Richard A. *The reports of the Historical Manuscripts Commission* (Helps for Students of History, no. 22). 1922. An introduction to the Commission's work and the principal collections.

63 Routledge, Frederick J. 'Manuscripts at Oxford relating to the later Tudors (1547–1603)', *TRHS*, 3rd ser., 8 (1914), 119–59. More satisfactory than (39).

64 Somerville, Robert (ed.). *Handlist of record publications* (British Record Association, pamphlet no. 3). 1951.

65 *The bulletins of the National Register of Archives*. 1948–. Particularly informative about local collections.

66 *The subject index to periodicals*. 1915–. The best guide to periodicals containing articles on English history.

67 Thomson, Theodore R. (ed.). *A catalogue of British family histories*, 1935.

68 Winfield, Percy H. *The chief sources of English legal history*. Cambridge, Mass., 1925. The best introduction to the subject.

III GENERAL SURVEYS

69 Bindoff, Stanley T. *Tudor England*. Harmondsworth, 1950. This minor classic is the best brief survey. It is esp. good on economic matters.

70 Black, John B. *The reign of Elizabeth, 1558–1603*. 2nd ed., Oxford, 1959. This and (81) are the Tudor vols. in *The Oxford history of England*. Black's is pedestrian but has a good bibliography.

71 Brett, S. Read. *The Tudor century, 1485–1603*. 1962.

72 Cahen, Léon and Maurice Braure. *L'Evolution politique de l'Angleterre moderne, 1485–1660*. Paris, 1960. Narrative weak and out of date.

73 Churchill, Winston S. *A history of the English-speaking peoples*, II, *The New World*. New York, 1956. Worth reading for the interesting views and magnificent prose of a very great amateur historian.

74 Elton, Geoffrey R. *England under the Tudors*. 1955; reprinted with a new bibliography, 1962. The best general survey. Stresses the importance of the work of Thomas Cromwell and the changes of the 1530s. Sees Elizabeth's reign as essentially a period of consolidation. The critical bibliography is a model.

75 Fisher, Herbert A. L. *The history of England from the accession of Henry VII to the death of Henry VIII, 1485–1547*. 1928. With (87) covers Tudor England in *The political history of England*. Though dated on many matters, they still constitute the best longer survey.

76 Froude, James A. *The history of England from the fall of Wolsey to the defeat of the Spanish Armada*. Revised ed. 1862–70, 12 vols. It is time to stop recommending this major classic of historical writing to beginners. It has too many inaccuracies, is strongly anti-Catholic, romanticizes and overestimates Henry VIII, and underestimates Elizabeth.

77 Harrison, David. *Tudor England*. 1953, 2 vols.

78 Innes, Arthur D. *England under the Tudors*. 1905. Replaced as vol. IV of *A history of England*, ed. Charles W. C. Oman, by (74).

79 Lingard, John. *A history of England from the first invasion by the Romans to the Revolution of 1688*, vols. IV–V. 1820–3. This dated Catholic account is still useful for documents.

80 Lockyer, Roger. *Tudor and Stuart Britain, 1471–1714*. 1964. An introductory survey that takes into account recent interpretations.

81 Mackie, John D. *The earlier Tudors, 1485–1558*. Oxford, 1952. Good for Henry VII, foreign affairs, and bibliography; otherwise ordinary.

82 Meissner, Paul. *England im Zeitalter von Humanismus, Renaissance und Reformation*. Heidelberg, 1952. Strong on the cultural side.

83 Morpurgo, Jack E. (ed.). *Life under the Tudors*. 1950. Introductory essays on various aspects of Tudor England by competent scholars.

84 Morris, Christopher. *The Tudors*. 1955. A series of interesting portraits, the outstanding one being that of Henry VII.

85 Myers, A. R. *England in the late middle ages*. Harmondsworth, 1952. Carries the medieval period to *c.* 1536. This is essentially in agreement with Elton's interpretation. See (74).

86 Pollard, Albert F. *Factors in modern history*. 1907. A collection of lectures, mainly on Tudor history, setting forth large interpretations which won nearly general acceptance for several decades. For a penetrating critique see Jack H. Hexter, 'Factors in modern history', in *Reappraisals*, pp. 26–44.

87 —— *The history of England from the accession of Edward VI to the death of Elizabeth, 1547–1603*. 1910. See (75).

88 Read, Conyers. *The Tudors: personalities and practical politics in sixteenth century England*. New York, 1936. Some of the views expressed in this small masterpiece are now out of date, but it is still well worth reading.

89 Traill, Henry D. and James S. Mann (eds.). *Social England*. Illustrated ed., vols. II–III, 1902. Articles by various authors cover all aspects of Tudor England. The selection of illustrations is excellent.

90 Williams, Charles H. *The making of Tudor despotism*. 1935.

91 Williamson, James A. *The Tudor age*. 1953. Good on maritime and naval history; otherwise average.

92 Woodward, George W. O. *Reformation and resurgence, 1485–1603*. 1963.

93 Wright, Louis B. and Virginia A. LaMar (eds.). *Life and letters in Tudor and Stuart England*. Ithaca, N.Y., 1962. Introductory essays on various aspects of Tudor and Stuart civilization. The essays vary in quality, but most of them contain useful bibliographies.

IV CONSTITUTIONAL AND ADMINISTRATIVE HISTORY

1 Printed sources

94 *A calendar of proceedings in chancery in the reign of Queen Elizabeth, to which are prefixed examples of earlier proceedings . . .* , ed. John Bayley. 1827–32, 3 vols.

95 *A collection of ordinances and regulations for the government of the royal household . . . .* Society of Antiquaries, 1790.

96 *Acts of the privy council of England*, ed. John R. Dasent. 1890–1907, 32 vols. Covers 1542–1604 with some gaps. See Read (24), p. 98.

97 Archbold, William A. J. (ed.). 'A manuscript treatise on the coinage by John Pryse, 1553', *EHR*, **12** (Oct. 1898), 709–10. Extracts.

98 Baldwin, Frances E. 'Proceedings in chancery under Wolsey', *BIHR*, **8** (June 1930), 17–20.

99 Bayne, Charles G. and William H. Dunham, Jr. (eds.). *Select cases in the council of Henry VII* (Selden Society, LXXV). 1958. Bayne's introduction, though not taking into account work since 1947, replaces that of Leadam (127). Bayne maintains that Henry VII's star chamber was mainly a civil rather than a criminal court.

100 Bradford, Gladys (ed.). *Proceedings in the court of star chamber in the reigns of Henry VII and Henry VIII* (Somerset Record Society, XXVII). 1911. Transcripts of Somerset cases at the Public Record Office.

101 Brooks, Frederick W. (ed.). *Supplementary Stiffkey papers* (Camden Miscellany, XVI, 3rd ser., LII). 1936. Supplements (147).

102 Cobbett, William, Thomas B. Howell *et al.* (eds.). *A complete collection of*

state trials and proceedings for high treason and other crimes and misdemeanors. 1816–98, 42 vols.

103 Coke, Edward. *The reports* . . . , ed. George Wilson. 1777, 7 vols. Coke, Dyer (107), and Plowden (136) are the best law reports for the Tudor period.

104 Davis, Elizabeth J. (ed.). 'Journal of the House of Lords for April and May, 1559', *EHR*, **28** (July 1913), 531–42.

105 D'Ewes, Simonds (ed.). *The journals of all the parliaments during the reign of Queen Elizabeth.* 1682. Still very valuable, but must now be supplemented by Neale (525).

106 Dugdale, William (ed.). *A perfect copy of all summons of the nobility to the great councils and parliaments of this realm from XLIX of King Henry III* . . . . 1685.

107 Dyer, James. *Reports of cases in the reigns of Hen. VIII, Edw. VI, Q. Mary, and Q. Elizabeth,* trans. and ed. John Vaillant. 1794, 3 vols.

108 Elton, Geoffrey R. (ed.). *The Tudor constitution: documents and commentary.* Cambridge, 1960. The selection and organization of documents are better than Tanner's (152). The introductions to the several sections add up to the fullest and most up-to-date survey of Tudor government.

109 Fishwick, Henry (ed.). *Pleadings and depositions in the duchy court of Lancaster* (Lancashire and Cheshire Record Society, XXXII, XXXV, XL). 1896–9. Covers Henry VII through Mary for an important court.

110 Fleetwood, William. *The office of a justice of the peace.* 1658. Written in 1565.

111 Gough, John W. (ed.). *Mendip mining laws and forest bounds* (Somerset Record Society, XLV). 1931.

112 Gross, Charles and Hubert Hall (eds.). *Select cases concerning the law merchant* (Selden Society, XXIII, XLVI, XLIX). 1908–32. Cases heard in the fair, staple, and tolsey courts and in the royal courts.

113 Hake, Edward. *Epiekeia, a dialogue on equity in three parts,* ed. David E. C. Yale. New Haven, 1953. An Elizabethan work on equity. On its significance see Prall (366), pp. 15–19.

114 Hawarde, John. *Les reportes del cases in camera stellata, 1593–1609,* ed. William P. Baildon. 1894.

115 Hearne, Thomas (ed.). *A collection of curious discourses written by eminent antiquaries upon several heads on our English antiquities.* 1775, 2 vols. Includes late Tudor treatises on law and related subjects.

116 Hemmant, Mary (ed.). *Select cases in the exchequer chamber,* II, *1461–1509* (Selden Society, LXIV). 1948.

117 Hughes, Charles (ed.). 'Nicholas Faunt's discourse touching the office of principal secretary of estate &c., 1592', *EHR*, **20** (July 1905), 499–508.

118 Hughes, Paul L. and James F. Larkin (eds.). *Tudor royal proclamations,* I, *The early Tudors (1485–1553).* New Haven, 1964. Gives full texts except for formulae. For an important discussion and critique of this work see Geoffrey R. Elton's review article in *Hist. J.,* **8** (no. 2, 1965), 266–71.

119 *Inventory and calendar of the contents of the Baga de secretis,* in *Reports of the deputy keeper of the public records,* **3,** 1842, app. II, no. 6; IV, 1843, app. II, no. 7. Unsatisfactory but accurate records of state trials.

120 Jack, Sybil and R. S. Schofield (eds.). 'Four early Tudor financial memoranda', *BIHR,* **36** (Nov. 1963), 189–206. Revealing for practices and abuses of financial administration.

121 *Journals of the House of Commons,* I. 1803. 1547–1628; this and (122) give some idea of what happened in each session but do not contain debates.

122 *Journals of the House of Lords,* I–II. 1846. 1510–1614.

123 Kingsford, Charles L. (ed.). 'Proceedings in the court of star chamber, Stonor v. Dormer and others, 1491', *EHR,* **35** (July 1920), 421–32.

124 Lambarde, William. *Archeion: or, a discourse upon the high courts of justice in England,* ed. Charles H. McIlwain and Paul L. Ward. Cambridge, Mass., 1957. A contemporary account of the secular court system in the late sixteenth century, particularly valuable for the star chamber.

125 —— *Eirenarcha, or the office of the justice of the peace,* 1602. The best sixteenth-century handbook for J.P.s.

126 Leadam, Isaac S. (ed.). *Select cases in the court of requests, 1497–1559* (Selden

Society, XII), 1898. The introduction contains the most satisfactory longer account of the history and procedure of this court. For a good short account see Elton (108), pp. 184–7.

127 —— Select cases before the king's council in star chamber (Selden Society, XVI, XXV). 1903–11. 1477–1544. See (99).

128 Marsden, Reginald G. (ed.). Select pleas in the court of admiralty (Selden Society, VI, XI). 1892–7. 1527–1602.

129 Maynard, John (ed.). Les reports des cases en les ans des roys Edward V, Richard III, Henri VII et Henri VIII touts qui par cydevant ont est publies. 1678–80, 11 parts. The best available collection of Year Books for the Tudor period. The last surviving Year Book is for 1536.

130 Mellows, William T. and Daphne H. Gifford (eds.). Peterborough local administration (Northampton Record Society, IX, X, XII, XIII, XVIII). Northampton, 1939–56. Documents relating to parochial administration, the last days of Peterborough monastery, the foundation of Peterborough Cathedral, and the dean and chapter as lords of the city. The best printed source collection for any Tudor city.

131 Merson, A. L. (ed.). The third book of remembrance of Southampton, 1514–1602 (Southampton Records Series, II, III, VIII). Southampton, 1951–65. Documents illuminating the growth of municipal government. A fourth vol. is still to come.

132 Milnes, Nora. 'Mint Records of Henry VIII', EHR, 32 (Apr. 1917), 270–3.

133 Monro, Cecil (ed.). Acta cancellaria, or selections from the records of the court of chancery (1558–1624). 1847.

134 Neale, John E. (ed.). 'The lord keeper's speech to the parliament of 1592–3', EHR, 31 (Jan. 1916), 128–37. A statement of Elizabeth's attitude on freedom of speech in parliament and its limitations by John Puckering.

135 Nef, John U. (ed.). 'Richard Carmarden's "A caveat for the quene" (1570)', Journal of Political Economy, 41 (Feb. 1933), 33–57. Deals with corruption in the collection of customs.

136 Plowden, Edmund. The commentaries, or reports . . . containing diverse cases . . . in the several reigns of King Edward VI, Queen Mary, King and Queen Philip and Mary, and Queen Elizabeth. 1792, 2 vols.

137 Pollard, Albert F. (ed.). 'An early parliamentary election petition', BIHR, 8 (Feb. 1931), 156–66.

138 Pollard, Albert F. and Marjorie Blatcher (eds.). 'Hayward Townshend's journals', BIHR, 12 (June 1934), 1–31.

139 Proceedings and ordinances of the privy council of England, 1368–1542, ed. N[icholas] H[arris] Nicolas. 1834–7, 7 vols. Vol. VII covers 1540–42; vol. VI ends in 1460. On the eighty years' gap see (295).

140 Prothero, George W. (ed.). Select statutes and other documents of the reigns of Elizabeth and James I. 4th ed., Oxford, 1913. The introduction is out of date.

141 Pugh, Thomas B. (ed.). The marcher lordships of South Wales, 1415–1536. Cardiff, 1963. An important collection of documents with useful introductions. The best thing we have for administration in the Marches of Wales during the period before that covered by (241).

142 Ramsay, George D. (ed.). Two sixteenth century taxation lists, 1545 and 1576 (Wiltshire Archaeological and Natural History Society, Records Branch, X). Devizes, 1954. Wiltshire tax lists which illustrate the development of the Tudor subsidy with an illuminating introduction.

143 Read, Conyers (ed.). William Lambarde and local government: his 'Ephemeris' and twenty-nine charges to juries and commissions. Ithaca, 1962. Lambarde's diary as a J.P. plus his charges illustrating the conduct of local government in late Elizabethan times.

144 Return of the name of every member of the lower house of the parliaments of England, Scotland, and Ireland . . . 1213–1874, in Parliamentary papers, 62, (1878), pts. I–III. Not complete but the fullest list available. On additions and corrections see Read (24), p. 89.

145 Robinson, Richard. A briefe collection of the queenes majesties most high and honourable courtes of recordes, ed. R. L. Rickard (Camden Miscellany, XX,

3rd ser., LXXXIII). 1953. A short late Elizabethan treatise on the royal courts.

146   *Rotuli parliamentorum ut et petitiones et placita in parliamento*. 1832, 6 vols. This work stops in 1504. Continued in vol. I of (122).

147   Saunders, Herbert W. (ed.). *The official papers of Sir Nathaniel Bacon of Stiffkey, Norfolk, as justice of the peace, 1580–1620* (Camden Society, 3rd ser., XXVI). 1915. Papers illustrating the working of local government. For additional Stiffkey papers see (101).

148   Smith, Thomas. *De republica anglorum*, ed. Leonard Alston. Cambridge, 1906. An authoritative contemporary account of English government. Also interesting as an example of contemporary political thought, though by no means profound.

149   Stanford, William. *An exposition of the king's prerogative*. 1567.

150   Steele, Robert (ed.). *Tudor and Stuart proclamations, 1485–1714*, vol. I. Oxford, 1910. Brief summaries. Now replaced for 1485–1553 by (118).

151   Steuart, A. Francis (ed.). *Trial of Mary queen of Scots*. 2nd ed., 1951.

152   Tanner, Joseph R. (ed.). *Tudor constitutional documents, A.D. 1485–1603, with an historical commentary*. Cambridge, 1940. The commentary reflects older views on Tudor government. Now replaced by Elton (108) except for a few documents.

153   *The border papers: calendar of letters and papers relating to the affairs of the borders of England and Scotland ... (1560–1603)*. Edinburgh, 1894–6, 2 vols. Consists mainly of the reports of the border wardens.

154   *The statutes of the realm*, ed. Alexander Luders *et al.* 1810–28, 11 vols. Vols. II–IV cover Tudor period; vols. X–XI provide useful indexes.

155   Thorne, Samuel E. (ed.). *A discourse upon the exposicion and understanding of statutes*. San Marino, 1942. Thorne's introduction contains the best discussion of statutes and their interpretation in the sixteenth century. On the authorship of the *Discourse* see (349).

156   —— *Prerogativa regis: tertia lectura Roberti Constable de Lyncolnis Inne anno 11 H. 7.* New Haven, 1949. Illustrative of the expansion of the royal prerogative under Henry VII. Thorne's introduction is an excellent study of the law of the prerogative.

157   Townshend, Hayward. *Historical collections, an exact account of the last four parliaments of Elizabeth*. 1680. 1598–1601. For an indication of the faults of this valuable private diary see Neale (525), II, 327, 404, 427, 436.

158   Willan, Thomas S. (ed.). *A Tudor book of rates*. Manchester, 1962. The 1582 issue of the book of rates with an analysis of Tudor economic policy by the editor.

159   Williams, W. Ogwen (ed.). *The calendar of Caernarvonshire quarter sessions records*, vol. I. Caernarvon, 1956. This first vol. of what promises to be an important series covers 1541–58.

2 Surveys

160   Hallam, Henry. *Constitutional history of England from the accession of Henry VII to the death of George II*, vol. I. 1846. Mainly interesting as a pioneer work.

161   Holdsworth, William S. *A history of English law*. 1922–52, 13 vols.; vol. I of 7th ed., revised by Stanley B. Chrimes, 1956. This very great work contains much on constitutional history as well as being the fullest legal history of England. Vols. IV–V deal with the sixteenth century; vol. I of the 7th ed. has the best survey of the various courts.

162   Keir, David L. *Constitutional history of modern Britain, 1485–1937*, 3rd ed. 1947. Has a good but somewhat dated survey of the Tudor period.

163   McIlwain, Charles H. *Constitutionalism ancient and modern*, revised ed., Ithaca, N.Y., 1947. Chapter 5, 'The transition from medieval to modern', deals mainly and brilliantly with Tudor England.

164   Maitland, Frederic W. *The constitutional history of England*. Cambridge, 1908. Still quite useful on the Tudor period.

165 Marcham, Frederick G. *A constitutional history of modern England, 1485 to the present.* New York, 1960. Generally sound though not brilliant on the Tudor period.

166 Plucknett, Theodore F. T. *A concise history of the common law.* 5th ed., 1956. The best short legal history.

167 Taswell-Langmead, Thomas P. *English constitutional history,* 11th ed. by Theodore F. T. Plucknett. Boston, 1960. This up-to-date version of an old standard is quite detailed and well documented for the Tudor period.

3 Monographs

168 Baldwin, James F. *The king's council in England during the middle ages.* Oxford, 1913. This great work on the medieval council contains a misleading epilogue which sees the early Tudor council as relatively unimportant and inactive. See Elton (295), pp. 269–70.

169 Beard, Charles A. *The office of justice of the peace in England.* New York, 1904. Useful only as an introduction.

170 Bell, Henry E. *An introduction to the history and records of the court of wards and liveries.* Cambridge, 1953. An excellent and thorough study of the organization of the court of wards that should be supplemented with (200).

171 —— *Maitland: a critical examination and assessment,* Cambridge, Mass., 1965. Chapter IX, 'The sixteenth century', gives a valuable appraisal of Maitland's views on Tudor constitutional, legal, and religious history in light of recent scholarship.

172 Bonner, George A. *The office of the king's remembrancer, showing the connexion with the old exchequer and the modern treasury.* 1931.

173 Brooke, George C. *English coins from the seventh century to the present.* 1955.

174 Brooks, Frederick W. *The council of the north* (Historical Association Pamphlets, general series, no. 25). 1953. A good short account. For a fuller study see (219).

175 —— *York and the council of the north* (St Anthony's Hall Publications, V). 1954.

176 Craig, John H. M. *The mint: a history of the London mint from A.D. 287 to 1948.* Cambridge, 1953.

177 Dawson, John P. *A history of lay judges.* Cambridge, Mass., 1960. The larger part of this work deals with English courts, royal and local, and is important for the Tudor period.

178 Dicey, Albert V. *The privy council.* 1887. Brief and out of date.

179 Dietz, Frederick C. *English government finance 1485–1558* (University of Illinois Studies in the Social Sciences, vol. IX, no. 3). Urbana, Ill., 1920. This, (180), (181), and (182) are the only detailed studies of government finance during the Tudor period. A reconsideration of Dietz's figures and their interpretation is needed.

180 —— *English public finance, 1558–1641.* New York, 1932.

181 —— *Finances of Edward VI and Mary* (Smith College Studies in History, III, no. 2). Northampton, Mass., 1918.

182 —— *The exchequer in Elizabeth's reign* (Smith College Studies in History, VIII, no. 2). Northampton, Mass., 1923.

183 Dowell, Stephen. *A history of taxation and taxes in England from the earliest times to the present day,* I. 1884. Still a standard work.

184 Dunham, William H., Jr. *Lord Hastings' indentured retainers, 1461–1483: the lawfulness of livery and retaining under the Yorkists and Tudors* (Transactions of the Connecticut Academy of Arts and Sciences, XXXIX). New Haven, 1955. Chapter V of this important study of 'bastard feudalism' shows Tudor policy towards retaining as one of connivance and control.

185 Eagleston, Arthur J. *The Channel Islands under Tudor government, 1485–1642.* Cambridge, 1949.

186 Elton, Geoffrey R. *The Tudor revolution in government.* Cambridge, 1953. Deals with Thomas Cromwell's administrative reforms, indicating that they mark a change from medieval to modern. Though still considered

controversial by some, this book has stood up well under fire. It is essential for financial administration, the main officials of the crown, the council, and the royal household.

187 Elton, Geoffrey R. *Star chamber stories*. 1958.

188 Evans, Florence M. G. *The principal secretary of state: a survey of the office from 1558 to 1680*. Manchester, 1923. See also (186) and (853) on the office of secretary.

189 Feavearyear, Albert E. *The pound sterling: a history of English money*. Oxford, 1931. Good on the coinage and its manipulation. Cf. (371).

190 Gladish, Dorothy M. *The Tudor privy council*. Retford, 1915. Of use for the Elizabethan council; otherwise best ignored.

191 Gras, Norman S. B. *The early English customs system* (Harvard Economic Studies, xviii). Cambridge, Mass., 1918. Deals mainly with the earlier period, but prints some sixteenth-century documents including the 'Book of rates'.

192 Gray, Charles M. *Copyhold, equity, and the common law* (Harvard Historical Monographs, no. 53). Cambridge, Mass., 1963. A sound study of the Tudor development of remedies for copyholders in equity and at common law.

193 Gray, Howard L. *The influence of the Commons on early legislation* (Harvard Historical Studies, xxiv). Cambridge, Mass., 1932. Mainly fifteenth century, but useful for procedure at the beginning of the Tudor period.

194 Hall, Hubert. *A history of the custom-revenue in England from the earliest times to the year 1827*. 1885, 2 vols.

195 Head, Ronald E. *The royal supremacy and the trial of bishops, 1558–1725*. 1962. Shows the crown's use of the royal supremacy in taking disciplinary action against bishops.

196 Henderson, Edith G. *Foundations of English administrative law*. 1963. Primarily a discussion of the origins and use of the writs of *mandamus* and *certiorari* by individuals against illegal government action. Mainly seventeenth century, but some reference to the sixteenth.

197 Hodgkin, Thomas. *The wardens of the northern marches*. 1908.

198 Hornemann, Karl. *Das Privy Council von England zur Zeit der Königin Elisabeth*. Hanover, 1912.

199 Hudson, William. *A treatise on the court of star chamber*, in Francis Hargrave (ed.). *Collectanea juridica*, vol. ii. 1792, 1–239. Apparently written late in James I's reign, this is the soundest early treatise on the court.

200 Hurstfield, Joel. *The queen's wards: wardship and marriage under Elizabeth I*. 1958. An important study of the effects of the administration of wardships by the court of wards on Elizabethan government and society.

201 Kay, Frederick G. *Royal mail: the story of the posts in England from the time of Edward IV to the present day*. 1951.

202 Lewis, Ada H. *A study of Elizabethan ship-money, 1558–1603*. Philadelphia, 1928.

203 McIlwain, Charles H. *The high court of parliament and its supremacy*. New Haven, 1910. Mainly medieval but of use for the Tudor period. The argument that parliament was a court and not a legislature is now questionable, certainly for Tudor parliaments.

204 Maitland, Frederic W. *English law and the Renaissance*. Cambridge, 1901. Maitland's thesis that Roman law nearly triumphed over the common law in sixteenth-century England is no longer tenable. See Holdsworth (161), iv, 253–85, Elton (2305), pp. 78–9, and Bell (171), pp. 131–6.

205 —— *Equity, also the forms of action at common law*. Cambridge, 1909.

206 —— *Justice and police*. 1885.

207 Maxwell-Lyte, Henry C. *Historical notes on the use of the great seal of England*. 1926.

208 Neale, John E. *The Elizabethan House of Commons*. 1949. Considers the House of Commons as an institution: its members, elections, and procedures. This and (525) constitute a peerless contribution to Elizabethan history and are leading to a significant reappraisal of early Stuart history.

209 Ogilvie, Charles. *The king's government and the common law, 1471–1641*.

Oxford, 1958. An account of the conflicts between the common lawyers and the king's government that is quite critical of the former. Somewhat dated on the political and constitutional side.

210 Oman, Charles W. C. *The coinage of England.* 1931.

211 Osborne, Bertram. *Justices of the peace, 1361–1848.* Shaftesbury, Dorset, 1960. Contains a useful introduction to Tudor J.P.s.

212 Percy, Eustace. *The privy council under the Tudors.* Oxford, 1907. Short and of little use.

213 Pickthorn, Kenneth. *Early Tudor government: Henry VII.* Cambridge, 1934. The only book devoted to the subject and a good one.

214 —— *Early Tudor government: Henry VIII.* Cambridge, 1934. Abandons the topical approach of (213) for a chronological approach. Less satisfactory but still useful, perhaps more so for political history than constitutional.

215 Pike, Luke O. *The constitutional history of the House of Lords.* 1894. This standard work is rather slight on the Tudor period.

216 Pollard, Albert F. *The evolution of parliament,* 2nd ed. 1926. This rather controversial work contains valuable information and interesting ideas on the Tudor period but must be read with some caution.

217 Putnam, Bertha H. *Early treatises on the practice of the justices of the peace in the fifteenth and sixteenth centuries* (Oxford Studies in Social and Legal History, VII). Oxford, 1924. A pioneer study revealing much about the procedure and powers of the justices. Supplemented in (370).

218 Price, William H. *The English patents of monopoly* (Harvard Economic Studies, I). Cambridge, Mass., 1906. This well-documented work covers 1558–1640.

219 Reid, Rachel R. *The king's council in the north.* 1921. Full and sound. See also (174).

220 Reith, Charles. *A new study of police history.* Edinburgh, 1956.

221 Reynolds, Ernest E. *The trial of St Thomas More.* 1964. Of little independent value. See (275) for a better analysis of the constitutional and legal significance of More's trial.

222 Richardson, Walter C. *The history of the court of augmentations, 1536–1554.* Baton Rouge, 1962. A detailed study of what became the most important of the revenue courts under Henry VIII.

223 —— *Tudor chamber administration, 1485–1547.* Baton Rouge, 1952. A very important work, somewhat at variance with Elton (186). Sees near revolutionary, though still feudal, developments in revenue administration under Henry VII. Cf. (303).

224 Robinson, Howard. *The British post office: a history.* Princeton, 1948. A standard work.

225 Roskell, John S. *The Commons and their speakers in English parliaments, 1367–1523.* Manchester, 1965. Mainly a study of speakers, Peter de la Mare to Thomas More.

226 Scofield, Cora L. *A study of the court of star chamber.* Chicago, 1900. A pioneer work. For a brief up-to-date account see Elton (108), pp. 158–63.

227 Senior, William. *Doctors' commons and the old court of admiralty: a short history of the civilians in England.* 1922. A civil law survey.

228 Simpson, Alfred W. B. *An introduction to the history of the land laws.* Oxford, 1961. Important, esp. chapters 6–8, for the sixteenth century.

229 Skeel, Caroline A. J. *The council in the marches of Wales.* 1904. Now replaced by (241).

230 Somerville, Robert. *History of the duchy of Lancaster,* I, *1265–1603.* 1953. Useful both for the peculiar institution of the duchy and as an introduction to its records.

231 Spence, George. *The equitable jurisdiction of the court of chancery.* 1846, 2 vols. Most useful as a history of the court.

232 Squibb, Q. C. *The high court of chivalry: a study of the civil law in England.* Oxford, 1959. An important study, but rather slight on the Tudor period.

233 Thomas, James H. *Town government in the sixteenth century.* 1933. Good on practical aspects of town administration such as streets and their cleaning, lighting, water supply, and fire-fighting.

234 Thomson, G[ladys] S[cott]. *Lords lieutenants in the sixteenth century: a study in Tudor local administration.* 1923. A sound study.

235 Usher, Roland G. *The institutional history of the House of Commons, 1547–1641* (Washington University Studies, vol. XI, humanistic series, no. 2). St Louis, Mo., 1924.

236 Vocht, Henry de. *Acta Thomae Mori: history of the reports of his trial and death with an undated contemporary narrative* (Humanistica Lovaniensia, VII). Louvain, 1947.

237 Webb, Sidney and Beatrice. *English local government: the story of the king's highway.* 1913. In the early part there are chapters on road legislation and road administration relevant to the Tudor period.

238 Wellington, Richard H. *The king's coroner, being a complete collection of the statutes relating to the office, together with a short history of the same.* 1905–6, 2 vols.

239 Wilkinson, Bertie. *The coronation in history* (Historical Association Pamphlets, general series, no. 23). 1953. A good survey.

240 Willcox, William B. *Gloucestershire: a study in local government, 1590–1640.* New Haven, 1940. Good as a study of local administration in Gloucestershire; fails in applying the subject to the larger scene.

241 Williams, Penry. *The council in the marches of Wales under Elizabeth I.* Cardiff, 1958. Excellent, with a good account of the council's earlier life.

242 Williams, W. Llewelyn. *The making of modern Wales: studies in the Tudor settlement of Wales.* 1919. Studies important for political and religious as well as constitutional history. Chapter 4, 'The king's court of great sessions', is particularly valuable.

243 Williams, W. Ogwen. *Tudor Gwynedd: The Tudor age in the principality of Wales.* 1958. Indicates that Henry VIII's legislation had little effect on government and society in Wales.

244 Woodworth, Allegra. *Purveyance for the royal household in the reign of Queen Elizabeth* (Transactions of the American Philosophical Society, new ser., XXXV, pt. I). Philadelphia, 1945. A study of the administrative and financial aspects of purveyance and of the grievances that arose out of purveyance.

4 Biographies

245 Dunkel, Wilbur. *William Lambarde, Elizabethan jurist 1536–1601.* New Brunswick, N.J. 1965. The life of a learned, able, and loyal Elizabethan jurist.

246 Lehmberg, Stanford E. *Sir Walter Mildmay and Tudor government.* Austin, Texas, 1964. Particularly valuable for financial administration, Henry VIII through Elizabeth. Also of some significance for Elizabeth's parliaments.

247 Wright, Herbert G. *Life and works of Arthur Hall of Grantham.* Manchester, 1919. Important for cases of parliamentary privilege.

5 Articles

248 Adair, Edward R. 'The first clerk of the privy council', *LQR*, **39** (Apr. 1923), 240–4. Maintains that the first clerk was Thomas Derbye, not William Paget.

249 —— 'The privy council registers', *EHR*, **30** (Oct. 1915), 698–704. See (355).

250 —— 'The statute of proclamations', *EHR*, **32** (Jan. 1917), 34–46. Denies that the statute of 1539 was intended to give proclamations the force of laws; it was only concerned with the manner of trying offenders against them. See (287).

251 Adair, Edward R. and Florence M. G. Evans. 'Writs of assistance from 1558 to 1700', *EHR*, **36** (July 1921), 356–72. Deals with summons to parliament.

252 Anderson, Andrew H. 'Henry, Lord Stafford (1501–1563) in local and central government', *EHR*, **78** (Apr. 1963), 225–42. A study of the public service of a conservative member of the old nobility under Mary and Elizabeth.

253 Barnes, Thomas G. 'Due process and slow process in the late Elizabethan-

early Stuart star chamber', *AJLH*, **6** (July–Oct. 1962), 221–49, 315–46. Excellent for star chamber procedure and development.

254 —— 'Star chamber mythology', *AJLH*, **5** (Jan. 1961), 1–11. Both a demolition of the commonly accepted myths about star chamber and a defence of that court.

255 —— 'The archives and archival problems of the Elizabethan and early Stuart star chamber', *Journal of the Society of Archivists*, **2** (Oct. 1963), 345–60. Deals with star chamber records.

256 Barnes, Thomas G. and A. Hassell Smith. 'Justices of the peace from 1558–1688—a revised list of sources', *BIHR*, **32** (Nov. 1959), 221–42. A revision of the list of sources provided in (369), an assessment of their value, and a study of the procedure of appointment of J.P.s.

257 Bayne, Charles G. 'The first House of Commons of Queen Elizabeth', *EHR*, **23** (July–Oct. 1908), 455–76, 643–82. A pioneer study of elections, composition, etc. Now superseded by Neale (208).

258 Beresford, Maurice W. 'The common informer, the penal statutes, and economic regulation', *EcHR*, 2nd ser., **10** (Dec. 1957), 221–38. A useful statistical study. See (288).

259 Bindoff, Stanley T. 'Parliamentary history, 1529–1688', in *The Victoria history of the counties of England: a history of Wiltshire*, v (1957), 111–70. An important study of Wiltshire members and elections.

260 —— 'The making of the statute of artificers', in *Govt. & Soc.*, pp. 59–94. Indicative of the Commons' influence on the making of an important statute.

261 Blatcher, Marjorie. 'Touching the writ of Latitat: an act "of no great moment"', in *Govt. & Soc.*, pp. 188–212. Discusses the use of the writ of *latitat* by the King's Bench to take legal business from other courts.

262 Brown, Louise F. 'Ideas of representation from Elizabeth to Charles II', *JMH*, **11** (Mar. 1939), 23–40.

263 Cam, Helen M. 'The decline and fall of English feudalism', *History*, new ser., **25** (Dec. 1940), 216–33. Sees feudalism as dying in the early Tudor period. Cf. (312).

264 Cheyney, Edward P. 'The court of star chamber', *AHR*, **18** (July 1912), 727–50. Mainly late Elizabethan.

265 Churchill, E. F. 'Dispensations under the Tudors and Stuarts', *EHR*, **34** (July 1919), 409–15.

266 —— 'The dispensing power of the crown in ecclesiastical affairs', *LQR*, **38** (July–Oct. 1922), 297–316, 420–34.

267 —— 'The dispensing power and the defence of the realm', *LQR*, **37** (Oct. 1921), 412–41.

268 Collier, John P. 'On Sir Nicholas Bacon, lord keeper, with extracts from some of his unprinted papers and speeches', *Arch.*, **36** (1865), 339–48.

269 Cooper, J. P. 'A revolution in Tudor history?', *PP*, no. 26 (Nov. 1963), 110–12. A communication on (399).

270 —— 'The supplication against the ordinaries reconsidered', *EHR*, **72** (Oct. 1957), 616–41. A critique of (290). At issue is the history of the supplication of 1532 and particularly the government's part in its passage. Also see (318).

271 Davies, C. S. L. 'Provision for armies, 1509–50: a study in the effectiveness of early Tudor government', *EcHR*, 2nd ser., **17** (no. 2, 1964), 234–48.

272 Davies, D. Seaborn. 'Acontius, champion of toleration, and the patent system', *EcHR*, **7** (Nov. 1936), 63–6.

273 —— 'The early history of the patent specification', *LQR*, **50** (Jan.–Apr. 1934), 86–109, 260–74. Supplements (306).

274 Derrett, J. Duncan M. 'Neglected versions of the contemporary account of the trial of Sir Thomas More', *BIHR*, **33** (Nov. 1960), 202–23.

275 —— 'The trial of Sir Thomas More', *EHR*, **79** (July 1964), 449–77. A valuable account. See (221).

276 Dietz, Frederick C. 'Elizabethan customs administration', *EHR*, **45** (Jan. 1930), 35–58.

277 Duncan, James L. 'The end and aim of law, II, Legal theories in England in the sixteenth and seventeenth centuries', *Juridical Review*, **50** (Sept. 1938), 257–81.

278 Dunham, William H., Jr. 'Henry VIII's whole council and its parts', *HLQ*, 7 (Feb. 1943), 7–46. This, (280), (281), and (282) are important contributions to our knowledge of the council, but the term 'whole council' is more than questionable. See Elton (295), pp. 272–73.

279 —— 'Regal power and the rule of law: a Tudor paradox', *JBS*, 3 (May 1964), 24–56. An interesting discussion of the development of the rule of law under the Tudor 'despots'.

280 —— 'The Ellesmere extracts from the "Acta consilii" of King Henry VIII', *EHR*, 58 (July 1943), 301–18.

281 —— 'The members of Henry VIII's whole council, 1509–27', *EHR*, 59 (May 1944), 187–210.

282 —— 'Wolsey's rule of the king's whole council', *AHR*, 49 (July 1944), 644–62.

283 Edwards, J. Goronwy. 'The emergence of majority rule in English parliamentary elections', *TRHS*, 5th ser., 14 (1964), 175–96. Nearly half of this interesting paper refers to Tudor England.

284 Elton, Geoffrey R. 'A further note on parliamentary drafts in the reign of Henry VIII', *BIHR*, 27 (Nov. 1954), 189–200.

285 —— 'A revolution in Tudor history?', *PP*, no. 32 (Dec. 1965), 103–9. Answers (400). The concluding article of an interesting and useful debate.

286 —— 'Constitutional development and political thought in Western Europe', *NCMH*, II, 438–63. Useful for seeing English developments in terms of the larger Western European scene.

287 —— 'Henry VIII's act of proclamations', *EHR*, 75 (Apr. 1960), 208–22. Agrees in part with Adair (250), but disagrees with his contention that the act was not concerned with the validity of proclamations.

288 —— 'Informing for profit: a sidelight on Tudor methods of law enforcement', *Camb. Hist. J.*, 11 (no. 2, 1954), 149–67. This and (258) are important studies of law enforcement and law effectiveness. Also see (187).

289 —— 'Parliamentary drafts, 1529–1540', *BIHR*, 25 (Nov. 1952), 117–32. Classifies drafts into government and private drafts.

290 —— 'The Commons' supplication of 1532: parliamentary manœuvres in the reign of Henry VIII', *EHR*, 66 (Oct. 1951), 507–34. See (270).

291 —— 'The Elizabethan exchequer: war in the receipt', in *Govt. & Soc.*, pp. 213–48. Discusses a battle for power and fees among exchequer officials that impaired efficient administration.

292 —— 'The evolution of a Reformation statute', *EHR*, 64 (Apr. 1949), 174–97. An important study of the act of appeals and Cromwell's role in drafting legislation.

293 —— 'The problems and significance of administrative history in the Tudor period', *JBS*, 4 (May 1965), 18–28. A plea for more administrative history, defending the importance of studying the machinery of government.

294 —— 'The Tudor revolution: a reply', *PP*, no. 29 (Dec. 1964), 26–49. A reply to (399) that gives no ground on major issues.

295 —— 'Why the history of the early-Tudor council remains unwritten', *Annali della Fondazione italiana per la storia amministrativa*, 1 (1964), 268–96. An appraisal of previous works and an analysis of the evidence for and the obstacles to a better reconstruction.

296 Emmison, Frederick G. 'A plan of Edward VI and secretary Petre for reorganizing the privy council's work, 1552–3', *BIHR*, 31 (Nov. 1958), 203–10.

297 Evans, E. 'Of the antiquity of parliaments in England: some Elizabethan and early Stuart opinions', *History*, new ser., 23 (Dec. 1938), 206–21.

298 George, M. D. 'Notes on the origin of the declared account', *EHR*, 31 (Jan. 1916), 41–58. On exchequer accounts of all revenue that was neither ancient nor crown land.

299 Glazebrook, P. R. 'Misprision of felony—shadow or phantom?', *AJLH*, 8 (July–Oct. 1964), 189–208, 283–302. Finds the origin of the 'crime' of misprision of treason in a small mistake occurring in Staunford's *Plees de Coron* of 1557.

300 Gleason, John H. 'The personnel of the commissions of the peace, 1554–

1564', *HLQ*, **18** (Feb. 1955), 169–77. Maintains 1554–64 saw no purge of J.P.s for religious reasons. Cf. (385).

301 Harriss, G. L. 'Aids, loans, and benevolences', *Hist. J.*, **6** (no. 1, 1963), 1–19. Though mainly concerned with the later middle ages, of some relevance for the early Tudor period.

302 Hinton, Raymond W. K. 'The decline of parliamentary government under Elizabeth I and the early Stuarts', *Camb. Hist. J.*, **12** (no. 2, 1957), 116–32.

303 Hooker, James R. 'Some cautionary notes on Henry VII's household and chamber "system"', *Speculum*, **33** (Jan. 1958), 69–75. Maintains that general organizational theories about the chamber and household, such as Richardson's (223), are misleading.

304 Housden, J. A. J. 'Early posts in England', *EHR*, **18** (Oct. 1903), 713–18.

305 —— 'The merchant strangers' post in the sixteenth century', *EHR*, **21** (Oct. 1906), 739–42.

306 Hulme, Edward W. 'The history of the patent system under the prerogative and at the common law', *LQR*, **12** (Apr. 1896), 141–54; **16** (Jan. 1900), 44–56. Contains lists and summaries of many Elizabethan patents. See also (273).

307 Hurstfield, Joel. 'Corruption and reform under Edward VI and Mary: the example of wardship', *EHR*, **68** (Jan. 1953), 22–36. Much of this, (309), (310), (311), and (312) has been incorporated into (200), though each retains independent value.

308 —— 'County government, c. 1530–c. 1660', in *The Victoria history of the counties of England: a history of Wiltshire*, v (1957), 80–110.

309 —— 'Lord Burghley as master of the court of wards', *TRHS*, 4th ser., **31** (1949), 95–114.

310 —— 'The Greenwich tenures of the reign of Edward VI', *LQR*, **65** (Jan. 1949), 72–81.

311 —— 'The profits of fiscal feudalism, 1541–1602', *EcHR*, 2nd ser., **8** (Aug. 1955), 53–61.

312 —— 'The revival of feudalism in early Tudor England', *History*, new ser., **37** (Jan. 1952), 131–45.

313 Ives, E. W. 'Promotion in the legal profession of Yorkist and early Tudor England', *LQR*, **75** (July 1959), 348–63.

314 —— 'The reputation of the Commons lawyers in English society, 1450–1550', *University of Birmingham Historical Journal*, **7** (no. 2, 1960), 130–42. Argues that their evil reputation was not entirely deserved.

315 Jones, William J. 'An introduction to petty bag proceedings in the reign of Elizabeth I', *California Law Review*, **51** (Dec. 1963), 882–905. Deals with the common law side of the court of chancery.

316 —— 'Conflict or collaboration? Chancery attitudes in the reign of Elizabeth I', *AJLH*, **5** (Jan. 1961), 12–54. Finds that chancery and the common law courts were 'less competing jurisdictions than collaborating dispensers of justice' during Elizabeth's reign.

317 —— 'Due process and slow process in the Elizabethan chancery', *AJLH*, **6** (Apr. 1962), 123–50. Excellent for chancery procedure.

318 Kelly, Michael. 'The submission of the clergy', *TRHS*, 5th ser., **15** (1965), 97–119. An important augmentation of the Elton–Cooper debate over the Commons' supplication (270). It emphasizes the extent of clerical opposition, indicates no clear government policy, and sees the king's victory as 'narrow, blundering, and legally suspect'.

319 Koebner, Richard. '"The imperial crown of the realm": Henry VIII, Constantine the Great, and Polydore Vergil', *BIHR*, **26** (May 1953), 29–52. An important discussion of the concept of empire in Tudor England with particular reference to Polydore Vergil and the act of appeals of 1533.

320 Labaree, Leonard W. and R. E. Moody. 'The seal of the privy council', *EHR*, **43** (Apr. 1928), 190–202.

321 Lapsley, Gaillard T. 'The problem of the north', *AHR*, **5** (Apr. 1900), 440–66. Concerned with the north and relations with Scotland.

322 Lehmberg, Stanford E. 'Star chamber: 1485–1509', *HLQ*, **24** (May 1961), 189–214. Concludes that the bulk of cases heard in Henry VII's star

chamber had to do with land tenure, and in most riot or forcible entry was alleged.

323 Levine, Mortimer. 'A more than ordinary case of "rape"', 13 and 14 Elizabeth I', *AJLH*, 7 (Apr. 1963), 159–64. Considers the question of the 'Englishry' of a Scot as well as the development of the law of rape.

324 —— 'A parliamentary title to the crown in Tudor England', *HLQ*, 25 (Feb. 1962), 121–7. Maintains that Mary and/or Elizabeth had such a title.

325 —— 'Richard III—usurper or lawful king?', *Speculum*, 34 (July 1959), 391–401. Maintains the validity of the Yorkist title of Henry VIII and his successors.

326 Mackenzie, William M. 'The debateable land', *SHR*, 30 (Oct. 1951), 109–25.

327 Magee, Brian. 'The first parliament of Queen Elizabeth', *Dublin Review*, 200 (Jan. 1937), 60–78. Claims Catholics were not fairly represented and that parliamentary opposition to religious change was strong. Cf. Neale (525), I, 38–9, 51–84.

328 Marsden, Reginald G. 'Early prize jurisdiction and prize law in England', *EHR*, 24 (Oct. 1909), 675–97; 25 (Apr. 1910), 243–63; 26 (Jan. 1911), 34–56. Mainly Tudor and Stuart periods.

329 Miller, Helen. 'London and parliament in the reign of Henry VIII', *BIHR*, 35 (Nov. 1962), 128–49.

330 —— 'Subsidy assessments of the peerage in the sixteenth century', *BIHR*, 28 (May 1955), 15–34.

331 Milsom, Stroud F. C. 'Richard Hunne's "Praemunire"', *EHR*, 76 (Jan. 1961), 80–2.

332 Milligan, Burton. 'Counterfeiters and coin clippers in the sixteenth and seventeenth centuries', *NQ*, 182 (Feb. 1942), 100–5.

333 Neale, John E. 'Commons journals of the Tudor period', *TRHS*, 4th ser., 3 (1920), 136–70. Much of this and the following important articles by Neale has been incorporated into (208) and (525).

334 —— 'More Elizabethan Elections', *EHR*, 61 (Jan. 1946), 18–44.

335 —— 'Parliament and the succession question in 1562/3 and 1566', *EHR*, 36 (Oct. 1921), 497–520.

336 —— 'Peter Wentworth', *EHR*, 39 (Jan.–Apr. 1924), 36–54, 175–205.

337 —— 'Queen Elizabeth's quashing of bills in 1597–8', *EHR*, 34 (Oct. 1919), 586–8; 36 (July 1921), 480.

338 —— 'The authorship of Townshend's "Historical collections"', *EHR*, 36 (Jan. 1921), 96–9.

339 —— 'The Commons' privilege of free speech in parliament', in *Tud. Stud.*, pp. 257–87.

340 —— 'Three Elizabethan elections', *EHR*, 46 (Apr. 1931), 209–39.

341 Newton, Arthur P. 'The establishment of the great farm of the customs', *TRHS*, 4th ser., 1 (1918), 129–56.

342 —— 'The king's chamber under the early Tudors', *EHR*, 32 (July 1917), 348–72.

343 —— 'Tudor reforms in the royal household', in *Tud. Stud.*, pp. 231–57.

344 Notestein, Wallace. 'The winning of the initiative by the House of Commons', *PBA*, 11 (1924), 125–75. Though mainly concerned with the seventeenth century, good for late Elizabethan procedural changes.

345 Oman, Charles W. C. 'The Tudors and the currency, 1526–60', *TRHS*, 2nd ser., 9 (1895), 167–88. Also see (371) and the excellent discussions in (246).

346 Parmiter, Geoffrey de C. 'Saint Thomas More and the oath', *Downside Review*, 78 (Winter 1959–60), 1–13.

347 —— 'Tudor indictments, illustrated by the indictment of St Thomas More', *Rec. Hist.*, 6 (Oct. 1961), 140–56.

348 Perceval, R. W. 'Henry VIII and the origin of the royal assent by commission', *Parliamentary Affairs*, 3 (Spring 1950), 307–15.

349 Plucknett, Theodore F. T. 'Ellesmere on statutes', *LQR*, 60 (July 1944), 242–9. Identifies Thomas Egerton as the author of the *Discourse upon statutes* (155).

350 —— 'Some proposed legislation of Henry VIII', *TRHS*, 4th ser., **19** (1936), 119–44. See (377).

351 Pollard, Albert F. 'A changeling member of parliament', *BIHR*, **10** (June 1932), 20–7.

352 —— 'A protean clerk of the Commons', *BIHR*, **18** (Nov. 1940), 49–51.

353 —— 'Council, star chamber, and privy council under the Tudors', *EHR*, **37** (July–Oct. 1922), 337–60, 516–39; **38** (Jan. 1923), 42–60. Clears up some of the earlier misconceptions on the early Tudor period.

354 —— 'Hayward Townshend's journals', *BIHR*, **13** (June 1935), 9–34; **14** (Feb. 1937), 149–65; **15** (June 1937), 1–18.

355 —— 'Lords' journals', *EHR*, **30** (April 1915), 304. This and (249) consider the presence among the Lords' journals of a page from the privy council register.

356 —— 'Queen Elizabeth's under-clerks and their Commons' journals', *BIHR*, **17** (June 1939), 1–12.

357 —— 'Receivers of petitions and clerks of parliament', *EHR*, **57** (Apr. 1942), 202–26.

358 —— 'The authenticity of the "Lords' journals" in the sixteenth century', *TRHS*, 3rd ser., **8** (1914), 17–40.

359 —— 'The clerical organization of parliament', *EHR*, **57** (Jan. 1942), 31–85.

360 —— 'The clerk of the crown', *EHR*, **57** (July 1942), 312–33.

361 —— 'The De Facto act of Henry VII', *BIHR*, **7** (June 1929), 1–12. Good on an act that too much has been read into.

362 —— 'The growth of the court of requests', *EHR*, **56** (Apr. 1941), 300–3.

363 —— 'The under-clerks and the Commons' journals (1509–1558)', *BIHR*, **16** (Feb. 1939), 144–67.

364 —— 'Thomas Cromwell's parliamentary lists', *BIHR*, **9** (June 1931), 31–43.

365 —— 'Wolsey and the Great Seal', *BIHR*, **7** (Nov. 1929), 85–97.

366 Prall, Stuart E. 'The development of equity in Tudor England', *AJLH*, **8** (Jan. 1964), 1–19. Discusses Tudor writings on equity and concludes that equity developed out of the common law tradition, that its development is no evidence of a 'reception' of Roman law, and that there was no issue of common law versus equity but one of 'the rule of law versus rule by administrative fiat'.

367 Prothero, George W. 'On two petitions presented by parliament to Queen Elizabeth', *EHR*, **2** (Oct. 1887), 741–6.

368 Pugh, Thomas B. '"Indenture for the marches" between Henry VII and Edward Stafford (1477–1521), duke of Buckingham', *EHR*, **71** (July 1956), 436–41.

369 Putnam, Bertha H. 'Justices of the peace for 1558–1688', *BIHR*, **4** (Feb. 1927), 144–56. See (256).

370 —— 'Sixteenth century treatises for justices of the peace', *University of Toronto Law Journal*, **7** (no. 1, 1947), 137–61. Supplements (217).

371 Read, Conyers. 'Profits on the recoinage of 1560–1', *EcHR*, **6** (Apr. 1936), 186–93. Corrects Feavearyear's figures (189), but cf. Lehmberg (246), p. 59 n.

372 —— 'Walsingham and Burghley in Queen Elizabeth's privy council', *EHR*, **28** (Jan. 1913), 34–58. Development of factions in the privy council, 1570–90, mainly on matters of foreign policy.

373 Rees, James F. 'Tudor policy in Wales', in *Studies in Welsh History* (Cardiff, 1947), pp. 26–47. Good on Tudor legislation on Wales.

374 Rees, William. 'The Union of England and Wales', *Transactions of the Honourable Society of Cymmrodorion* (1937), pp. 27–100. Of some use for political history but stronger on the administrative and judicial effects of the Act of Union.

375 Rezneck, Samuel. 'The trial of treason in Tudor England', in *Essays in history and political theory in honor of Charles Howard McIlwain* (Cambridge, Mass., 1936), pp. 258–88.

376 Richardson, Walter C. 'Some financial expedients of Henry VIII', *EcHR*, 2nd ser., **7** (Aug. 1954), 33–48.

377 —— 'The Court of the Commonweal', *Papers of the Michigan Academy of Science, Arts and Letters*, **19** (1933), 459–76. Deals with a new administrative

court allegedly proposed by Cromwell. See also (350) and (289), which shows this was not a Cromwell scheme.

378 Richardson, Walter C. 'The surveyor of the king's prerogative', *EHR*, **56** (Jan. 1941), 52–75. A study of a unique revenue office created by Henry VII and dropped by Henry VIII.

379 Roskell, John S. 'Perspectives in English parliamentary history', *BJRL*, **46** (Mar. 1964), 448–75. Contains a critique of Pollard, Elton, and Neale for maintaining that 'parliament entered upon its proper career in the sixteenth century'.

380 Ruddock, Alwyn A. 'The earliest records of the high court of admiralty (1515–1558)', *BIHR*, **22** (Nov. 1949), 139–51.

381 Schoeck, Richard J. 'Canon law in England on the eve of the Reformation', *Mediaeval Studies*, **25** (1963), 124–47. Indicates the importance of canon law in early Tudor legal and political history and political thought largely through an examination of Thomas More and the canon law.

382 —— 'Early Anglo-Saxon studies and legal scholarship in the Renaissance', *Studies in the Renaissance*, **5** (1958), 102–10.

383 Simpson, H. B. 'The office of constable', *EHR*, **10** (Oct. 1895), 625–41.

384 Skeel, Caroline A. J. 'The council of the west', *TRHS*, 4th ser., **4** (1921), 62–80. See (404).

385 Smith, A. Hassell. 'The personnel of the commissions of the peace, 1554–1564: A reconsideration', *HLQ*, **22** (Aug. 1959), 301–12. Argues against (300) that the early years of Elizabeth's reign saw a 'purge' of J.P.s.

386 Smith, Goldwin. 'Elizabeth and the apprenticeship of parliament', *University of Toronto Quarterly*, **8** (July 1939), 431–9.

387 Smith, Lacey B. 'English treason trials and confessions in the sixteenth century', *JHI*, **15** (Oct. 1954), 471–98. Shows an unedifying side of Tudor justice.

388 Snow, Vernon F. 'Proctorial representation and conciliar management during the reign of Henry VIII', *Hist. J.*, **9** (no. 1, 1966), 1–26. Deals with the development of the proxy system and its use by the privy council in managing the House of Lords.

389 Somerville, Robert. 'Henry VIII's "Council learned in the law"', *EHR*, **54** (July 1939), 427–42. Deals with a special committee of the council concerned with enforcing the penal legislation.

390 —— 'The duchy of Lancaster council and court of duchy chamber', *TRHS*, 4th ser., **23** (1941), 159–77. The standard authority on an important court.

391 Thomson, G[ladys] S[cott]. 'The origin and growth of the office of deputy-lieutenant', *TRHS*, 4th ser., **5**, (1922), 150–67.

392 Thorne, Samuel E. 'The equity of a statute and Heydon's case', *Illinois Law Review*, **31** (1936), 202–17. Deals with judicial interpretation of statute, mid-fourteenth century to 1580.

393 Thornley, Isabel D. 'The treason legislation of Henry VIII (1531–1534)', *TRHS*, 3rd ser., **11** (1917), 87–124. Predates Cromwell's influence on policy-making. See Elton (186), p. 95 n.

394 Usher, Roland G. 'The significance and early interpretation of the statute of uses', *Washington University Studies*, **1**, pt. II (Oct. 1913), 42–53. Shows how a statute designed to abolish uses was so interpreted by the common law courts as to perpetuate the same.

395 Vinogradoff, Paul. 'Reason and conscience in sixteenth century jurisprudence', *LQR*, **24** (Oct. 1908), 373–84. Through a study of St German's *Dialogues* (2204) shows the influence of the later schoolmen and canon lawyers on English jurisprudence.

396 Wallace, H. M. 'Berwick in the reign of Queen Elizabeth', *EHR*, **46** (Jan. 1931), 79–88.

397 Williams, Charles H. 'The so-called star chamber act', *History*, new ser., **15** (July 1930), 129–35. On this Act of 1487, which did not create the court of star chamber, also see Pollard (353), **37**, 520–9.

398 Williams, Penry. 'The star chamber and the council in the marches of Wales, 1558–1603', *Bulletin of the Board of Celtic Studies*, **16** (May 1956),

287–97. Suggests that the increase in star chamber suits was due to an increase in litigation, not to disorder or to shortcomings of the council in the marches.

399 Williams, Penry and G. L. Harriss. 'A revolution in Tudor history?' *PP*, no. 25 (July 1963), 3–58. A two-front attack on Elton's interpretation of Tudor history from the viewpoints of a fifteenth-century specialist and an Elizabethan specialist. Stimulating but not convincing. Cf. (294).

400 —— 'A revolution in Tudor history?', *PP*, no. 31 (July 1965), 87–96. Replies to (294). Adds little to the controversy.

401 Wilson, Jean S. 'Sheriff's rolls of the sixteenth and seventeenth centuries', *EHR*, **47** (Jan. 1932), 31–45.

402 Wolffe, B. P. 'Henry VII's land revenues and chamber finance', *EHR*, **79** (Apr. 1964), 225–54. Criticizes figures given in Dietz (179) and some commentaries of Tudor specialists.

403 Woodward, George W. O. 'The role of parliament in the Henrician revolution', *Schweizer Beiträge zur allgemeinen Geschichte*, **16** (1958), 56–65. Denies that parliament's role was revolutionary from a constitutional point of view.

404 Youings, Joyce A. 'The council of the west', *TRHS*, 5th ser., **10** (1960), 41–60. Shows the council of the west to have been a short-lived Cromwellian project.

V POLITICAL HISTORY

1 Printed Sources

405 Archbold, William A. J. (ed.). 'Sir William Stanley and Perkin Warbeck', *EHR*, **14** (July 1899), 529–34. Reports of their trials, missing from the *Baga de secretis*.

406 Bateson, Mary (ed.). 'The pilgrimage of grace, and Aske's examination', *EHR*, **5** (Apr.–July 1890), 330–45, 550–73.

407 Bémont, Charles (ed.). *Le premier divorce de Henri VIII et le schisme d'Angleterre*. Paris, 1917. Prints and translates into French an anonymous fragment of a Latin chronicle written *c.* 1556–7. Attributes it to Nicholas Harpsfield.

408 Birch, Thomas (ed.). *Memoirs of the reign of Queen Elizabeth from the year 1581 till her death*. 1754, 2 vols. Primarily letters.

409 Bruce, John (ed.). 'Inedited documents relating to the imprisonment and condemnation of Sir Thomas More', *Arch.*, **27** (1838), 361–74.

410 —— *Correspondence of King James VI of Scotland with Sir Robert Cecil and others in England during the reign of Queen Elizabeth* (Camden Society, old ser., LXXVIII). 1861. Important for Robert Cecil's paving the way for James's accession in England and for the Essex conspiracy. For additional letters between Cecil and James see (440).

411 Burgoyne, Frank J. (ed.). *History of Queen Elizabeth, Amy Robsart, and the earl of Leicester, being a reprint of 'Leycesters Commonwealth'*. 1904. A contemporary attack on Robert Dudley, earl of Leicester. Completely unreliable. On its authorship see (689).

412 Byrne, M[uriel] St C[lare] (ed.). *The letters of King Henry VIII*. 1936. Valuable mainly for Henry's love letters to Anne Boleyn and an appendix giving the various dates assigned by different authorities to those significant letters.

413 *Cabala, sive scrinia sacra*. 1691, 2 pts. Has many letters of the reigns of Henry VIII and Elizabeth.

414 *Calendar of inquisitions post mortem . . . , Henry VII*. 1898–1955. 3 vols.

415 *Calendar of state papers, domestic*, ed. Robert Lemon and Mary A. E. Green. 1856–72, 12 vols. Edward VI through Elizabeth. The first two vols. are little more than a catalogue; the rest are more satisfactory.

416 *Calendar of the close rolls . . . , Henry VII*. 1955–63, 2 vols.

417 *Calendar of the fine rolls . . . , Henry VII*. 1962.

418 *Calendar of the patent rolls . . . , Edward VI*. 1924–9, 5 vols.

419 *Calendar of the patent rolls ...*, *Elizabeth.* 1939–. Vol. IV, appearing in 1964, goes through 1569.

420 *Calendar of the patent rolls ...*, *Henry VII.* 1914–16, 2 vols.

421 *Calendar of the patent rolls ...*, *Philip and Mary.* 1936–9, 4 vols.

422 Camden, William. *The historie of the most renowned and virtuous Princess Elizabeth, late queen of England.* 1630. The best account of Elizabeth's reign by a contemporary.

423 Campbell, William E. and Arthur W. Reed (eds.). *The English works of Sir Thomas More ...* 1931, 2 vols. Incomplete and being replaced by the Yale edition of the complete works of St Thomas More.

424 Cavendish, George. *The life and death of Cardinal Wolsey,* ed. Richard S. Sylvester (E.E.T.S., orig. ser., CCXLIII), 1959. The best ed. of a valuable source. Though written by a partisan, Wolsey's servant, much of what is said rings true.

425 Clapham, John. *Elizabeth of England: certain observations concerning the life and reign of Queen Elizabeth,* ed. Evelyn and Conyers Read. Philadelphia, 1951. Written by a servant of Lord Burghley, this also contains short accounts of the reigns of the earlier Tudors.

426 Collier, John P. (ed.). *The Egerton papers ...* (Camden Society, old ser., XII). 1840. Contains letters and papers of figures of Elizabeth's reign.

427 ——— *Trevelyan Papers* (Camden Society, old ser., LXVII, LXXXIV, CV). 1863–72. Of use for the early Tudor period.

428 Cramer, John A. (ed.). *The second book of the travels of Nicander Nucius of Corcyra* (Camden Society, old ser., XVII). 1841. The largest part of this work, translated from the Greek, is an untrustworthy chronicle of the reign of Henry VIII.

429 Crosby, Allan J. and John Bruce (eds.). *Accounts and papers relating to Mary, Queen of Scots* (Camden Society, old ser., XCIII). 1867. The expenses of Mary's maintenance in England and of her funeral plus an anonymous treatise, *A justification of Queen Elizabeth in relacion to the affaire of Mary Queene of Scottes.*

430 Dickens, Arthur G. (ed.). 'New records of the pilgrimage of grace', *Yorks. Arch. J.,* **33** (pt. 131, 1937), 298–308. Four letters of Henry VIII.

431 ——— 'The Yorkshire submissions to Henry VIII, 1541', *EHR,* **53** (Apr. 1938), 267–75. An aftermath of the pilgrimage of grace.

432 Ehses, Stefan (ed.). *Römische Dokumente zur Geschichte der Ehescheidung Heinrichs VIII von England.* Paderborn, 1893. Very important for Henry's divorce. For Ehses' conclusions summarized in English see (678).

433 Ellis, Henry (ed.). *Original letters, illustrative of English history.* 1824–46, 11 vols. in three series. Mainly useful for the reigns of Henry VIII and Elizabeth.

434 Elton, Geoffrey R. (ed.). 'Two unpublished letters of Thomas Cromwell', *BIHR,* **22** (May 1949), 35–8.

435 Fabyan, Robert. *The new chronicles of England and France,* ed. Henry Ellis. 1811. Of use for Henry VII's reign.

436 Forest, William. *The history of Grisild the Second: a narrative, in verse, of the divorce of Katharine of Aragon,* ed. William D. Macray. 1875. Written at the end of Mary's reign.

437 Gairdner, James (ed.). 'The draft dispensation for Henry VIII's marriage with Anne Boleyn', *EHR,* **5** (July 1890), 544–50.

438 Grafton, Richard. *Grafton's chronicle; or history of England.* 1809.

439 Guaras, Antonio de. *The accession of Queen Mary,* ed. Richard Garnett. 1892. An account by a Spanish merchant living in London at the time.

440 Hailes, David Dalrymple, Lord (ed.). *The secret correspondence of Sir Robert Cecil with James I,* Edinburgh, 1766. Also see (410).

441 Hall, Edward. *The triumphant reigne of Kyng Henry the VIII,* ed. Charles Whibley. 1904, 2 vols. Very partial to Henry, but the best contemporary account.

442 Harington, John. *Nugae antiquae: being a miscellaneous collection of original papers ... written during the reigns of Henry VIII, Edward VI, Queen Mary, Elizabeth, and King James,* ed. Thomas Park. 1804, 2 vols.

443 Harpsfield, Nicholas. *A treatise on the pretended divorce between Henry VIII and Catharine of Aragon*, ed. Nicholas Pocock (Camden Society, new ser., XXI). 1878. Written in Mary's reign.

444 —— *The life and death of Sir Thomas Moore, knight* . . . , ed. Elsie V. Hitchcock and Raymond W. Chambers (E.E.T.S., orig. ser., CLXXXVI). 1932. Written in Mary's reign and based in part on Roper (489), this is the first complete life of More. A Marian propaganda piece, but more objective than Stapleton (620).

445 Harrison, George B. (ed.). *Letters of Queen Elizabeth*. 1935. Convenient but there are many omissions.

446 Hay, Denys (ed.). *The anglica historia of Polydore Vergil, 1485–1537* (Camden Society, 3rd ser., LXXIV). 1950. Basic for the reign of Henry VII.

447 Haynes, Samuel and William Murdin (eds.). *Collection of state papers* . . . *left by William Cecil, Lord Burghley* . . . 1740–59, 2 vols. Still useful despite (448).

448 Historical Manuscripts Commission. *Calendar of the manuscripts of the* . . . *marquis of Salisbury* . . . *preserved at Hatfield House, Hertfordshire*. 1883–1940, 18 vols. A calendar of the most valuable private collection for Elizabeth's reign. For Hatfield MSS in the Commission's reports see Read (24), pp. 16–17. Many of the MSS in this collection are printed in full in (447).

449 Holinshed, Raphael. *Chronicles of England, Scotland, and Ireland*, ed. Henry Ellis. 1807–8, 6 vols. Mainly based on Stow (494). Useful for Elizabeth's reign to 1586.

450 Hopper, Clarence (ed.). *London chronicle during the reigns of Henry the Seventh and Henry the Eighth* (Camden Miscellany, IV, old ser., LXXIII). 1859. Brief and of little use.

451 Hume, Martin A. S. (trans. and ed.). *Chronicle of King Henry VIII of England*. 1889. A contemporary account by an unknown Spaniard of events in England from the beginning of Henry VIII's divorce suit to Protector Somerset's fall. Must be used with caution.

452 Jerdan, William (ed.). *Rutland papers: original documents illustrative of the courts and times of Henry VII and Henry VIII* (Camden Society, old ser., XXI). 1842.

453 Jones, Howard V. (ed.). 'The journal of Levinus Munck', *EHR*, **68** (Apr. 1953), 234–58. A journal of 1595–1605 by a servant of Robert Cecil.

453a Jordan, Wilbur K. (ed.). *The chronicle and political papers of King Edward VI*. Ithaca, N.Y., 1966. The *Journal* (471) plus six papers with a valuable critical introduction and notes.

454 Kennedy, William P. M. (ed.). 'The imperial embassy of 1553/4 and Wyatt's rebellion', *EHR*, **38** (Apr. 1923), 251–8.

455 Kingsford, Charles L. (ed.). *Two London chronicles from the collection of John Stow* (Camden Miscellany, XII, 3rd ser., XVIII). 1910. The first chronicle covers 1523–40; the second, 1548–55.

456 Lanfranc, Pierre (ed.). 'Un inédit de Ralegh sur la succession', *Etudes anglaises*, XIII (Jan.–Mar.1960), 38–46. A letter and memorandum of 1593, written by Raleigh to Elizabeth, arguing against determining the succession.

457 *Letters and papers, foreign and domestic, of the reign of Henry VIII*, ed. John S. Brewer, James Gairdner and Robert H. Brodie. 1862–1910, 21 vols. in 33 pts.; vol. I revised in 3 pts. plus a 2-pt. addenda by Brodie, 1920–32. The main source for internal and foreign affairs.

458 *Letters and papers illustrative of the reigns of Richard III and Henry VII*, ed. James Gairdner (Rolls Series, no. 24). 1861–3, 2 vols.

459 Lodge, Edmund (ed.). 'An account of the insurrection in the county of York in 1536', *Arch.*, **16** (1812), 330–4. A report of the Lancaster Herald.

460 —— *Illustrations of British history* . . . *in the reigns of Henry VIII, Edward VI, Mary, Elizabeth, and James I* . . . 1838, 3 vols.

461 McClure, Norman E. (ed.). *The letters of John Chamberlain* (American Philosophical Society Memoirs, XII, pts. I–II). Philadelphia, 1939, 2 vols. Letters of a London gossip of Elizabeth's reign. Useful for social as well as political life.

462 Madden, Frederick (ed.). 'Documents relating to Perkin Warbeck with remarks on his history', *Arch.*, **27** (1838), 153–210.

463 Malfatti, C. V. (trans. and ed.). *The accession, coronation, and marriage of Mary Tudor as related in four manuscripts in the Escorial.* Oxford, 1956.

464 Malkiewicz, A. J. A. (ed.). 'An eye-witness's account of the coup d'état of October 1549', *EHR*, **70** (Oct. 1955), 600–9. An account of Somerset's fall by a sympathizer.

465 Martin, Charles T. (ed.). *Journal of Sir Francis Walsingham, from December 1570 to April 1583* (Camden Miscellany, VI, old ser., CIV). 1871. A diary plus a catalogue of correspondence.

466 *Materials for a history of the reign of Henry VII*, ed. William Campbell (Rolls Series, no. 60). 1873, 2 vols. Documents for 1485–90.

467 *Memorials of King Henry VII*, ed. James Gairdner (Rolls Series, no. 10). 1858. Includes Bernard André's *Vita Henrici Septimi*, his *Annales Henrici Septimi*, and the *Journals* of Roger Machado.

468 Muller, James A. (ed.). *Letters of Stephen Gardiner.* Cambridge, 1933.

469 Neale, John E. (ed.). 'Proceedings in parliament relative to the sentence on Mary, Queen of Scots', *EHR*, **35** (Jan. 1920), 103–13.

470 Nichols, John G. (ed.). *Chronicle of the Grey Friars of London* (Camden Society, old ser., LIII). 1852. Of independent value for 1503–56, but no longer so for Wyatt's rebellion. See (749).

471 —— *Literary remains of Edward VI.* 1857. Contains Edward's *Journal*, a revealing document on the young king's character.

472 —— *The chronicle of Queen Jane, and of two years of Queen Mary, and especially of the rebellion of Sir Thomas Wyat* (Camden Society, old ser., XLVIII). 1850. The chronicle is a basic source for July 1553–October 1554. Equally valuable are the documents printed in the appendix.

473 —— *The diary of Henry Machyn . . . , 1550–63* (Camden Society, old ser., XLII). 1848. Useful for dating events, particularly deaths.

474 —— 'The second patent appointing Edward duke of Somerset protector, *temp.* King Edward the Sixth; introduced by an historical review of the various measures connected therewith', *Arch.*, **30** (1844), 463–89.

475 Nicolas, N[icholas] H[arris] (ed.). *Memoirs of the Life and Times of Sir Christopher Hatton . . .* 1847. Mainly correspondence.

476 Osborn, James M. (ed.). *The Quenes maiesties passage through the citie of London to Westminster the day before her coronacion* (Elizabethan Club Series, I). New Haven, 1960. A contemporary account of Elizabeth's entry into London. According to John E. Neale's introduction, the first propaganda piece for the Elizabethan régime and probably officially inspired.

477 Peck, Francis (ed.). *Desiderata curiosa.* 1732–5, 2 vols. Letters and tracts, a great many of them Elizabethan.

478 Pocock, Nicholas (ed.). *Records of the Reformation, the divorce 1527–1533.* Oxford, 1870, 2 vols.

479 —— *Troubles connected with the prayer-book of 1549* (Camden Society, new ser., XXXVIII). 1884. Letters and other documents.

480 Pollard, Albert F. (ed.). *The reign of Henry VII from contemporary sources* (University of London Historical Series, no. 1). 1913–14, 3 vols. A collection covering political, constitutional, social, economic, diplomatic, and religious history.

481 Pollen, John H. (ed.). *Mary Queen of Scots and the Babington plot* (Scottish History Society, 3rd ser., III). Edinburgh, 1922. Documents plus an introduction in which Father Pollen accepts the official version of Mary's incriminating letter to Babington. Cf. (531).

482 Proctor, John. *The history of Wyat's rebellion*, in *Tud. Tr.*, pp. 199–257. The fullest contemporary account by a partisan of Mary. Probably based in large part on Mychell. See (749).

483 Raine, James (ed.). *Depositions and other ecclesiastical proceedings from the courts of Durham* (Surtees Society, XXI). 1845. Important for depositions concerning the Rebellion of 1569.

484 Raviglio Rosso, Giulio. *I svccessi d'Inghilterra dopo la morte di Odoardo Sesto fino alla givnta in qvel regno de sereniss. don Filippo d'Austria, principe di*

Spagna. Ferrara, 1560. By an Italian who came to England in 1554. Useful for Lady Jane Grey and Mary's accession.

485 Read, Conyers (ed.). *The Bardon papers: documents relating to the imprisonment and trial of Mary, Queen of Scots* (Camden Society, 3rd ser., XVII). 1909.

486 Rice, George P., Jr. (ed.). *The public speaking of Queen Elizabeth: selections from her official addresses*. New York, 1951. Handy but does not always reproduce the best versions.

487 Rogers, Elizabeth F. (ed.). *St Thomas More: selected letters* (The works of St Thomas More, modernized series, 1). New Haven, 1961.

488 —— *The correspondence of Sir Thomas More*. Princeton, 1947. The standard ed. and a model of editing.

489 Roper, William. *The lyfe of Sir Thomas More, knighte*, ed. Elsie V. Hitchcock (E.E.T.S., orig. ser., CXCVII), 1935. Written by More's son-in-law, this very fine little biography is a main source for all subsequent lives of More.

490 Schmidt, Albert J. (ed.). 'A treatise on England's perils, 1578', *Archiv für Reformationsgeschichte*, **46** (no. 2, 1955), 243–9. By Thomas Wilson, Elizabeth's principal secretary.

491 Sharp, Cuthbert (ed.). *Memorials of the rebellion of 1569*. 1840.

492 Sidney, Philip. *Defence of the earl of Leicester*, in Albert Feuillerat (ed.). *The complete works of Sir Philip Sidney*. Cambridge, 1923, III, 61–71. An answer to *Leycesters Commonwealth* (411).

493 *State papers of King Henry VIII*. 1830–52, 11 vols. Prints in full many of the documents summarized in (457).

494 Stow, John. *Annales, or, a generall chronicle of England*, ed. Edmond Howes. 1631.

495 Thomas, Arthur H. and Isobel D. Thornley (eds.). *The great chronicle of London*. 1938. Stops in 1512 and attributed to Robert Fabyan.

496 Tytler, Patrick F. (ed.). *England under the reigns of Edward VI and Mary*. 1839, 2 vols. A useful collection of documents.

497 Wright, Thomas (ed.). *Queen Elizabeth and her times*. 1838, 2 vols. A good collection of correspondence.

498 Wriothesley, Charles. *A chronicle of England during the reigns of the Tudors*, ed. William D. Hamilton (Camden Society, new ser., XI, XX). 1875–7. Covers 1485–1559, but slight until 1533.

499 Yorke, Philip, 2nd earl of Hardwicke (ed.). *Miscellaneous state papers from 1501 to 1726 ... 1778*, 2 vols. Commonly cited as 'Hardwicke State Papers'. Useful for Elizabeth's reign.

2 Surveys

500 Brewer, John S. *The reign of Henry VIII from his accession to the death of Wolsey*, ed. James Gairdner. 1884, 2 vols. A very full account tending to overestimate Wolsey.

501 Busch, Wilhelm. *England under the Tudors*, I, *Henry VII*, trans. Alice M. Todd. 1895. Still the best detailed survey of the reign, but dated on its institutional and financial aspects.

502 Chauviré, Roger. *Le temps d'Elisabeth*. Paris, 1960. Interesting as a presentation of a French viewpoint.

503 Cheyney, Edward P. *History of England from the defeat of the Armada to the death of Elizabeth*. 1914–26, 2 vols. Meant to continue Froude (76). Lacks Froude's literary merit, but is the best detailed survey of 1588–1603. Particularly good on political institutions.

504 Chrimes, Stanley B. *Lancastrians, Yorkists, and Henry VII*, 1964. Brief but excellent on Henry VII, taking into account recent scholarship.

505 Godwin, Francis. *Annales of England, containing the reigns of Henry the Eighth, Edward the Sixt, and Queene Mary*, trans. and ed. Morgan Godwyn. 1630. A rather puritan account by a bishop.

506 Neale, John E. *The Elizabethan age*. 1951. A brief and suggestive attempt to explain what made the age a great one, by the greatest living authority.

507   Nobbs, Douglas. *England and Scotland, 1560–1707.* 1952. An interesting survey of politico-religious developments in England and Scotland.

508   Pollard, Albert F. *England under the Protector Somerset.* 1900. Overly sympathetic to Somerset, but still the best work on the first part of Edward VI's reign.

3 Monographs

509   Adlard, George. *Amye Robsart and the earl of Leycester . . .* 1870.

510   Bekker, Ernst. *Elizabeth und Leicester: Beiträge zur Geschichte Englands in den Jahren 1560 bis 1562* (Giessener Studien aus dem Gebiet der Geschichte, v). Giessen, 1890. Cf. (679).

511   Bindoff, Stanley T. *Ket's rebellion* (Historical Association Pamphlets, general series, no. 12). 1949. Brief and sound. For a fuller account see (529).

512   Chastelain, J. D. *L'imposture de Perkin Warbeck.* Brussels, 1955.

513   Crabitès, Pierre. *Clement VII and Henry VIII.* 1936. A Catholic defence of Clement based mainly on secondary sources.

514   Dodds, Madeleine H. and Ruth. *The pilgrimage of grace, 1536–37, and the Exeter conspiracy, 1538.* Cambridge, 1915, 2 vols. A detailed and standard account.

515   Ferrière-Percy, Hector de la. *Les projets de mariage de la reine Elizabeth.* Paris, 1882. As good as anything on Elizabeth's French courtships.

516   Froude, James A. *The divorce of Catherine of Aragon.* 1897. A justification of Henry VIII. Extremely hostile to Anne Boleyn.

517   Hayward, John. *Annals of the first four years of the reign of Queen Elizabeth,* ed. John Bruce (Camden Society, old ser., VII). 1840. A glorification of the young Elizabeth written in 1612.

518   Hicks, Leo. *An Elizabethan problem: some aspects of the careers of two exile-adventurers.* New York, 1964. Thomas Morgan and Charles Paget, close associates of Mary Stuart, who were really agents of Elizabeth's councillors.

519   Hume, Martin A. S. *Treason and plot. Struggles for Catholic supremacy in the last years of Queen Elizabeth.* 1901.

520   Le Grand, Joachim. *Histoire du divorce de Henry VIII.* Paris, 1688, 3 vols. An answer to Burnet (1687).

521   Levine, Mortimer. *The early Elizabethan succession question, 1558–1568.* Stanford, 1966. The only detailed study. Treats the politics, law, and ideas involved.

522   Loades, David M. *Two Tudor conspiracies.* Cambridge, 1965. A study of opposition to the Marian régime centring on Wyatt's rebellion of 1554 and the Dudley conspiracy of 1556.

523   Lowers, James K. *Mirror for rebels: a study of polemical literature relating to the northern rebellion, 1569.* Berkeley, 1953.

524   Naunton, Robert. *Fragmenta regalia: or observations on the late Queen Elizabeth, her times and favourites,* ed. Edward Arber. 1895. Written about 1630, this contains some interesting information and recollections.

525   Neale, John E. *Elizabeth I and her parliaments.* 1953–57, 2 vols. A narrative history of Elizabeth's parliaments. Very important for constitutional and religious history as well as political. See (208).

526   Ogle, Arthur. *The tragedy of the Lollards' tower.* Oxford, 1949. An important study that deals convincingly with the murder of Richard Hunne and the effect of his case on the Commons.

527   Rose-Troup, Frances. *The western rebellion of 1549.* 1913. A scholarly account of the insurrections in Devonshire and Cornwall against the Edwardian Reformation.

528   Rowse, A[lfred] L[eslie]. *Bosworth field: from medieval to Tudor England.* New York, 1966. Unconvincing as an attempt to restore Bosworth as a great turning-point.

529   Russell, Frederick W. *Kett's rebellion in Norfolk.* 1859. An old standard. Also see (511).

530 Rutton, William L. *Three branches of the family of Wentworth.* 1891. Contains useful information on Paul and Peter Wentworth.

531 Smith, Alan G. C. G. *The Babington plot.* 1936. A revision of Pollen (481) back to the older Catholic view. Accuses Walsingham of adding an incriminating sentence to Mary's letter to Babington.

532 Stafford, Helen G. *James VI of Scotland and the throne of England.* New York, 1940. A detailed study of the late Elizabethan succession question. Should be supplemented with (694).

533 Tressler, Victor G. A. *Die politische Entwickelung Sir Robert Cecils bis zum Tode Burleighs.* Leipzig, 1901.

534 Van Dyke, Paul. *Renascence portraits.* New York, 1905. Contains a fair portrait of Thomas Cromwell and in the appendix an article, 'Reginald Pole and Thomas Cromwell: an examination of the Apologia ad Carolum Quintum', in which Pole's portrait of Cromwell is properly rejected.

535 Zeeveld, W. Gordon. *Foundations of Tudor policy.* 1948. A study of the propagandist writings which defended the actions of Henry VIII and Cromwell. An important contribution though it may overestimate the writers involved.

4 Biographies

536 Abbot, Edwin A. *Bacon and Essex: a sketch of Bacon's earlier life,* 1877. Hostile to Bacon in the matter of Essex.

537 Bacon, Francis. *History of the reign of King Henry VII,* ed. J. Rawson Lumby. Cambridge, 1902. Bacon used his sources carelessly in this work which has greatly influenced modern accounts of Henry VII. See Busch (501), pp. 417–23.

538 Beckingsale, B. W. *Elizabeth I.* 1963. A sound biography and perhaps the cautious beginning of a break from the now traditional Neale interpretation (601).

539 Belloc, Hilaire. *Elizabeth, creature of circumstance.* New York, 1942. A prejudiced and sometimes perverse Catholic account.

540 Bertie, Georgina. *Five generations of a loyal house.* 1845. Only deals with the lives of Richard and Peregrine Bertie. Richard married the puritan Catherine of Suffolk and Peregrine commanded Elizabeth's forces in the Low Countries and France.

541 Boas, Frederick S. *Sir Philip Sidney.* 1955.

542 Bourne, H. R. Fox. *Memoir of Sir Philip Sidney.* 1862. An old standard but see (629).

543 Bowle, John. *Henry VIII.* 1964. Contains errors and is rather weak in interpretation.

544 Bowen, Catherine D. *Francis Bacon: the temper of a man.* Boston, 1963. Very good on Bacon's career during Elizabeth's reign.

545 —— *The lion and the throne: the life and times of Sir Edward Coke, 1552–1634.* 1957. Satisfactory on Coke's personal and political life; disappointing on the legal side.

546 Bridgett, Thomas E. *Life and writings of Thomas More.* 1891. A competent Catholic life.

547 Brooks, Eric St J. *Sir Christopher Hatton: Queen Elizabeth's favourite.* 1946.

548 Brown, M. C. *Mary Tudor, queen of France.* 1911.

549 Cardinal, Edwin V. *Cardinal Lorenzo Campeggio, legate to the courts of Henry VIII and Charles V.* Boston, 1935.

550 Casady, Edwin. *Henry Howard, earl of Surrey.* New York, 1938.

551 Cecil, Algernon. *A life of Robert Cecil, first earl of Salisbury.* 1915. The only full life, but unsatisfactory. See (693).

552 Chamberlin, Frederick. *The private character of Queen Elizabeth.* 1921. Largely Elizabeth's medical history, on which (588) is better.

553 Chambers, Raymond W. *Thomas More.* 1935. Easily the best life. Sympathetic to More.

554 Chapman, Hester W. *Lady Jane Grey.* Boston, 1962. Semi-scholarly but the best available biography.

555 Chapman, Hester W. *The last Tudor king: a study of Edward VI.* 1958. Non-professional but better and more objective than (590).

556 —— *Two Tudor portraits: Henry Howard, earl of Surrey, and Lady Katherine Grey.* 1960.

557 Chastenet, Jacques. *Elisabeth I.* Paris, 1953.

558 Creighton, Mandell. *Cardinal Wolsey.* 1898. Favourable to Wolsey.

559 —— *Queen Elizabeth.* 1899. Well worth reading as an antidote to later encomia.

560 Davey, Richard P. B. *The nine days' queen, Lady Jane Grey and her times.* 1909. See (554).

561 —— *The sisters of Lady Jane Grey, and their wicked grandfather.* 1911. Overly prejudiced against Charles Brandon, duke of Suffolk.

562 Devereux, Walter B. *Lives and letters of the Devereux, earls of Essex . . . , 1540–1646.* 1853, 2 vols. The letters are more valuable than the lives, particularly those of Robert, earl of Essex.

563 Dewar, Mary. *Sir Thomas Smith: a Tudor intellectual in office.* 1964. Deals mainly with Smith's political career. A future vol. on Smith as a writer is promised.

564 Edwards, Edward. *The life of Sir Walter Ralegh . . . together with his letters.* 1868, 2 vols. The life is obsolete but the letters are useful.

565 Elton, Geoffrey R. *Henry VIII: an essay in revision* (Historical Association Pamphlets, general series, no. 51). 1962. Froude's hero and Pollard's great king deflated.

566 Emmison, Frederick G. *Tudor secretary: Sir William Petre at court and home.* 1961. Excellent on Petre's home life. Though enlightening on the general scene, somewhat disappointing on the role of this rather ordinary official in political affairs.

567 Fatta, Conrado. *Il regno di Enrico VIII d'Inghilterra.* Florence, 1938, 2 vols. An impartial and sound account.

568 Ferguson, Charles H. *Naked to mine enemies: the life of Cardinal Wolsey.* Boston, 1958. Of uneven quality. The interpretation is mainly Pollard's (605).

569 Fiddes, Richard. *The life of Cardinal Wolsey.* 1726. Still useful for its appendix of documents.

570 Friedmann, Paul. *Anne Boleyn, a chapter of English history, 1527–1536.* 1884, 2 vols. Still the fullest and best life, though dated on some matters.

571 Gairdner, James. *Henry the Seventh.* 1889. Long the standard biography. A new life is in order.

572 —— *History of the life and reign of Richard the Third,* revised ed. Cambridge, 1898. The appendix contains an account of the adventures of Perkin Warbeck.

573 Garvin, Katherine (ed.). *The great Tudors.* 1935. A collection of short sketches by an unusual assortment of authors.

574 Gordon, M. A. *Life of Queen Katherine Parr.* Kendal, England, 1952.

575 Green, Mary A. E. *The lives of the princesses of England,* vol. v. 1854. Contains still useful biographies of Margaret and Mary Tudor, sisters of Henry VIII.

576 Handover, Phyllis M. *Arbella Stuart: royal lady of Hardwick and cousin to King James.* 1957. A good semi-popular life.

577 —— *The second Cecil: the rise to power, 1563–1604, of Sir Robert Cecil.* 1959. Insufficient. Robert Cecil awaits his biographer.

578 Harrison, George B. *The life and death of Robert Devereux, earl of Essex.* 1937.

579 Hayward, John. *The life and raigne of King Edward the Sixt . . .* 1636. Of some interest as an early life; otherwise of little value.

580 Herbert of Cherbury, Edward, Lord. *The life and raigne of King Henry the Eighth.* 1672. Mainly of interest as the first biography.

581 Hurstfield, Joel. *Elizabeth I and the unity of England.* 1960. A neat little political biography showing English unity as Elizabeth's governing ideal.

582 Innes, Arthur D. *Ten Tudor statesmen.* 1906. Particularly interesting for the sketch of Cromwell, which anticipates recent estimates of the man.

583 Jenkins, Elizabeth. *Elizabeth and Leicester: a biography*. New York, 1962.
584 —— *Elizabeth the Great*. New York, 1959. The main contribution of this much-acclaimed work is proof that Elizabeth was not bald.
585 Kendall, Paul M. *Richard the Third*. New York, 1955. In an appendix on the murder of the princes absolves Henry VII and inadvertently leaves Richard as the most likely murderer. On Kendall's charge of illegitimacy against Elizabeth of York, cf. (325).
586 Lindsay, Philip. *The queenmaker: a portrait of John Dudley . . . , duke of Northumberland*. 1951. Most unsatisfactory. Northumberland awaits a biography. For a sketch of his rise which is much sounder, see (644).
587 Maclean, John. *Life of Thomas Seymour*. 1869. Adequate for the lord admiral.
588 MacNalty, Arthur S. *Elizabeth Tudor: the lonely queen*. 1954. Good on Elizabeth's medical history.
589 —— *Henry VIII: a difficult patient*. 1953. Interesting on Henry's medical history.
590 Markham, Clements R. *King Edward VI, an appreciation*. 1907. See (555).
591 —— *Richard III: his life and character*. 1906. Elaborates on earlier accusation that Henry VII killed the princes (710). Cf. (675), (743), and (585).
592 Mattingly, Garrett. *Catherine of Aragon*. Boston, 1941. An outstanding biography. May overestimate Catherine's strength in England.
593 Maynard, Theodore. *Bloody Mary*. Milwaukee, Wis. 1955. This, (594), (595), (596), and (597) are popular Catholic biographies varying somewhat in degree of bias.
594 —— *Henry the Eighth*. Milwaukee, Wis., 1949.
595 —— *Humanist as hero: the life of Sir Thomas More*. New York, 1947.
596 —— *Queen Elizabeth*. Milwaukee, Wis., 1940.
597 —— *The Crown and the cross: a biography of Thomas Cromwell*. New York, 1950. Practically ignores Cromwell's career outside matters religious and is very prejudiced there. For a sane account see Dickens (1850).
598 Merriman, Roger B. *The life and letters of Thomas Cromwell*. Oxford, 1902, 2 vols. The letters are useful but the life is obsolete. A full and up-to-date biography is needed.
599 More, Cresacre. *The life of Thomas More*, ed. Joseph Hunter. 1828. By More's great-grandson. Based on Roper (489), Harpsfield (444), and Stapleton (620), with the author's embellishments.
600 Muller, James A. *Stephen Gardiner and the Tudor reaction*. 1926. Valuable but inclined to excuse Gardiner's inconsistency amd ambition.
601 Neale, John E. *Queen Elizabeth*. 1934. The standard life. Rather eulogistic.
602 Nicolas, N[icholas] H[arris]. *Life of William Davison, secretary of state and privy councillor to Queen Elizabeth*. 1823. Useful for letters and documents.
603 —— *Memoirs and literary remains of Lady Jane Grey*. 1832. Useful for letters and documents.
604 Pollard, Albert F. *Henry VIII*. 1905; 1966. Still the best life, though it tends to overestimate Henry. A Harper Torchbooks ed. of 1966 contains an introduction by Arthur G. Dickens appraising the work in light of recent research.
605 —— *Wolsey*. 1929; 1965. A great biography and still the best work on its subject. For an important estimate of Pollard and his *Wolsey* see Geoffrey R. Elton's introduction to the Fortuna Library ed. of 1965.
606 Prescott, Hilda F. M. *A Spanish Tudor: the life of 'Bloody Mary'*. New York, 1940. The best biography. Sound and readable.
607 Read, Conyers. *Mr Secretary Cecil and Queen Elizabeth*. 1955; *Lord Burghley and Queen Elizabeth*. 1960. Really a two-vol. study. Very detailed and particularly strong on diplomacy. Sees Cecil's relationship with Elizabeth as a partnership.
608 Reynolds, Ernest E. *Saint Thomas More*. 1953.
609 —— *Thomas More and Erasmus*. 1965. A study of their relationship.
610 Richardson, Aubrey. *The lover of Queen Elizabeth, being the life and character of Robert Dudley, earl of Leicester . . .* 1907. Unsatisfactory. There is no scholarly biography.
611 Ro. Ba. *The lyfe of Syr Thomas More . . .* , ed. Elsie V. Hitchcock and

Philip E. Hallett (E.E.T.S., orig. ser., CCXXII). 1945. Essentially Harpsfield (444) with additions from Stapleton (620).

612 Round, John H. *The early life of Anne Boleyn.* 1886. Primarily a contentious attack on the scholarship of Brewer (500). Cf. Gairdner (677).

613 Routh, Enid M. G. *Lady Margaret, mother of Henry VII.* 1925. As good as anything on Lady Margaret Beaufort.

614 —— *Sir Thomas More and his friends, 1477–1535.* Oxford, 1934.

615 Rowse, A[lfred] L[eslie]. *Ralegh and the Throckmortons.* 1962. Published in the United States as *Sir Walter Ralegh: his family and private life.* Mainly a sometimes brilliant but too brief sketch of Ralegh as a politician and an account of Sir Arthur Throckmorton, an Elizabethan gentleman, that is useful for social history.

616 Sergeant, Philip W. *Anne Boleyn: a study.* 1934. Adds little to Friedmann (570).

617 Slavin, Arthur J. *Politics and profit: a study of Sir Ralph Sadler, 1507–47.* Cambridge, 1966. A study of an able and successful politician, civil servant, and diplomatist whose career extended to 1587.

618 Smith, Lacey B. *A Tudor tragedy: the life and times of Catherine Howard.* 1961. Necessarily brief on Catherine, but interesting on Henry VIII.

619 Smith, Logan P. *The life and letters of Sir Henry Wotton.* Oxford, 1907, 2 vols. The letters are more useful than the life.

620 Stapleton, Thomas. *The life and illustrious martyrdom of Sir Thomas More,* trans. Philip E. Hallett. 1928. First published at Douai in 1588. Based on Roper (489), on More's English works, on recollections of Catholic exiles fifty years after More's execution, and on 'letters' which have since disappeared. Strongly biased.

621 Stone, Jean M. *The history of Mary I, queen of England.* 1901. Scholarly but marred by a strong Catholic bias.

622 Strachey, Lytton. *Elizabeth and Essex.* 1928. Interesting but must be used with caution.

623 Strickland, Agnes. *Lives of the Tudor and Stuart princesses,* revised ed. 1888. Dated but still necessary in several cases.

624 Strype, John. *The life of the learned Sir John Cheke . . .* Oxford, 1821. Still the only life.

625 Strype, John. *The life of the learned Sir Thomas Smith . . .* Oxford, 1820. Corrected by Dewar (563).

626 Temperley, Gladys. *Henry VII.* 1918. As good as Gairdner (571).

627 Thomson, Patricia. *Sir Thomas Wyatt and his background.* Stanford, 1964. Contains a sane and likely assessment of Wyatt's relationship with Anne Boleyn.

628 Tucker, Melvin J. *The life of Thomas Howard, earl of Surrey and second duke of Norfolk, 1443–1524.* The Hague, 1964.

629 Wallace, Malcolm W. *Sir P. Sidney.* Cambridge, 1915. The best life from a historical standpoint.

630 Wallace, Willard M. *Sir Walter Raleigh.* Princeton, 1959. As good as any of the many lives.

631 White, Beatrice M. I. *Mary Tudor.* 1935. Second to Prescott (606).

632 Williams, E. Carleton. *Bess of Hardwick.* 1959.

633 Williams, Neville. *Thomas Howard, fourth duke of Norfolk.* 1964. Sound political history.

634 Wilson, Mona. *Sir Philip Sidney.* New York, 1932.

635 Woodhouse, Reginald I. *The life of John Morton, archbishop of Canterbury.* 1895. A new biography is needed.

636 Wyatt, George. *The life of the virtuous, Christian, and renowned Queen Anne Boleigne,* in George Cavendish. *The life of Cardinal Wolsey,* ed. Samuel W. Singer. 1827. An Elizabethan eulogy of Anne, answering Sander (1665).

5 Articles

637 Aird, Ian. 'The death of Amy Robsart', *EHR*, **71** (Jan. 1956), 69–79. Concludes cancer of the breast is the real explanation.

638 Anglo, Sydney. 'The *British History* in early Tudor propaganda', *BJRL*, **44** (Sept. 1961), 17–48.

639 Antheunis, Louis. 'La succession au trône d'Elisabeth Ière d'Angleterre et les catholiques', *Rev. d'hist. ecc.*, **49** (no. 1, 1954), 157–67.

640 Ashe, Geoffrey. 'An Elizabethan adventurer: the career of Sir Anthony Standen', *Month*, new ser., **8** (Aug.–Oct. 1952), 81–92, 218–29. See also (873).

641 Barrington, Michael. 'Queen Mary (Tudor)', *NQ*, **195** (Jan. 1950), 4–7. Indicates Mary was not, as is often claimed, merciful.

642 —— '"The Mercury of peace, the Mars of war": Robert Devereux, second earl of Essex', *Essex Review*, **59** (Oct. 1950), 165–81; **60** (Jan.–Oct. 1951), 7–11, 76–80, 116–23, 169–78; **61** (Jan. 1952), 1–10.

643 Batho, G. R. 'The execution of Mary, Queen of Scots', *SHR*, **39** (Apr. 1960), 35–42. Argues from a letter of Elizabeth that she was split with her council over Mary's execution and that her anger at its taking place was genuine.

644 Beer, Barrett L. 'The rise of John Dudley, duke of Northumberland', *History Today*, **15** (Apr. 1965), 269–77.

645 Behrens, Betty. 'A Note on Henry VIII's divorce project of 1514', *BIHR*, **11** (Feb. 1934), 163–4. Corroborating evidence for the existence of such a project.

646 Bindoff, Stanley T. 'A kingdom at stake, 1553,' *History Today*, **3** (Sept. 1953), 642–8. A brief account of Northumberland's attempt to change the succession.

647 Booth, Kevin. 'The problem of the breach with Rome, 1529–34', *Month*, new ser., **10** (Aug. 1953), 85–93. A discussion of modern works on the subject. Partial to Hughes (1695).

648 Breen, Quirinus. 'Celcio Calcagnini (1479–1541)', *Church History*, **21** (Sept. 1952), 225–38. Of some relevance to the question of Henry VIII's divorce.

649 Brett, S. Read. 'Queen Elizabeth's legacy to the Stuarts', *Quarterly Review*, **292** (Apr. 1954), 202–14.

650 Brodie, Dorothy M. 'Edmund Dudley: minister of Henry VII', *TRHS*, 4th ser., **15** (1932), 133–61.

651 Brown, J. Mainwaring. 'Henry VIII's book, "Assertio septem sacramentorum", and the royal title of "Defender of the Faith"', *TRHS*, 1st ser., **8** (1880), 242–61.

652 Busch, Wilhelm. 'Der Sturz des Cardinals Wolsey im Scheidungshandel König Heinrichs VIII von England', *Historisches Taschenbuch*, 6th ser., **9** (1890), 39–114.

653 —— 'Der Ursprung der Ehescheidung König Heinrichs VIII von England', *Historisches Taschenbuch*, 6th ser., **8** (1889), 271–327.

653a Bush, M. L. 'The Lisle–Seymour land disputes: a study of power and influence in the 1530s', *Hist. J.*, **9** (no. 3, 1966), 255–74. Sheds light on the workings of Henrician politics and reveals the future Protector Somerset as a rather different man than Pollard's noble character (508).

654 Chambers, D. S. 'Cardinal Wolsey and the papal tiara', *BIHR*, **38** (May 1965), 20–30. Shows that Wolsey's aspirations to become pope were not as great as assumed by Pollard (605).

655 Cheney, A. Denton. 'The holy maid of Kent', *TRHS*, 2nd ser., **18** (1904), 107–30.

656 Constant, Gustave. 'Clément VII et le divorce d'Henri VIII (1527–1533)', in *Mélanges Albert Dufourcq*. Paris, 1932, pp. 145–62.

657 Cooper, J. P. 'Henry VII's last years reconsidered', *Hist. J.*, **2** (no. 2, 1959), 103–29. Rejects Elton's view (670) that Henry's reputation for rapacity was undeserved.

658 Cross, M. Claire. 'The third earl of Huntingdon and Elizabethan Leicestershire', *Transactions of the Leicestershire Archaeological and Historical Society*, **36** (1960), 6–21. Good on the puritan earl as a local magnate.

659   Cussans, John E. 'Notes on the Perkin Warbeck insurrection', *TRHS*, 1st ser., **1** (1875), 61–77. Isn't sure Warbeck was an impostor.

660   Davis, Elizabeth J. 'The authorities for the case of Richard Hunne', *EHR*, **30** (July 1915), 477–88.

661   Derrett, J. Duncan M. 'Henry Fitzroy and Henry VIII's "Scruple of conscience"', *Renaissance News*, **16** (Spring 1963), 1–9. Henry's consideration of making his bastard son his heir prior to his falling in love with Anne Boleyn.

662   Dickens, Arthur G. 'Sedition and conspiracy in Yorkshire during the later years of Henry VIII', *Yorks. Arch. J.*, **34** (pt. 4, 1939), 379–98. Shows unrest rather than quiet in Yorkshire after the collapse of the pilgrimage of grace.

663   —— 'Some popular reactions to the Edwardian reformation in Yorkshire', *Yorks. Arch. J.*, **34** (pt. 2, 1939), 151–69. Especially valuable for the Yorkshire rising of 1549.

664   Dimmock, Arthur. 'The conspiracy of Dr Lopez', *EHR*, **9** (July 1894), 440–72. Argues that Lopez was guilty. Cf. (692).

665   Dodd, Arthur H. 'North Wales in the Essex revolt of 1601', *EHR*, **59** (Sept. 1944), 348–70. An important and interesting study of local factions.

666   Ehses, Stefan. 'Die päpstliche Dekretale in dem Scheidungsprozesse Heinrichs VIII', *Historisches Jahrbuch*, **9** (1888), 28–48, 209–50, 609–49. This and (667) give the results of researches documented in (432).

667   —— 'Papst Klemens VII in dem Scheidungsprozesse Heinrichs VIII', *Historisches Jahrbuch*, **13** (1892), 470–88.

668   Elton, Geoffrey R. 'A High Road to Civil War?', in *Ren. to C.-Ref.*, pp. 325–47. Shows that the Tudor constitution did not die with Elizabeth and that late Elizabethan developments did not make the Civil War inevitable.

669   —— 'Henry VII: a restatement', *Hist. J.*, **4** (no. 1, 1961), 1–29. A reply to (657), defending the position taken in (670).

670   —— 'Henry VII: Rapacity and remorse', *Hist. J.*, **1** (No. 1, 1958), 21–39. Rejects the traditional view that Henry's last years were characterized by rapacity and illegality.

671   —— 'King or minister? The man behind the Henrician reformation', *History*, new ser., **39** (Oct. 1954), 216–32. Assigns to Cromwell the chief responsibility for the ideas and policies which underlay the break with Rome.

672   —— 'Thomas Cromwell', *History Today*, **6** (Aug. 1956), 528–35. A brief and interesting summary of Cromwell's life and work.

673   —— 'Thomas Cromwell's decline and fall', *Camb. Hist. J.*, **10** (no. 2, 1951), 150–85. Presents a fair picture of a controversial figure.

674   Feret, Pierre. 'Le premier divorce de Henri VIII', *Revue des questions historiques*, **64** (1898), 53–89.

675   Gairdner, James. 'Did Henry VII murder the princes?', *EHR*, **6** (July 1891), 444–64. Says no in reply to (710).

676   —— 'Henry VIII', in *CMH*, **11**, 416–73.

677   —— 'Mary and Anne Boleyn', *EHR*, **8** (Jan.–Apr. 1893), 53–60, 299–300. Argues against Round (612) that Mary was the elder sister.

678   —— 'New lights on the divorce of Henry VIII', *EHR*, **11** (Oct. 1896), 673–702; **12** (Jan.–Apr. 1897), 1–16, 237–53. The 'new lights' come from Ehses (432).

679   —— 'The death of Amy Robsart', *EHR*, **1** (Apr. 1885), 235–59; **13** (Jan. 1897), 83–90. Maintains her death was accidental.

680   —— 'The early Tudors', in *CMH*, **1**, 643–92.

681   —— 'The fall of Cardinal Wolsey', *TRHS*, 2nd ser., **13** (1899), 75–102.

682   Gairdner, James and Isaac S. Leadam. 'A supposed conspiracy against Henry VII', *TRHS*, 2nd ser., **18** (1904), 157–94. Critique of Leadam (699) by Gairdner and reply by Leadam.

683   Gammon, Samuel R., III. 'Mary Tudor's tragedy of conscience', *Emory University Quarterly*, **9** (Mar. 1953), 39–47.

684   Gumbley, Walter. '"Cecil over England: Philip over Spain"', *Blackfriars*, **19** (Mar. 1938), 186–93. A Roman Catholic view of Burghley's policy.

685   Hall, Hubert. 'The imperial policy of Elizabeth, from the state papers,

foreign and domestic', *TRHS*, 2nd ser., **3** (1886), 205–41. Critical of Elizabeth's foreign and domestic policies.

686 Hay, Denys. 'The "Narratio historica" of P. Vincentius, 1553', *EHR*, **63** (July 1948), 350–6.

687 Hicks, Leo. 'Father Robert Persons, S. J. and the book of succession', *Rec. Hist.*, **4** (Oct. 1957), 104–37. Concludes that Parsons was not the sole author of Doleman's *Conference* (2185), that he was not irrevocably committed to the idea of the Infanta succeeding Elizabeth, and that he had no intention of making England subject to Spain.

688 —— 'Sir Robert Cecil, Father Parsons, and the succession, 1600–1', *Archivum Historicum Societatis Iesu*, **24** (July–Dec. 1955), 95–139.

689 —— 'The growth of a myth: Father Robert Parsons, S.J. and Leicester's Commonwealth', *Studies*, **46** (Spring 1957), 91–105. Considers Sir Charles Arundell the probable author.

690 Hughes, Philip. 'A hierarchy that fought, 1554–9', *Clergy Review*, **18** (Jan. 1940), 25–39.

691 —— 'The pilgrimage of grace: 1536–1936', *Clergy Review*, **12** (Oct. 1936), 261–79.

692 Hume, Martin A. S. 'The so-called conspiracy of Dr Ruy Lopez', *Transactions of the Jewish Historical Society of England*, **6** (1908–10), 32–55. Presents a good case for the innocence of Lopez. Cf. (664).

693 Hurstfield, Joel. 'Robert Cecil, earl of Salisbury: minister of Elizabeth and James I', *History Today*, **7** (May 1957), 279–89. A brief but fine survey.

694 —— 'The succession struggle in late Elizabethan England', in *Govt. & Soc.*, pp. 369–96. An excellent discussion. Emphasizes Robert Cecil's role in smoothing the way for James I's accession.

695 Jackson, John E. 'Wulfhall and the Seymours', *Wiltshire Archaeological and Natural History Magazine*, **15** (1875), 140–207. Contains material on Protector Somerset and on the clandestine marriage of his son with Lady Catherine Grey.

696 Jenkins, Gladys. 'Ways and means in Elizabethan propaganda', *History*, new ser., **26** (Sept. 1941), 105–14. Discusses use of proclamations, speeches in parliament and star chamber, sermons, pamphlets, and plays.

697 Kocher, Paul H. 'Francis Bacon and his father', *HLQ*, **21** (Feb. 1958), 133–58.

698 Lander, J. R. 'Attainder and forfeiture, 1453 to 1509', *Hist. J.*, **4** (no. 2, 1961), 119–51. A judicious examination of the problem. Shows Henry VII to have been more severe than Edward IV in these matters.

699 Leadam, Isaac S. 'An unknown conspiracy against Henry VII', *TRHS*, 2nd ser., **16** (1902), 133–51. Cf. (682).

700 Lee, Sidney. 'The last years of Elizabeth', in *CMH*, III, 328–63.

701 Levine, Mortimer. 'The last will and testament of Henry VIII: a reappraisal appraised', *Historian*, **26** (Aug. 1964), 471–85. A critique of (738).

702 Loades, David M. 'The enforcement of reaction, 1553–1558', *JEH*, **16** (Apr. 1965), 54–66. A good study of Marian policy.

703 —— 'The press under the early Tudors: a study in censorship and sedition', *Transactions of the Cambridge Bibliographical Society*, **4** (pt. 1, 1964), 29–50.

704 MacCaffrey, Wallace T. 'Elizabethan politics: the first decade, 1558–1568', *PP*, no. 24 (Apr. 1963), 25–42. A good discussion of a confusing and critical decade.

705 —— 'England: The crown and the new aristocracy, 1540–1600', *PP*, no. 30 (Apr. 1965), 52–64. Sees the period as one in which the 'new aristocracy' advanced its political power at the expense of the crown. A convincing presentation with important ideas and implications.

706 —— 'Place and patronage in Elizabethan politics', in *Govt. & Soc.*, pp. 95–126.

707 —— 'Talbot and Stanhope: an episode in Elizabethan politics', *BIHR*, **33** (May 1960), 73–85. An interesting account of a feud in the early 1590s.

708 McManaway, James. 'Elizabeth, Essex, and James', in Herbert Davis and Helen Gardner (eds.). *Elizabethan and Jacobean studies presented to Percy Francis Wilson*. Oxford, 1959, pp. 219–30.

709 Manning, Roger B. 'Catholics and local office holding in Elizabethan Sussex', *BIHR*, **35** (May 1962), 47–61. Finds that many Catholics continued to hold office throughout Elizabeth's reign.

710 Markham, Clements R. 'Richard III: a doubtful verdict reviewed', *EHR*, **6** (Apr. 1891), 250–83. Claims Henry VII murdered the princes in 1486. Cf. (675).

711 Mattingly, Garrett. 'William Allen and Catholic propaganda in England', in *Aspects de la propagande religieuse*. Geneva, 1957, pp. 325–39.

712 Mullinger, James B. 'Philip and Mary', in *CMH*, II, 512–49.

713 Myers, A. R. 'The character of Richard III', *History Today*, **4** (Aug. 1954), 511–21. An understanding portrait of Richard which contains an apologia for Henry VII.

714 Neale, John E. 'Sir Nicholas Throckmorton's advice to Queen Elizabeth on her accession to the throne', *EHR*, **65** (Jan. 1950), 91–8.

715 —— 'The Elizabethan political scene,' *PBA*, **34** (1948), 97–117. A brilliant essay on the nature of Elizabethan politics.

716 Oman, Charles W. C. 'The personality of Henry the Eighth', *Quarterly Review*, **269** (July 1937), 88–144.

717 Parker, Thomas M. 'Was Thomas Cromwell a Machiavellian?', *JEH*, **1** (Jan.–Apr. 1950), 61–75. Maintains he was. Cf. Elton (2305). But agrees with Elton (671) that Cromwell was the directing genius in the Henrician Reformation.

718 Pike, Clement E. 'The intrigue to deprive the earl of Essex of the lord lieutenancy of Ireland', *TRHS*, 3rd ser. **5** (1911), 89–104.

719 Pineas, Rainer. 'Robert Barnes's polemical use of history', *Bibliothèque d'Humanisme et Renaissance*, **26** (no. 1, 1964), 55–69.

720 Pollen, John H. 'The accession of James I', *Month*, **101** (June 1903), 572–85.

721 —— 'The politics of English Catholics during the reign of Queen Elizabeth', *Month*, **99** (Jan.–June 1902), 43–60, 131–48, 290–305, 394–411, 600–18; **100** (July–Aug. 1902), 71–87, 176–88.

722 —— 'The question of Elizabeth's successor', *Month*, **101** (May 1903), 517–32. Useful but assumes the validity of Mary Stuart's claim without question.

723 Read, Conyers. 'Good Queen Bess', *AHR*, **31** (July 1926), 647–61.

724 —— 'William Cecil and Elizabethan public relations', in *Govt. & Soc.*, pp. 21–55.

725 Reid, Rachel R. 'The political influence of the "north parts" under the later Tudors', in *Tud. Stud.*, pp. 208–30.

726 —— 'The rebellion of the earls, 1569', *TRHS*, 2nd ser., **20** (1906), 171–203.

727 Rowse, A[lfred] L[eslie]. 'Eminent Henrician: Thomas Wriothesley, first earl of Southampton', *History Today*, **15** (June–July 1965), 382–90, 468–74. A sketch of a mainly successful but second-rate political career. Also see (729).

728 —— 'Sir Nicholas Throckmorton', *History Today*, **12** (Jan.–Feb. 1962), 3–12, 125–31.

729 —— 'Thomas Wriothesley, first earl of Southampton', *HLQ*, **28** (Feb. 1965), 105–29.

730 Rutton, William L. 'Lady Katharine Grey and Edward Seymour, earl of Hertford', *EHR*, **13** (Apr. 1898), 302–7. Corrects old errors.

731 Scarisbrick, J. J. 'Henry VIII and the Vatican library', *Bibliothèque d'Humanisme et Renaissance*, **24** (1962), 211–16. Attempts of Henry VIII to obtain evidence for his divorce in the Vatican library and of Clement VII to obtain ancient texts in England. Introduces new evidence on Henry's claim of an imperial title.

732 —— 'The pardon of the clergy, 1531', *Camb. Hist. J.*, **12** (no. 1, 1956), 22–39. A careful consideration of an important episode that others have read too much into.

733 Schmidt, Albert J. 'Thomas Wilson, Tudor scholar-statesman', *HLQ*, **20** (May 1957), 205–18.

734 Skeel, Caroline A. J. 'Wales under Henry VII', in *Tud. Stud.*, pp. 1–25.

735 Slavin, Arthur J. 'Sir Ralph Sadler and Master John Hales at the Hanaper: a sixteenth-century struggle for property and profit', *BIHR*, **38** (May 1965), 31–47. An interesting illustration of Tudor patronage.

736 Smith, Alan G. B. 'Portrait of an Elizabethan: the career and character of Sir Michael Hicks', *History Today*, **14** (Oct. 1964), 716–25. A sketch of a servant and ally of the Cecils.

737 Smith, Edward O., Jr. 'The Elizabethan doctrine of the prince as reflected in the sermons of the episcopacy, 1559–1603', *HLQ*, **28** (Nov. 1964), 1–18.

738 Smith, Lacey B. 'The last will and testament of Henry VIII: a question of perspective', *JBS*, **2** (Nov. 1962), 14–27. A rejection of the traditional view that Henry drew up his will with the idea of ruling from the grave. Cf. (701).

739 Smith, Preserved. 'German opinion and the divorce of Henry VIII', *EHR*, **27** (Oct. 1912), 671–81.

740 —— 'Luther and Henry VIII', *EHR*, **26** (Oct. 1910), 656–69. Relations during the periods of the *Assertio* and the divorce.

741 Stevenson, Joseph. 'Perkin Warbeck', *Month*, **75** (Aug. 1892), 508–19.

742 Strong, Roy C. 'The popular celebration of the accession day of Queen Elizabeth I', *Journal of the Warburg and Courtauld Institutes*, **21** (1958), 86–103.

743 Tanner, Lawrence E. and William Wright. 'Recent investigations regarding the fate of the princes in the tower', *Arch.*, **84** (1934), 1–26. Clearly points to an acquittal for Henry VII.

744 Thompson, W. D. J. Cargill. 'The sixteenth-century editions of *A supplication unto King Henry the Eighth* by Robert Barnes, D.D.: a footnote to the history of the royal supremacy', *Transactions of the Cambridge Bibliographical Society*, **3** (no. 2, 1960), 133–42.

745 Thurston, Herbert. 'The canon law of divorce', *EHR*, **19** (Oct. 1904), 632–45. Henry VIII's negotiations with Clement VII for a divorce.

746 Vallance, Aymer. 'Hollingbourne Manor and the Culpepers', *Archaeologia Cantiana*, **49** (1938), 189–94. Refers to Thomas Culpeper and Queen Catherine Howard.

747 Ward, B. M. 'Queen Elizabeth and William Davison', *EHR*, **44** (Jan. 1929), 104–6.

748 Wernham, Richard B. 'The disgrace of William Davison', *EHR*, **46** (Oct. 1931), 632–6.

749 Wiatt, William H. 'The lost history of Wyatt's rebellion', *Renaissance News*, **15** (Summer 1962), 128–33. On a contemporary account by John Mychell which was the source of much in other such accounts.

750 Williams, Charles H. 'In search of the queen', in *Govt. & Soc.*, pp. 1–22. Discusses changing attitudes of historians towards Elizabeth.

751 —— 'The rebellion of Humphrey Stafford in 1486', *EHR*, **43** (Apr. 1928), 181–90.

752 Williams, Neville. 'The duke in his country: Thomas Howard, 4th duke of Norfolk, 1536–1572', *History Today*, **14** (Jan. 1964), 14–24. The role of a great magnate in local politics.

753 Williams, Penry. 'The Welsh borderland under Queen Elizabeth', *Welsh Historical Review*, **1** (no. 1, 1960), 19–36. Discusses the limitations of Tudor success in establishing law and order in Wales and the extent to which Welsh society was assimilated to English by 1603.

754 Wolf, Lucien. 'The Jews in Elizabethan England', *Transactions of the Jewish Historical Society of England*, **11** (1924–27), 1–91. Deals mainly with the political and diplomatic activities of the English Marranos, esp. Hector Nuñez and Alvaro Mendez.

VI FOREIGN RELATIONS

1 Printed sources

755 Albèri, Eugenio (ed.). *Relazione degli ambasciatori Veneti al senato durante il secolo decimo sesto*. Florence, 1839–63, 15 vols. The first six vols. deal mainly with English affairs.

756 Birch, Thomas (ed.). *An historical view of the negotiations between the courts*

of England, France, and Brussels from the year 1592 to 1617. 1749. Mainly extracts from the state papers of Sir Thomas Edmondes and Anthony Bacon.

757 Blok, Pieter J. (ed.). *Correspondance inédite de Robert Dudley, comte de Leycester, et de François et Jean Hotman.* Haarlem, 1911. Leicester's intrigues with Dutch factions.

758 Bourrilly, V. L. and Pierre de Vaissière (eds.). *Ambassades en Angleterre de Jean du Bellay.* Paris, 1905. September 1527–February 1529.

759 Bruce, John (ed.). *Correspondence of Robert Dudley, earl of Leycester, during his government of the Low Countries, in the years 1585 and 1586* (Camden Society, old ser., XXVII). 1844.

760 —— *Letters of Queen Elizabeth and King James VI of Scotland* (Camden Society, old ser., XLVI). 1849. 1582–1603.

761 Brugmans, Hajo (ed.). *Correspondentie van Robert Dudley, graaf van Leycester, en andere documenten betreffende zijn gouvernement-generaal in de Nederlanden, 1585–1588.* Utrecht, 1931, 3 vols.

762 Butler, Geoffrey G. (ed.). *The Edmondes Papers,* 1913. Mainly Anglo-French relations, 1592–99.

763 *Calendar of state papers, foreign,* ed. William B. Turnbull *et al.* 1863–1950, 23 vols. The accession of Edward VI to July 1589. Continued in (789).

764 *Calendar of state papers, Milan,* ed. Allen B. Hinds. 1912.

765 *Calendar of state papers relating to Ireland,* ed. Hans C. Hamilton and Robert P. Mahaffy. 1860–1912, 11 vols. Henry VIII through Elizabeth.

766 *Calendar of state papers relating to Scotland and Mary Queen of Scots, 1457–1603,* ed. Joseph Bain *et al.* Edinburgh and Glasgow, 1898–. Vol. XII, published in 1952, stops in 1597.

767 *Calendar of state papers, Rome,* ed. James M. Rigg. 1916–26, 2 vols.

768 *Calendar of state papers, Spanish,* ed. Gustav A. Bergenroth *et al.* 1862–1954, 15 vols. in 20. 1485–1558.

769 *Calendar of state papers, Spanish, Elizabeth,* ed. Martin A. S. Hume. 1892–9, 4 vols. Incomplete. Must be supplemented by (785) and (794).

770 *Calendar of state papers, Venetian,* ed. Rawdon Brown, G. Cavendish Bentinck, and Horatio F. Brown, vols. I–IX. 1864–98. Useful for the earlier Tudor period; somewhat slight for Elizabeth's reign.

771 Cameron, Annie I. (ed.). *Warrender papers* (Scottish History Society, 3rd ser., XVIII–XIX). Edinburgh, 1931–2. 1527–1603. Useful for Anglo-Scottish relations.

772 Castelnau, Michel de. *Memoirs of the reigns of Francis II and Charles IX of France,* 1724. Covers 1559–70 of French history and of some value for Anglo-French relations.

773 Clifford, Arthur (ed.). *The state papers and letters of Sir Ralph Sadler.* Edinburgh, 1809, 2 vols. Important for Anglo-Scottish relations, 1539–47, and for Mary Stuart in England.

774 Clifford, Henry. *The life of Jane Dormer, duchess of Feria,* ed. Joseph Stevenson. 1887. The life of the wife of the Spanish ambassador in England under Mary and at Elizabeth's accession by her servant. Of use for domestic as well as foreign affairs.

775 Collins, Arthur (ed.). *Letters and memorials of state, in the reigns of Queen Mary, Queen Elizabeth . . .* 1746, 2 vols. Commonly referred to as the Sidney papers, their chief value is for Anglo-Irish and Anglo-Dutch relations.

776 Crump, Lucy (trans.). *A Huguenot family in the sixteenth century: the memoirs of Philippe de Mornay, Sieur du Plessis Marly, written by his wife.* 1926. A full translation to 1590. Of use for Anglo-French relations.

777 Digges, Dudley (ed.). *The compleat ambassador.* 1655. Correspondence of Francis Walsingham during his embassies in France, 1570–3 and 1581.

778 Doutrepont, Georges and Omer Jodogne (eds.). *Chroniques de Jean Molinet.* Brussels, 1935–7, 3 vols. Important for Anglo-French relations, 1474–1506.

779 Ferrière-Percy, Hector de la (ed.). *Lettres de Catherine de Médicis.* Paris, 1880–1909, 10 vols. Useful for Anglo-French relations, 1558–88.

780 *Foedera . . . ,* ed. Thomas Rymer and Robert Sanderson. 1727–35, 20 vols. Primarily a collection of treaties and other diplomatic documents.

781 Forbes, Patrick (ed.). *A full view of the public transactions in the reign of Q. Elizabeth.* 1740–1, 2 vols. Mainly Anglo-French relations, 1558–63.

782 Gachard, Louis P., and Joseph Lefevre (eds.). *La correspondance de Philippe II sur les affaires des Pays-Bas.* 1st pt., Brussels, 1848–79, 5 vols.; 2nd pt., Brussels, 1940–56, 3 vols. This important collection is now complete to 1591.

783 Giustinian, Sebastian. *Four years at the court of Henry VIII ..., January 12th 1515, to July 26th 1519,* trans. Rawdon Brown. 1854, 2 vols. The dispatches of a Venetian ambassador.

784 Kaulek, Jean (ed.). *Correspondance politique de MM. de Castillon et de Marillac, ambassadeurs de France en Angleterre.* Paris, 1885. Covers 1537–42.

785 Kervyn de Lettenhove, Joseph M. B. C., Baron and L. Gilliodts van Severen (eds.). *Relations politiques des Pays-Bas et de l'Angleterre sous le règne de Philippe II.* Brussels, 1882–1900, 11 vols. The main source for English relations with the Low Countries, 1555–79.

786 Klarwill, Victor von (ed.). *Queen Elizabeth and some foreigners,* trans. Thomas H. Nash. 1928. Mainly correspondence relative to the projected marriage between Elizabeth and Archduke Charles.

787 Labanoff, Alexandre (ed.). *Lettres, instructions, et mémoires de Marie Stuart.* Paris, 1844, 7 vols. Does not include all letters. For additional ones see (799).

788 Lefèvre-Pontalis, Germain (ed.). *Correspondance politique de Odet de Selve, ambassadeur de France en Angleterre.* Paris, 1888. 1546–9.

789 *List and analysis of state papers foreign series, Elizabeth I,* 1, *August 1589–June 1590,* ed. Richard B. Wernham. 1964. The first vol. of a series designed to continue the *Calendar* (763). A list of MSS and then a consolidated summary of their contents. Actually works better than the traditional system thanks to Wernham's masterly editing.

790 *List of despatches of ambassadors from France to England, 1509–1714,* ed. Armand Baschet, in *Reports of the deputy keeper of the public records,* **39,** 1878, app. 1, 573–826.

791 Loomie, Albert J. (ed.). 'Richard Stanyhurst in Spain: two unknown letters of August 1593', *HLQ,* **28** (Feb. 1965), 145–55. Two letters of an Anglo-Irish Catholic convert.

792 Maclean, John (ed.). *Letters from Sir Robert Cecil to Sir George Carew* (Camden Society, old ser., LXXXVIII), 1864. Letters concerning Ireland, January 1600 to February 1603.

793 Murray, James A. H. (ed.). *The Complaynt of Scotlande* (E.E.T.S., extra ser., XVII–XVIII), 1872–3. The *Complaynt* and the appended English tracts are very important for Anglo-Scottish relations, 1542–9.

794 Navarrete, Fernández de et al. (eds.). *Colección de documentos inéditos para la historia de España.* Madrid, 1842–95, 112 vols. Particularly vols. LXXXVII, LXXXIX, XC, XCI, and XCII.

795 Pollen, John H. (ed.). *A letter from Mary Queen of Scots to the duke of Guise, Jan. 1562* (Scottish History Society, XLIII). Edinburgh, 1904. Contains documents of importance for Anglo-Scottish relations.

796 Stevenson, Joseph (ed.). *The correspondence of Robert Bowes of Aske, Esq., ambassador of Queen Elizabeth to the court of Scotland* (Surtees Society, XIV). 1842. July 1577–September 1583.

797 Talbot, C. H. (ed.). *Elisabetha I Angliae regnante conscriptae ex archivis publicis Londiniarum* (Elementa ad Fontium Editiones, IV). Rome and Oxford, 1961. 170 papers from the state papers, foreign series, Poland.

798 Teulet, Alexandre (ed.). *Correspondance diplomatique de B. Salaignac de la Mothe Fénelon.* Paris and London, 1838–40, 7 vols. The best source for Anglo-French relations, 1568–75.

799 —— *Lettres de Marie Stuart.* Paris, 1859. Supplements Labanoff (787).

800 —— *Relations politiques de la France et de l'Espagne avec l'Écosse au XVIᵉ siècle.* Paris, 1862, 5 vols. Particularly useful for Anglo-French relations.

801 *The Hamilton papers: letters and papers illustrating the political relations of England and Scotland in the sixteenth century,* ed. Joseph Bain. Edinburgh, 1890–2, 2 vols.

802 Vertot d'Aubeuf, René A. and Claude Villaret (eds.). *Ambassades de messieurs de Noailles en Angleterre.* Leyden, 1763, 5 vols. 1553–7 and 1559.
803 Weiss, Charles (ed.). *Papiers d'état du cardinal de Granvelle.* Paris, 1841–52, 9 vols. 1500–65.
804 Winwood, Ralph. *Memorials of affairs of state in the reigns of Queen Elizabeth and King James I,* ed. Edmund Sawyer, vol. I. 1725. 1597–1603. Of use for Anglo-French relations.

2 Surveys

805 Mattingly, Garrett. *Renaissance diplomacy.* 1955. This, Mattingly's best and least-read book, is the only satisfactory account of the forms and techniques of Renaissance diplomacy. It contains much of value on England's foreign relations, esp. with Spain.
806 Seeley, John R. *The growth of British policy,* I. Cambridge, 1913. The first 250 pp. of this famous work deal with Elizabeth's reign. Dated but still worth reading.
807 Wernham, Richard B. *Before the Armada: the growth of English foreign policy, 1485–1588.* 1966. Fills a long need for an adequate survey.
808 Zeller, Gaston. *Histoire des relations internationales,* II, *Les temps modernes: de Christophe Colomb à Cromwell.* Paris, 1953. The best general survey of the period.

3 Monographs

809 Armstrong Davison, Meredith H. *The casket letters.* Washington, 1965. Acquits Mary Stuart.
810 Bayne, Charles G. *Anglo-Roman relations, 1558–1565* (Oxford Historical and Literary Studies, II). Oxford, 1913. Discussion plus a useful appendix of documents.
811 Black, John B. *Elizabeth and Henry IV.* Oxford, 1914.
812 Blok, Pieter J. *History of the Netherlands,* trans. and abridged, O. A. Bierstadt and Ruth Putnam. New York, 1898–1912, 5 vols.
813 Busch, Wilhelm. *Cardinal Wolsey und die kaiserlich-englische Allianz, 1522–1525.* Bonn, 1886.
814 —— *Drei Jahre englischer Vermittlungspolitik, 1518–1521.* Bonn, 1884.
815 Conway, Agnes. *Henry VII's relations with Scotland and Ireland, 1485–98.* Cambridge, 1932.
816 Dupuy, Antoine. *Histoire de la réunion de la Bretagne à la France.* Paris, 1880, 2 vols. Good for early relations of Henry VII with France.
817 Fernández Alvarez, Manuel. *Tres embajadores de Felipe II en Inglaterra.* Madrid, 1951. Claims Philip could have gained control over Elizabeth if he had followed the advice of his ambassadors in England, 1558–68. A doubtful thesis derived from taking the reports of the ambassadors at face value.
818 Ferrière-Percy, Hector de la. *Le XVI⁰ siècle et les Valois, d'après documents inédits du British Museum et du Record Office.* Paris, 1879. Anglo-French relations, mainly 1558–74.
819 Gairdner, James and James Spedding. *Studies in English history.* Edinburgh, 1881. Contains an article by Spedding on the negotiations with Spain concerning Catherine of Aragon's first marriage and one by Gairdner on her second marriage.
820 Geyl, Pieter. *The revolt of the Netherlands,* 2nd ed. 1958.
821 Hamy, Alfred. *Entrevue de François I⁰ʳ avec Henry VIII à Boulogne-sur-mer en 1532.* Paris, 1898.
822 Harbison, E. Harris. *Rival ambassadors at the court of Queen Mary.* Princeton, 1940. The activities of the French and Imperial ambassadors. Of use for domestic politics as well as foreign affairs.
823 Heidrich, Paul. *Der geldrische Erbfolgestreit.* Kassel, 1896. The negotiations for Henry VIII's marriage with Anne of Cleves.
824 Henderson, Thomas F. *The casket letters and Mary Queen of Scots.* 2nd ed.,

Edinburgh, 1890. The best case for the genuineness of the casket letters. On the voluminous literature of this subject see Read (24), pp. 444–6.

825 Hosack, John. *Mary Queen of Scots and her accusers*. Edinburgh, 1870–4, 2 vols. The best case for the forgery of the casket letters.

826 Hume, Martin A. S. *Two English queens, Mary and Elizabeth, and Philip*. 1908.

827 Kervyn de Lettenhove, Joseph M. B. C., Baron. *Les Huguenots et les Gueux*. Bruges, 1883–5, 6 vols. Good for Elizabeth's relations with the Huguenots and the Dutch.

828 Kretzschmar, Johannes. *Die Invasionsprojekte der katholischen Mächte gegen England zur Zeit Elisabeths*. Leipzig, 1892. Based on the Vatican archives.

829 Laffleur de Kermaingant, Pierre P. *L'ambassade de France en Angleterre, sous Henri IV, 1598–1605*. Paris, 1886–95, 4 vols.

830 Lang, Andrew. *The mystery of Mary Stuart*. 1912. In this ed. Lang revises his previous views on the casket letters and accepts those of Henderson (824).

831 Loomie, Albert J. *The Spanish Elizabethans: the English exiles at the court of Philip II*. New York, 1963. A valuable but sometimes partisan study by a Jesuit of the English Catholic exiles in Spain and their lack of influence on Spanish policy.

832 Mahon, Reginald H. *Mary Queen of Scots: a study of the Lennox narrative in the university library at Cambridge*. Cambridge, 1924. A pro-Marian re-examination of the casket letters.

833 Mattingly, Garrett. *The defeat of the Spanish Armada*. 1959. Published in the United States as *The Armada*. Fine as this work is for the great encounter, it is more important for the diplomacy of the Anglo-Spanish war and the picture it gives of its European setting.

834 Merriman, Roger B. *The rise of the Spanish empire*. 1918–34, 4 vols. Contains much on Anglo-Spanish relations to 1598.

835 Meyer, Arnold O. *Die englische Diplomatie in Deutschland zur Zeit Eduards VI und Mariens*. Breslau, 1900.

836 Mignet, François A. M. *La rivalité de François I et de Charles Quint*. Paris, 1875, 2 vols. Of particular use for continental diplomacy during the period of Henry VIII's divorce.

837 Motley, John L. *History of the United Netherlands from the death of William the Silent to the synod of Dort*. 1860–7, 4 vols. This and (838) are very full on Anglo-Dutch relations. Motley's strong bias against Philip II must be taken into account. Should be supplemented with Geyl (820).

838 —— *The rise of the Dutch republic*. 1855, 3 vols.

839 Philippson, Martin. *Westeuropa im Zeitalter von Philip II, Elizabeth, und Heinrich IV*. Berlin, 1882.

840 Prueser, F. *England und die Schmalkaldener, 1535–40*. Leipzig, 1929. Henry VIII's negotiations with the German Protestant princes.

841 Rait, Robert S. and Annie I. Cameron. *King James's secret*. 1927. An interesting account of James's attitude towards the trial and execution of his mother, with documents.

842 Ruble, J. E. Alphonse, Baron de. *Le traité de Cateau-Cambrésis*. Paris, 1889.

843 Strong, Roy C. and J. A. Van Dorsten. *Leicester's triumph*. Leyden, 1964. Leicester's attempt to create an Anglo-Dutch state, 1585–6. Excellent on his progresses as attempts to propagate and popularize his régime.

844 Thompson, James W. *The wars of religion in France, 1559–76*. Chicago, 1909. Good for Anglo-French affairs.

845 Törne, Per O. von. *Don Juan d'Autriche et les projets de conquête de l'Angleterre*. Helsingfors, 1915–28, 2 vols.

4 Biographies

846 Armstrong, Edward. *The Emperor Charles V*. 1902–13, 2 vols. Contains much of use for English foreign affairs, Henry VIII through Mary's accession.

847 Chambers, D. S. *Cardinal Bainbridge in the court of Rome, 1509 to 1514*. New York, 1965. Henry VIII's loyal resident ambassador in Rome.

848 Fleming, David H. *Mary Queen of Scots from her birth to her flight into*

England. 1898. The detailed notes and references, which are longer than the text, are very useful.

849 Henderson, Thomas F. *Mary Queen of Scots*. 1905, 2 vols. Considered the best biography, but (848) is more useful for the period it covers.

850 Jensen, De Lamar. *Diplomacy and dogmatism: Bernardino de Mendoza and the French Catholic League*. Cambridge, Mass., 1964. Primarily the story of the diplomacy in France of an aggressive Spaniard which had important consequences for England.

851 Miller, Amos C. *Sir Henry Killigrew: Elizabethan soldier and diplomat*. Leicester, 1963. Mainly concerned with Killigrew's diplomatic activities.

852 Philippson, Martin. *Histoire du règne de Marie Stuart*. Paris, 1891–2, 3 vols. Still of use for its documentation.

853 Read, Conyers. *Mr Secretary Walsingham and the policy of Queen Elizabeth*. Oxford, 1925. 3 vols. The best study of Elizabethan foreign policy. Less appreciative of Elizabeth than (607). Also good for the office of secretary. In an appendix to vol. I prints Robert Beale, *A treatise of the office of a councellor and principall secretarie*, 1592.

854 Richardson, Walter C. *Stephen Vaughan, financial agent of Henry VIII: a study of financial relations with the Low Countries*. Baton Rouge, 1953.

855 Stählin, Karl. *Sir Francis Walsingham und seine Zeit*, I. Heidelberg, 1908. Useful for Anglo-French relations. 1570–3.

856 Tex, Jan den. *Oldenbarnevelt: Opgang, 1547–1588*. Haarlem, 1960. Of interest for Anglo-Dutch relations in the decade before 1588.

857 Wegg, Jervis. *Richard Pace: a Tudor diplomatist*. 1932.

5 Articles

858 Atkinson, Ernest G. 'The cardinal of Châtillon in England, 1568–71', *Hug. Soc. Proc.*, 3 (1888–91), 172–285.

859 Behrens, Betty. 'Origihs of the office of English resident ambassador in Rome', *EHR*, 49 (Oct. 1934), 640–56.

860 —— 'The office of the English resident ambassador: its evolution as illustrated by the career of Sir Thomas Spinelly, 1509–22', *TRHS*, 4th ser., 16 (1933), 161–95.

861 Black, John B. 'Queen Elizabeth, the sea beggars, and the capture of Brille, 1572', *EHR*, 46 (Jan. 1931), 30–47.

862 Bossy, John A. 'English Catholics and the French marriage, 1577–81', *Rec. Hist.*, 5 (Jan. 1959), 2–16.

863 Bourrilly, V. L. 'François Ier et Henry VIII, l'intervention de la France dans l'affaire du divorce à propos de travaux récents', *Revue d'histoire moderne et contemporaine*, 1 (1899), 271–84.

864 Cheyney, Edward P. 'England and Denmark in the later days of Queen Elizabeth', *JMH*, 1 (Mar. 1929), 9–39.

865 —— 'International law under Queen Elizabeth', *EHR*, 20 (Oct. 1905), 659–72.

866 Donaldson, Gordon. 'Foundations of Anglo-Scottish union', in *Govt. & Soc.*, pp. 282–314. Discusses the development of religious and cultural links between England and Scotland in the sixteenth century and maintains they paved the way for the later Union. Interesting, though the case may be overstated.

867 Elton, Geoffrey R. 'Anglo-French relations in 1522: a Scottish prisoner of war and his interrogation', *EHR*, 78 (Apr. 1963), 510–16.

868 Ferrière-Percy, Hector de la. 'La paix de Troyes avec l'Angleterre, 1563–4', *Revue des questions historiques*, 33 (1883), 36–75.

869 Grey, Ian. 'Ivan the Terrible and Elizabeth of England', *History Today*, 12 (Sept. 1962), 648–55. Ivan's attempts to achieve closer relations with England.

870 Hale, John R. 'International relations in the west: diplomacy and war', in *NCMH*, I, 259–91. A sound introduction to c. 1520.

871 Harbison, E. Harris. 'French intrigue at the court of Queen Mary', *AHR*, 45 (Apr. 1940), 533–51.

872 Harrison, Eric. 'Henry VIII's gangster: the affair of Ludovico da L'Armi', *JMH*, **15** (Dec. 1943), 265–74.

873 Hicks, Leo. 'The embassy of Sir Anthony Standen in 1603, part 1', *Rec. Hist.*, **5** (Oct. 1959), 91–127. Standen's career before the accession of James I.

874 Hume, Martin A. S. 'The visit of Philip II', *EHR*, **7** (Apr. 1892), 253–80.

875 Jensen, De Lamar. 'Franco-Spanish diplomacy and the Armada', in *Ren. to C.-Ref.*, pp. 205–29. An illuminating discussion of the success of Spanish diplomacy, 1586–8.

876 Kirchner, Walther. 'England and Denmark, 1558–1588', *JMH*, **17** (Mar. 1945), 1–15.

877 Lee, Maurice, Jr. 'The fall of the Regent Morton: a problem in satellite diplomacy', *JMH*, **28** (June 1956), 111–29. Explains Elizabeth's failure to intervene effectively in Morton's behalf in terms of the diplomatic situation on the Continent.

878 Levy, F. J. 'A semi-professional diplomat: Guido Cavalcanti and the marriage negotiations of 1571', *BIHR*, **35** (Nov. 1962), 211–20.

879 Mackie, John D. 'Henry VIII and Scotland', *TRHS*, 4th ser., **29** (1947), 93–114.

880 Mattingly, Garrett. 'A humanist ambassador', *JMH*, **4** (June 1932), 175–85. On Eustace Chapuys, Imperial ambassador in England, 1529–45.

881 —— 'An early non-aggression pact', *JMH*, **10** (Mar. 1938), 1–30. The treaty of London of 1518.

882 —— 'The reputation of Doctor de Puebla', *EHR*, **55** (Jan. 1940), 27–46. A vindication of the first resident ambassador in England and the negotiator of Catherine of Aragon's first marriage.

883 Merriman, Roger B. 'The Spanish embassy in Tudor England', *Massachusetts Historical Society Proceedings*, **65** (1940), 392–400.

884 Neale, John E. 'Elizabeth and the Netherlands, 1586–7', *EHR*, **45** (July 1930), 373–96. Discusses the financing of Leicester's expedition. Cf. (900).

885 —— 'The fame of Sir Edward Stafford', *EHR*, **44** (Apr. 1929), 203–20. Critique of Read (890).

886 Pears, Edwin. 'The Spanish Armada and the Ottoman Porte', *EHR*, **8** (July 1893), 439–66. Elizabeth's attempts to secure Turkish support against Spain.

887 Prestage, Edgar. 'The Anglo-Portuguese alliance', *TRHS*, 4th ser., **17** (1934), 69–100. Includes a good general survey of Anglo-Portuguese relations during the Tudor period.

888 Quinn, David B. 'Henry VIII and Ireland, 1509–34', *Irish Historical Studies*, **12** (Sept. 1961), 318–44. Sees Henry VIII's Irish policies as groping.

889 Read, Conyers. 'Queen Elizabeth's seizure of the duke of Alva's pay-ships', *JMH*, **5** (Dec. 1933), 443–64.

890 —— 'The fame of Sir Edward Stafford', *AHR*, **20** (Jan. 1915), 292–313. Maintains that Elizabeth's ambassador to France, 1583–9, was a traitor. Cf. Neale (885).

891 —— 'The fame of Sir Edward Stafford', *AHR*, **35** (Apr. 1930), 560–6. Answers Neale (885).

892 Robinson, Agnes M. F. 'Queen Elizabeth and the Valois princes', *EHR*, **2** (Jan. 1887), 40–77. Anglo-French diplomacy, esp. marriage projects, c. 1567–83.

893 Rogers, David M. '"The Catholic moderator": a French reply to Bellarmine and its English author, Henry Constable', *Rec. Hist.*, **5** (Oct. 1960), 224–35. A book by an English Catholic used to support Henry of Navarre's claim to the French crown. On Constable see also John A. Bossy, 'A propos of Henry Constable', *Rec. Hist.*, **6** (Apr. 1962), 228–37, and George Wickes, 'Henry Constable, poet and courtier (1562–1613)', *Biographical Studies*, **2** (no. 4, 1954), 272–300.

894 Rogers, Elizabeth F. 'Sir John Hackett, Henry VIII's ambassador in Malines', *Medievalia et Humanistica*, **6** (Jan. 1950), 89–100. Ambassador in the Low Countries, 1526–34.

895 Roth, Cecil. 'England and the last Florentine republic, 1527–30', *EHR*, **40** (Apr. 1925), 174–95.

896 Strong, Roy C. 'Sir Henry Unton and his portrait: an Elizabethan memorial picture and its history', *Arch.*, **99** (1965), 53–76. Contains an account of Unton's diplomatic career.

897 Sutherland, N. M. 'Queen Elizabeth and the conspiracy of Amboise, March 1560', *EHR*, **81** (July 1966), 474–89. Shows there is no evidence proving Elizabeth was implicated.

898 Wernham, Richard B. 'English policy and the revolt of the Netherlands', in John S. Bromley and Ernst H. Kossmann (eds.). *Britain and the Netherlands*, I, 1960, pp. 29–40. Sees Elizabeth's policy towards the Netherlands revolt inspired as much by fear of France as by fear of Spain.

899 —— 'The mission of Thomas Wilkes to the United Provinces in 1590', in J. Conway Davies (ed.). *Studies Presented to Sir Hilary Jenkinson*. 1957, pp. 423–55.

900 Woude, A. M. van der. 'De Staten, Leicester en Elizabeth in financiële verwikkelingen', *Tijdschrift voor Geschiedenis*, **74** (no. 1, 1961), 64–82. Critique of Neale (884). Rejects his figures on English financial contributions and his criticisms of Leicester and the Dutch.

VII SOCIAL HISTORY

1 Printed sources

901 Allison, K. J. 'An Elizabethan village "census"', *BIHR*, **36** (May 1963), 91–103. A 'census' of Ealing in Middlesex. The earliest census yet found.

902 Batho, G. R. (ed.). *The household papers of Henry Percy, ninth earl of Northumberland (1564–1632)* (Camden Society, 3rd ser., XCIII), 1962.

903 Bell, James. 'A narrative of the journey of Cecilia, princess of Sweden to the court of Queen Elizabeth', ed. Margaret Morison, *TRHS*, 2nd ser., **12** (1898), 181–224.

904 Bülow, Gottfried von (ed.). 'Journey through England and Scotland made by Liupold von Wedel in the years 1584 and 1585', *TRHS*, 2nd ser., **9** (1895), 223–70.

905 Bülow, Gottfried von and Walter Powell (eds.). 'Diary of the journey of Philip Julius, duke of Stettin-Pomerania, through England in the year 1602', *TRHS*, 2nd ser., **6** (1892), 1–67.

906 Byrne, M[uriel] St C[lare] (ed.). *The English home discovered in 2 dialogues*. 1924. Dialogues by Huguenot refugees who taught French in Elizabethan London.

907 Dickens, Arthur G. (ed.). *Clifford letters of the sixteenth century* (Surtees Society, CLXXII). Durham, 1962. Letters, mainly of the reign of Henry VIII, which shed much light on the society of northern England.

908 Dyce, Alexander (ed.). *Kemps nine daies wonder: performed in a daunce from London to Norwich* (Camden Society, old ser., XI). 1840. An incident of Elizabeth's reign that reminds one of modern stunts.

909 Eland, G. (ed.). *Thomas Wotton's letter-book, 1574–1586*. 1960. Letters of a nonconformist country gentleman.

910 Frere, F. (ed.). *A proper newe booke of cookerye*. Cambridge, 1913. First published in 1558.

911 Furnivall, Frederick J. (ed.). *Child-marriages, divorces, and ratifications . . . in the diocese of Chester, A.D. 1561–6* (E.E.T.S., orig. ser., CVIII). 1897. Depositions from the bishop's court and entries from the mayors' book.

912 Harrison, William. *Elizabethan England*, ed. Frederick J. Furnivall. 1876. A handy edition of the famous *Description of England*, the best Elizabethan account of Elizabethan England. Also in (449).

913 Hazlitt, William C. (ed.). *Inedited tracts: illustrating the manners, opinions, and occupations of Englishmen during the sixteenth and seventeenth centuries*. 1868.

914 Holles, Gervase. *Memorials of the Holles family, 1493–1656*, ed. A. C. Wood (Camden Society, 3rd ser., LV). 1937. A good family chronicle dated 1658.

915 Judges, Arthur V. (ed.). *The Elizabethan underworld.* 1930. A collection of Tudor and early Stuart tracts and ballads on thieves, rogues, vagabonds, etc.

916 Kirk, Richard E. G. and Ernest F. (eds.). *Return of aliens dwelling in the city and suburbs of London from the reign of Henry VIII to that of James I* (Huguenot Society of London, vol. X in 4 pts.). Aberdeen, 1900–8, 4 vols.

917 Malfatti, C. V. (trans. and ed.). *Two Italian accounts of Tudor England: a journey to London in 1497; a picture of English life under Queen Mary.* Barcelona, 1953. For a Greek account of England at the end of Henry VIII's reign see (428).

918 Meads, Dorothy M. (ed.). *Diary of Lady Margaret Hoby, 1599–1605.* Boston, 1930.

919 Moryson, Fynes. *The itinerary of Fynes Moryson.* Glasgow, 1907–8, 4 vols. A late Elizabethan traveller in Britain and Europe.

920 Nichols, John (ed.). *The progresses and public processions of Queen Elizabeth.* 1823, 3 vols.

921 Nichols, John G. and John Bruce (eds.). *Wills from doctors' commons: a selection from the wills of eminent persons proved in the prerogative court of Canterbury, 1495–1695* (Camden Society, old ser., LXXXIII), 1863. Wills are of great value for social history. Many indexes and calendars of wills have been published in the Index Library Series. See Mullins (53), pp. 104–14.

922 Page, William (ed.). *Letters of denization and acts of naturalization for aliens in England, 1509–1603* (Huguenot Society of London, VIII). Lymington, 1893.

923 Peyton, S. A. (ed.). 'The houses of correction at Maidstone and Westminster', *EHR,* **43** (Apr. 1927), 251–61.

924 Powell, Edgar (ed.). *The travels and life of Sir Thomas Hoby . . . . written by himself, 1547–1564* (Camden Miscellany, X, 3rd ser., IV). 1902.

925 Read, Conyers (ed.). 'Lord Burghley's household accounts', *EcHR,* 2nd ser., **9** (Dec. 1956), 343–8.

926 Rye, William B. (ed.). *England as seen by foreigners in the days of Elizabeth and James I.* 1865. Extracts from accounts of foreign visitors to England.

927 Simon, André L. (ed.). *The star chamber dinner accounts.* 1959. The accounts give the food and the prices of the same for star chamber dinners. Simon adds an interesting commentary on Tudor foods and some Tudor recipes.

928 Smith, L[ucy] T[oulmin] (ed.). *The itinerary of John Leland in or about the years 1535–1543.* 1907–10, 5 vols. Leland's travels in England.

929 Smith, William. *The particular description of England,* ed. Henry V. Wheatley and Edmund W. Ashbee. 1879. Probably written *c.* 1588.

930 Smith, William J. (ed.). *Herbert correspondence: the sixteenth and seventeenth century letters of the Herberts of Chirbury, Powis Castle, and Dolgoug.* Cardiff and Dublin, 1963.

931 Sneyd, Charlotte A. (ed.). *A relation, or rather a true account, of the island of England . . . about the year 1500* (Camden Society, old ser., XXXVII). 1847. Apparently the account of a Venetian. Of great value.

932 Stapleton, Thomas (ed.). *Plumpton correspondence: a series of letters, chiefly domestick, written in the reigns of Edward IV, Richard III, Henry VII, and Henry VIII* (Camden Society, old ser., IV). 1839. Correspondence of a Yorkshire gentry family. Useful for the social conditions of that class prior to the dissolution of the monasteries.

933 Stow, John. *A survey of London,* ed. Charles L. Kingsford. Oxford, 1908, 2 vols. The best ed. of a famous and valuable Elizabethan survey.

934 Thomson, G[ladys] S[cott] (ed.). 'Roads in England and Wales in 1603', *EHR,* XXXIII (Apr. 1918), 234–43. A contemporary manuscript.

935 Williams, Clare (ed.). *Thomas Platter's travels in England, 1599.* 1937. A translation of a German account of England.

936 Wilson, Thomas. *The state of England anno Dom. 1600,* ed. F. J. Fisher (Camden Miscellany, XVI, 3rd ser., LII). 1936. By the nephew of Elizabeth's principal secretary of the same name. Contains much on political history, but is more useful as a reflection of the social and economic ideas of an educated member of the gentry.

937 Wright, Louis B. (ed.). *Advice to a son: precepts of Lord Burghley, Sir Walter Raleigh, and Francis Osborne.* Ithaca, N.Y., 1962.

2 Surveys

938 Dodd, Arthur H. *Life in Elizabethan England*. 1961. This and (943) comprise a sound social history of Tudor England.

939 Palmer, Roger L. *English social history in the making: the Tudor revolution*. 1934. Introductions and extracts from documents.

940 Quennell, Marjorie and Charles H. B. *A history of everyday things in England*, revised ed. by Peter Quennell, vol. I. 1957.

941 Salzman, Louis F. *England in Tudor times*. 1926.

942 Trevelyan, George M. *English social history*. New York and Toronto, 1942. Chapters 4–7 of this great classic cover the Tudor period. Though dated in some respects, it remains the best survey.

943 Williams, Penry. *Life in Tudor England*. 1964. See (938).

3 Monographs

944 Atkinson, Tom. *Elizabethan Winchester*. 1963.

945 Aydelotte, Frank. *Elizabethan rogues and vagabonds*. Oxford, 1913. The standard account.

946 Baldwin, Frances E. *Sumptuary legislation and personal regulation in England*. Baltimore, 1926.

947 Bean, J. M. W. *The estates of the Percy family, 1416–1537*. Oxford, 1958. A very detailed survey of an aristocratic family during a critical period.

948 Bouch, C. M. L. and Gwilym P. Jones. *A short economic and social history of the Lake Counties, 1500–1830*. Manchester, 1961. Discusses religion, government, and culture as well as society and economy.

949 Byrne, M[uriel] St C[lare]. *Elizabethan life in town and country*. 7th ed., 1954. Semi-popular but worth while.

950 Camden, Carroll. *The Elizabethan woman: a panorama of English womanhood, 1540–1640*. 1952. Very good for English domestic relations.

951 Campbell, Mildred. *The English yeoman under Elizabeth and the early Stuarts*. New Haven, 1942. A sound study of the social, economic, and cultural aspects of an important class.

952 Chew, Samuel C. *The crescent and the rose: Islam and England during the Renaissance*. New York, 1937. Deals mainly with travel.

953 Cunnington, C[ecil] W[illett] and Phillis. *Handbook of English costume in the sixteenth century*. Philadelphia, 1954.

954 Drummond, Jack C. and Anne Wilbraham. *The Englishman's food: a history of five centuries of English diet*. 1939.

955 Dunlop, Ian. *Palaces and progresses of Elizabeth I*. 1962. Also of some use for architectural history.

956 Dutton, Ralph. *English court life from Henry VII to George II*. 1963. Nearly half is on Tudor court life.

957 Emmison, Frederick G. *Tudor food and pastimes: life at Ingatestone Hall*. 1965. Several chapters from (566) in somewhat different form.

958 Fairholt, Frederick W. *Costume in England*, ed. Harold A. Dillon. 1896, 2 vols. Still a standard reference work.

959 Ferguson, Arthur B. *The Indian summer of English chivalry*. Durham, N.C., 1960. Discusses the survival of chivalrous ideas among the aristocracy in the mid-sixteenth century.

960 Finberg, H. P. R. *The Gostwicks of Willington and other studies* (Bedfordshire Historical Record Society, XXXVI). Aspley Guise, 1956. The history of a gentry family. Particularly interesting on John Gostwick, administrative assistant to Thomas Cromwell. The other studies are transcripts of Bedfordshire documents by other scholars.

961 Finch, Mary A. *The wealth of five Northamptonshire families, 1540–1640*. Oxford, 1956. A pioneer work testing theories on the wealth of the gentry.

962 Fussell, George E. and K. R. *The English countryman: his life and work, A.D. 1500–1900*. 1955.

963 —— *The English countrywoman: a farmhouse social history*, A.D. *1500–1900*. 1953.
964 Grimble, Ian. *The Harington family*. 1957.
965 Hall, Hubert. *Society in the Elizabethan age*. 1886.
966 Hill, James W. F. *Tudor and Stuart Lincoln*. Cambridge, 1956. A balanced and interesting study of a town.
967 Howard, Clare M. *English travellers of the Renaissance*. 1913. A good general account with a useful bibliography.
968 Jackman, William T. *The development of transportation in modern England*. Cambridge, 1916, 2 vols. Vol. I of this standard work includes the sixteenth century.
969 James, Percival. *The Baths of Bath in the sixteenth and early seventeenth centuries*. 1938.
970 Jones, Paul V. B. *The household of a Tudor nobleman* (University of Illinois Studies, VI). Urbana, Ill., 1917.
971 Jordan, Wilbur K. *Philanthropy in England, 1480–1660: a study of the changing pattern of English social aspirations*. New York, 1959. In this and the following works Jordan, on the basis of a prodigious study of wills, conclusively shows the importance of private charity in Reformation England. His claim of a great increase in charitable bequests, 1540–1660, is weakened, though not destroyed, by his failure to take sufficient account of the price rise.
972 —— *Social institutions in Kent, 1480–1660* (Archaeologia Cantiana, LXXV). Ashford, 1961.
973 —— *The charities of London, 1480–1660: the aspirations and the achievements of the urban society*. New York, 1960.
974 —— *The charities of rural England: the aspirations and the achievements of the rural society*. 1961.
975 —— *The forming of the charitable institutions of the west of England: a study of the changing pattern of social aspirations in Bristol and Somerset, 1480–1660* (Transactions of the American Philosophical Society, new ser., vol. L, pt. 8). Philadelphia, 1960.
976 —— *The social institutions of Lancashire, 1480–1660*. Manchester, 1962.
977 Kelso, Ruth. *Doctrine for a lady of the Renaissance*. Urbana, Ill. 1929.
978 —— *The doctrine of the English gentleman in the sixteenth century*. Urbana, Ill. 1929.
979 Laver, James. *Early Tudor, 1485–1558* (Costume of the Western World, vol. III, no. 1). 1951. Beautifully illustrated.
980 Lemonnier, Léon. *La vie quotidienne en Angleterre sous Elisabeth*. Paris, 1950. Deals with social life and custom.
981 Leonard, E. M. *The early history of English poor relief*. Cambridge, 1900. 1514–1644. A dated standard work that should be replaced.
982 Leys, Mary D. R. *Catholics in England, 1559–1829: a social history*. 1961.
983 Linthicum, M. Channing. *Costume in the drama of Shakespeare and his contemporaries*. Oxford, 1936. Detailed and valuable.
984 MacCaffrey, Wallace T. *Exeter, 1540–1650: the growth of an English country town*. Cambridge, Mass., 1958. An excellent account of an important town that has wider implications.
985 Moir, Esther. *The Discovery of Britain: the English tourists, 1540–1840*. 1964. Good on English domestic tourists, with a useful catalogue of manuscript sources.
986 Murray, L. H. *The ideal of the court lady, 1561–1625*. Chicago, 1938.
987 O'Conor, Morreys J. *Godes peace and the queenes: vicissitudes of a house, 1539–1615*. Cambridge, Mass., 1934. The legal and extralegal battles of gentry and noble families over the ownership of an Oxfordshire manor.
988 Onions, Charles T. (ed.). *Shakespeare's England: an account of the life and manners of his age*. Oxford, 1916, 2 vols.
989 Owen, G. Dyfnalt. *Elizabethan Wales: the social scene*. Cardiff, 1962.
990 Parks, George B. *The English traveller to Italy*, I, *the middle ages (to 1525)*. Stanford, 1954.
991 Pearson, Lu E. *Elizabethans at home*. Stanford, 1957. Contains much interesting information on the daily life of Elizabethans and a useful bibliography.

992 Penrose, Boies. *Urbane travellers, 1581–1635*. Philadelphia, 1942. On Fynes Moryson and other English travellers abroad.

993 Powell, Chilton L. *English domestic relations, 1487–1653*. New York, 1917. Useful on marriage, divorce, and family relationships, with a valuable bibliography.

994 Reynolds, Graham. *Elizabethan and Jacobean, 1558–1625* (Costume of the Western World, vol. III, no. 2). 1951. A good general discussion and fine illustrations.

995 Robson-Scott, William D. *German travellers in England, 1400–1800*. Oxford, 1953.

996 Rowse, A[lfred] L[eslie]. *The England of Elizabeth: the structure of society*. 1951. A brilliant, though sometimes prejudiced, study of all aspects of the age: society, government, religion, etc.

997 —— *Tudor Cornwall: portrait of a society*, 1941.

998 Simpson, Alan. *The wealth of the gentry, 1540–1660: East Anglian studies*. Chicago, 1961. Centres around three scholarly and interesting case studies. The thesis of stability among the gentry despite the price rise is debatable.

999 Steinbicker, Carl R. *Poor relief in the sixteenth century* (Studia Facultas Theologica, XLVIII). Washington, 1937. A Catholic attempt to show that Catholic countries did better than Protestant countries in dealing with the problem of poor relief in the sixteenth century.

1000 Stone, Lawrence (ed.). *Social change and revolution in England, 1540–1640*. 1965. Extracts of articles and documents, many dealing with the gentry controversy. Stone's introduction summarizes and appraises the debate.

1001 Stone, Lawrence. *The crisis of the aristocracy, 1558–1641*. Oxford, 1965. A massive study of the peerage. Sees it in trouble, particularly financial, and losing ground to the gentry. Whatever the fate of its interpretations, this book will always be of value for its splendid detail.

1002 Tawney, Richard H. *Social history and literature*. Cambridge, 1950. Mainly deals with the Elizabethan age in discussing the significance of literature for social history.

1003 Tenison, Eva M. *Elizabethan England*. Leamington, England, 1933–61, 14 vols. Good for illustrations.

1004 Thomson, G[ladys] S[cott]. *Two centuries of family history*. 1930. The Russell family, sixteenth and seventeenth century.

1005 Trevor-Roper, Hugh R. *The gentry, 1540–1640* (Economic History Review Supplements, no. 1). Cambridge, 1953. Trevor-Roper's main contribution to the gentry debate. Maintains a declining gentry and directly attacks Tawney (1067).

1006 Webb, Sidney and Beatrice. *English local government: English poor law history*, pt. 1, *The old poor law*. 1927. The first two chapters deal with the sixteenth century.

1007 White, Beatrice M. I. *Royal nonesuch: a Tudor tapestry*. 1933. Good on court life and on Mary Tudor and Charles Brandon.

1008 White, Helen C. *Social criticism in popular religious literature of the sixteenth century*. New York, 1944. Mainly interesting for quotations.

1009 Wilson, Violet A. *Queen Elizabeth's maids of honour and ladies of the privy chamber*. 1922. Popular but the only book on the subject.

1010 Winchester, Barbara. *Tudor family portrait*. 1955. An interesting portrait of a puritan merchant and his family.

1011 Woodward, W. Arthur. *The countryman's jewel: days in the life of a sixteenth century squire*, ed. Marcus Woodward. 1934. Largely extracts from *Maison rustique* by Charles Estienne (1504–64).

4 Biographies

1012 Bradford, Charles A. *Blanche Parry, Queen Elizabeth's gentlewoman*. 1935.

1013 —— *Helena, marchioness of Northampton*. 1936.

1014 Chambers, Edmund K. *Sir Henry Lee: an Elizabethan portrait*. Oxford, 1936. The portrait of a courtier.

1015 James. M. E. *Change and continuity in the Tudor north: the rise of Thomas, first Lord Wharton.* York, 1965. A brief and significant study of the rise of a great northern family in the first half of the sixteenth century.

1016 Rawson, Maud S. *Bess of Hardwick and her circle.* New York, 1910.

1017 —— *Penelope Rich and her circle.* 1911.

1018 Sargent, Ralph M. *At the court of Queen Elizabeth: the life and lyrics of Sir Edward Dyer.* Oxford, 1935.

5 Articles

1019 Anglo, Sydney. 'The court festivals of Henry VII: a study based upon the account books of John Heron, treasurer of the chamber', *BJRL*, **43** (Sept. 1960), 12–45.

1020 —— 'The London pageants for the reception of Katharine of Aragon: November 1501', *Journal of the Warburg and Courtauld Institutes*, **26** (1963), 53–89. A masterpiece of London pageantry.

1021 Batho, Gordon R. 'The finances of an Elizabethan nobleman: Henry Percy, ninth earl of Northumberland (1564–1631)', *EcHR*, 2nd ser., **9** (Apr. 1957), 433–50.

1022 Butler, K. T. 'Giacopo Castelvetro, 1546–1616', *Italian Studies*, **5** (1950), 1–42. An Italian who taught Italian language and customs to the English.

1023 Burrell, Sidney A. 'Calvinism, capitalism, and the middle classes: some afterthoughts on an old problem', *JMH*, **32** (Mar. 1960), 129–41. Questions the objectivity of the 'gentry' controversialists.

1024 Cooper, J. P. 'The counting of manors', *EcHR*, 2nd ser., **8** (no. 3, 1956), 377–89. A penetrating critique of Tawney's statistical data (1067) and his defence of it (1068).

1025 Cornwall, Julian. 'English country towns in the fifteen twenties', *EcHR*, 2nd ser., **15** (no. 1, 1962), 54–69. A study of towns of Buckinghamshire, Rutland, and Sussex.

1026 —— 'The early Tudor gentry', *EcHR*, 2nd ser., **17** (no. 3, 1965), 456–75. An analysis of the gentry, greater and lesser, of five counties during the 1520s. Makes sensible definitions of gentry.

1027 Cross, M. Claire. 'An exchange of lands with the crown, 1587–1588', *BIHR*, **34** (Nov. 1961), 178–83. The earl of Huntingdon's apparently futile attempt to get out of debt by exchanging lands with the queen.

1028 Darivas, Basile. 'Etude sur la crise économique de 1593–7 en Angleterre et la loi des pauvres', *Revue d'histoire économique et sociale*, **30** (no. 4, 1952), 382–98. The economic crisis of 1593–7 and the poor law of 1597.

1029 Davies, K. G. 'The mess of the middle class', *PP*, no. 22 (July 1962), 77–83. An interesting appraisal of Hexter's *Reappraisals*.

1030 Davis, Eliza J. 'The transformation of London', in *Tud. Stud.*, pp. 287–314.

1031 Dickens, Bruce. 'The Gueveras of Stenigot: Spanish squires in Tudor Lincolnshire', *Bulletin of Hispanic Studies*, **37** (Oct. 1960), 215–21.

1032 Dodd, Arthur H. 'Elizabethan towns and cities', *History Today*, **11** (Feb. 1961), 136–44.

1033 —— 'Mr Myddelton the merchant of Tower Street', in *Govt. & Soc.*, pp. 249–81. The story of a successful London merchant.

1034 Elton, Geoffrey R. 'An early Tudor poor law', *EcHR*, 2nd ser., **6** (Aug. 1953), 55–67. Indicates the extent of Henry VIII's 'war against poverty'.

1035 Emmison, Frederick G. '1555 and all that: a milestone in the history of the English road', *Essex Review*, **64** (Jan. 1955), 15–25. About an act which was to set the parish as the unit of road maintenance for nearly three centuries.

1036 —— 'Poor relief accounts of two rural parishes in Bedfordshire, 1563–1598', *EcHR*, **3** (Jan. 1931), 102–16.

1037 —— 'The care of the poor in Elizabethan Essex: recently discovered records', *Essex Review*, **62** (Jan. 1953), 7–28.

1038 —— 'The "very naughty ways" of Elizabethan Essex', *Essex Review*, **64** (Apr. 1955), 85–91. An interesting little study of Essex 'roads'.

1039   Emmison, Frederick G. 'Was the highways act of 1555 a success?', *Essex Review*, **64** (Oct. 1955), 221–34. On parish execution of the Tudor highways acts in Essex.

1040   Everitt, Alan. 'Social mobility in early modern England', *PP*, no. 33 (Apr. 1966), 56–73. See also (1061).

1041   Gay, Edwin F. 'The rise of an English country family: Peter and John Temple, to 1603', *HLQ*, **1** (July 1938), 376–90.

1042   Harris, George. 'Domestic everyday life, manners, and customs in this country . . . , pt. v—from the commencement of the sixteenth century to the commencement of the eighteenth century', *TRHS*, **9** (1881), 224–53.

1043   Hexter, Jack H. 'Storm over the Gentry', in *Reappraisals*, pp. 117–62. A brilliant critique of both sides in the controversy, but somewhat more favourable to Trevor-Roper than to Tawney.

1044   —— 'The myth of the middle class in Tudor England', in *Reappraisals*, pp. 71–116. A brilliant demolition of the 'rise of the middle class' explanation of English history, 1500–1800. But see (1029).

1045   Hooper, Wilfred. 'The Tudor sumptuary laws', *EHR*, **30** (July 1915), 433–49. Laws regarding 'abuses' in apparel and their enforcement.

1046   Hoskins, William G. 'An Elizabethan provincial town: Leicester', in J. H. Plumb (ed.), *Studies in social history*, 1955, pp. 33–67.

1047   —— 'English provincial towns in the early sixteenth century', *TRHS*, 5th ser., **6** (1956), 1–20. Excellent on a little-known subject.

1048   —— 'The Elizabethan merchants of Exeter', in *Govt. & Soc.*, pp. 163–87.

1049   Jordan, Wilbur K. 'The English background of modern philanthropy', *AHR*, **66** (Jan. 1961), 401–8.

1050   Mousley, J. E. 'The fortunes of some gentry families of Elizabethan Sussex', *EcHR*, 2nd ser., **11** (Apr. 1959), 467–83. Sees connection between recusancy and economic decline.

1051   Notestein, Wallace. 'The English woman, 1580–1625', in J. H. Plumb (ed.), *Studies in social history*, 1955, pp. 69–107.

1052   Pinchbeck, Ivy. 'The state and the child in sixteenth-century England', *British Journal of Sociology*, **7** (Sept. 1956), 273–85; **8** (Mar. 1957), 59–74.

1053   Pollard, Albert F. 'The Reformation parliament as a matrimonial agency and its national effects', *History*, new ser., **21** (Dec. 1936), 219–29. Matrimonial alliances among families of M.P.s

1054   Pound, J. F. 'An Elizabethan census of the poor: the treatment of vagrancy in Norwich, 1570–1580', *University of Birmingham Historical Journal*, **8** (no. 2, 1962), 135–61.

1055   Rich, E. E. 'The population of Elizabethan England', *EcHR*, 2nd ser., **2** (no. 3, 1950), 247–65. Stresses the importance of population movement.

1056   Rowse, A[lfred] L[eslie]. 'Alltyrynys and the Cecils', *EHR*, **75** (Jan. 1960), 54–76.

1057   Scouloudi, Irene. 'Alien immigration into and alien communities in London, 1558–1640', *Hug. Soc. Proc.*, **16** (no. 1, 1938), 27–49.

1058   Sellers, Maud. 'The city of York in the sixteenth century', *EHR*, **9** (Apr. 1894), 275–304.

1059   Slavin, Arthur J. 'Parliament and Henry VIII's bigamous principal secretary', *HLQ*, **28** (Feb. 1965), 131–43. Sir Ralph Sadler's matrimonial difficulties.

1060   Stone, Lawrence. 'Marriage among the English nobility in the 16th and 17th centuries', *Comparative Studies in Society and History*, **3** (Jan. 1961), 182–206.

1061   —— 'Social mobility in England, 1500–1700', *PP*, no. 33 (Apr. 1966), 16–55. See also (1040).

1062   —— 'The anatomy of the Elizabethan aristocracy', *EcHR*, **18** (nos. 1–2, 1948), 1–53. Confirms Tawney (1067). Cf. Trevor-Roper (1069).

1063   —— 'The Elizabethan aristocracy—a restatement', *EcHR*, 2nd ser., **4** (no. 3, 1952), 302–21. Reply to Trevor-Roper (1069).

1064   —— 'The fruits of office: the case of Robert Cecil, first earl of Salisbury, 1596–1612', in *Ec. & Soc. Hist.*, pp. 89–116. Shows how Robert Cecil found high office a road to riches.

1065   —— 'The inflation of honours, 1558–1641', *PP*, no. 14 (Nov. 1958), 45–70.

Argues that Elizabeth's failure to give adequate rewards to her servants created a political system favourable to the sale of titles that took place under the early Stuarts.

1066 —— 'The nobility in business', in *The Entrepreneur*. Cambridge, Mass., 1957, pp. 14–21.

1067 Tawney, Richard H. 'The rise of the gentry, 1558–1640', *EcHR*, 11 (no. 1, 1941), 1–38. The initial presentation of the case for a rising gentry.

1068 —— 'The rise of the gentry: a postscript', *EcHR*, 2nd ser., 7 (no. 1, 1954), 91–7. Defends statistical data in (1067). Cf. Cooper (1024).

1069 Trevor-Roper, Hugh R. 'The Elizabethan aristocracy: an anatomy anatomized', *EcHR*, 2nd ser., 3 (no. 3, 1951), 279–98. An anatomization of Stone (1062).

1070 Wolf, Lucien. 'Jews in Tudor England', in *Essays in Jewish History*, ed. Cecil Roth. 1934, pp. 73–90. Deals with Jews in Tudor England before Elizabeth's accession.

1071 Wood, Alfred C. 'The Holles family', *TRHS*, 4th ser., 19 (1936), 145–65.

1072 Wrigley, E. A. 'Family limitation in pre-industrial England', *EcHR*, 2nd ser., 19 (Apr. 1966), 82–109. A demographic study, *c.* 1560–1837.

1073 Wyatt, Thomas. 'Aliens in England before the Huguenots', *Hug. Soc. Proc.*, 19 (no. 1, 1953), 79–94. A good general article.

1074 Zagorin, Perez. 'The social interpretation of the English revolution', *Journal of Economic History*, 19 (Sept. 1959), 376–401. Predominantly seventeenth century but relevant as a critique of the thesis of Trevor-Roper (1005).

VIII ECONOMIC HISTORY

1 Printed sources

1075 Bland, Alfred E., Philip A. Brown and Richard H. Tawney (eds.). *English economic history: select documents*. 1914. Pt. II contains Tudor documents with useful introductions.

1076 Carr, Cecil T. (ed.). *Select charters of trading companies, A.D. 1530–1707* (Selden Society, XXVIII). 1913.

1077 Cholmeley, William. *The request and suite of a true-hearted Englishman*, ed. William Thomas (Camden Miscellany, II, old ser., LV). 1853. A tract on economic conditions, written in 1553 and dealing mainly with the cloth trade.

1078 Lamond, Elizabeth (ed.). *A discourse of the common weal of this realm of England*. Cambridge, 1893. Maintains this important treatise, published in 1581, was probably written in 1549 and attributes it to John Hales. Others attribute it to Sir Thomas Smith. See Hughes (1215). Dewar (563) claims she will prove Smith the author in her next volume.

1079 Lingelbach, William E. (ed.). *The Merchant Adventurers of England: their laws and ordinances with other documents*. Philadelphia, 1902. Valuable documents; introduction now questionable in part.

1080 Lyell, Laetitia and Frank D. Whatney (eds.). *Acts of court of the Mercers' Company, 1453–1527*. Cambridge, 1936.

1081 McGrath, Patrick (ed.). *The marchants aviso*. Boston, 1957. A manual for merchants and factors engaged in overseas trade by John Browne, a Bristol merchant of Elizabeth's reign.

1082 Parsloe, Guy (ed.). *Wardens' accounts of the Worshipful Company of Founders of the city of London, 1497–1681*. 1964. The accounts of a lesser livery company.

1083 Pauli, Reinhold (ed.). *Drei volkswirthschaftliche Denkschriften aus der Zeit Heinrichs VIII von England*. Göttingen, 1878. 'A treatise concerning the staple and the commodities of the realme' (attributed to Clement Armstrong), 'How the comen people may be set to worke: an order of a comen welth', and 'How to reforme the realme in settyng them to worke and to restore tillage'.

1084 Ramsay, George D. (ed.). *John Isham, mercer and merchant adventurer: two account books of a London merchant in the reign of Elizabeth I* (Northamptonshire Record Society, XXI). Durham, 1962. Ramsay's introduction is a valuable study of a London merchant and of trade.

1085 Read, Conyers (ed.). 'English foreign trade under Elizabeth', *EHR*, **29** (July 1914), 515–24. A list of commodities traded, c. 1580.

1086 Rich, E. E. (ed.). *The ordinance book of Merchants of the Staple.* Cambridge, 1937. The ordinances of 1565. Rich's introduction is an excellent history of the Staplers in Tudor times.

1087 Sellers, Maud (ed.). *The acts and ordinances of the Eastland Company* (Camden Society, 3rd ser., XI). 1906.

1088 —— *The York mercers and merchant adventurers, 1356–1917* (Surtees Society, CXXIX). Durham, 1918. Valuable documents, largely from the Tudor period.

1089 Stevens, Henry (ed.). *The dawn of British trade to the East Indies as recorded in the minutes of the East India Company, 1599–1603.* 1886.

1090 Tawney, Richard H. and Eileen Power (eds.). *Tudor economic documents* (University of London Historical Series, no. 14). 1924, 3 vols. The main source collection for Tudor economic history.

1091 Tolstoy, George (ed.). *The first forty years of intercourse between England and Russia.* St Petersburg, 1875. Documents, 1553–93.

1092 Wilson, Thomas. *A discourse upon usury . . . ,* ed. Richard H. Tawney. New York, 1925. Tawney's introduction to this important Elizabethan treatise is the best account of sixteenth-century monetary theory and practice.

2 Surveys

1093 Clapham, John H. *A concise economic history of Britain from the earliest times to 1750.* Cambridge, 1949. The best introduction to the subject.

1094 Clark, George N. *The wealth of England from 1496 to 1760.* Oxford, 1946. A good survey of economic developments.

1095 Cunningham, William. *The growth of English industry and commerce,* revised ed. Cambridge, 1907–10, 2 vols. Still useful.

1096 Lipson, Ephraim. *The economic history of England.* 7th ed., 1937, vol. I, 5th ed., 1948–56, vols. II–III. The fullest general account.

1097 Ramsay, George D. *English overseas trade during the centuries of emergence.* 1957. The best general survey of English foreign trade.

1098 Ramsey, Peter. *Tudor economic problems.* 1963.

3 Monographs

1099 Bekker, Ernst. *Der Afrikahandel der Königin Elisabeth von England und ihr Handelskrieg mit Portugal, 1569–77.* Giessen, 1899.

1100 Beveridge, William H., Lord. *Prices and wages in England from the twelfth to the nineteenth century,* I, *Price tables: the mercantile era.* 1939. Replaces Rogers (1145) for prices, 1550–1830.

1101 Blagden, Cyprian. *The Stationers' Company: a history, 1403–1959.* 1960.

1102 Bowden, Peter J. *The wool trade in Tudor and Stuart England.* 1962. Excellent for internal aspects; weaker on foreign aspects. See also (1138) and (1142).

1103 Brentano, Lujo. *On the history and development of gilds, and the origin of trade-unions.* 1870. Interesting but not always reliable.

1104 Burwash, Dorothy. *English merchant shipping, 1460–1540.* Toronto, 1947.

1105 Carus-Wilson, Eleanora M. and Olvie Coleman. *England's export trade, 1275–1547.* Oxford, 1963. Tables, graphs, and appendices with an excellent introduction.

1106 Coleman, Donald C. *The British paper industry, 1495–1860.* Oxford, 1958.

1107 Connell-Smith, Gordon. *Forerunners of Drake: a study of English trade with Spain in the early Tudor period.* 1954. Thorough and sound.

1108 Davies, Margaret G. *The enforcement of English apprenticeship, 1563–1642.* 1956. A careful and useful study. See (1130).

1109 Deardorff, Neva R. *English trade in the Baltic during the reign of Elizabeth*, in *Studies in the history of English commerce in the Tudor period.* New York, 1912, pp. 219–332.

1110 De Smedt, Oskar. *De Engelse natie te Antwerpen in de 16ᵉ eeuw (1496–1582).* Antwerp, 1950–4, 2 vols. Important for the Merchant Adventurers.

1111 Dollinger, Philippe. *La Hanse.* Paris, 1964. A good small study, esp. for the sixteenth century.

1112 Dunlop, O[live] J[ocelyn] and Richard D. Denham. *English apprenticeship and child labour.* 1912.

1113 Ehrenberg, Richard. *Capital and finance in the age of the Renaissance*, trans. Mrs H. M. Lucas. New York, 1928. Good on the sixteenth-century money market.

1114 —— *Hamburg und England im Zeitalter der Königin Elisabeth.* Jena, 1896.

1115 Epstein, Mordecai. *The early history of the Levant Company.* 1908.

1116 Gerson, Armand J. *The organization and early history of the Muscovy Company*, in *Studies in the history of English commerce in the Tudor period.* New York, 1912, pp. 1–122.

1117 Gough, John W. *The mines of Mendip.* Oxford, 1930.

1118 Gross, Charles. *The gild merchant.* Oxford, 1890, 2 vols. An old standard with over a volume of documents.

1119 Hagedorn, Bernhard. *Ostfrieslands Handel- und Schiffahrt im 16. Jahrhundert* (Abhandlungen zur Verkehrs- und Seegeschichte, Bd. III). Berlin, 1910. This and (1120) are useful for English trade with Emden and for the Merchant Adventurers.

1120 —— *Ostfrieslands Handel- und Schiffahrt vom Ausgang des 16. Jahrhunderts bis zum westfälischen Frieden (1580–1648)* (Abhandlungen zur Verkehrs- und Seegeschichte, Bd. VI). Berlin, 1912.

1121 Hamilton, Henry. *The English brass and copper industries to 1800.* 1926. See also (1364).

1122 Hazlitt, William C. *The livery companies of the city of London.* 1892.

1123 Heaton, Herbert. *The Yorkshire woollen and worsted industries.* 1920.

1124 Heckscher, Eli F. *Mercantilism*, revised by E. F. Söderlund. 1956, 2 vols. Remains the standard work.

1125 Herbert, William. *The history of the twelve great livery companies of London.* 1837, 2 vols. Useful for documents.

1126 Hibbert, Francis A. *The influence and development of English gilds: as illustrated by the history of the craft gilds of Shrewsbury.* Cambridge, 1891.

1127 Hughes, Edward. *Studies in administration and finance, 1558–1825, with special reference to the history of salt taxation in England.* Manchester, 1934. Particularly chapter II, 'The Elizabethan salt patents'.

1128 Jenkin, A. K. Hamilton. *The Cornish miner.* 1927.

1129 Jenkins, James T. *The herring and herring fisheries.* 1927.

1130 Kelsall, Roger K. *Wage regulations under the statute of artificers.* 1938. This, (1108), and (1269), provide a full account of the working of the Statute of Artificers.

1131 Kernkamp, J. H. *De Handel op den Vijand, 1572–1609.* Utrecht, 1934, 2 vols. Dutch and English trade with Spain.

1132 Knoop, Douglas and Gwilym P. Jones. *The sixteenth century mason.* 1937.

1133 Kramer, Stella. *The English craft guilds: studies in their progress and decline.* New York, 1905. Rejects older view that the decline of the craft guilds was largely due to late medieval and Tudor legislation.

1134 Lewis, George R. *The Stannaries: a study of the English tin miner* (Harvard Economic Series, III). Cambridge, Mass., 1908.

1135 Lipson, Ephraim. *English woollen and worsted industries.* Revised ed., 1953.

1136 Lubimenko, Inna. *Les relations commerciales et politiques de l'Angleterre avec la Russie avant Pierre le Grand.* Paris, 1933.

1137 Lucas, Charles P. *The beginnings of English overseas enterprise: a prelude to*

49

empire. Oxford, 1917. A study of the Merchants of the Staple, the Merchant Adventurers, and the Eastland merchants.

1138 Mendenhall, Thomas C. *The Shrewsbury drapers in the XVIth and XVIIth centuries.* Oxford, 1953. This and (1142) are excellent for the wool trade.

1139 Nef, John U. *Industry and government in France and England, 1540–1640* (Memoirs of the American Philosophical Society, xv). Philadelphia, 1940. Argues that the decline in effectiveness of government control of industry in England was largely due to the first 'Industrial Revolution'. See (1415).

1140 —— *The rise of the British coal industry.* 1932, 2 vols.

1141 Pauli, Reinhold. *Der hansische Stalhof in London.* Bremen, 1856. The Steelyard was the main base of the Hansards in England.

1142 Ramsay, George D. *The Wiltshire woollen industry in the sixteenth and seventeenth centuries.* Oxford, 1943. See (1138).

1143 Richards, Richard D. *The early history of banking in England.* 1929.

1144 Robertson, Hector M. *Aspects of the rise of economic individualism.* Cambridge, 1933. A critique of the Weber thesis. For a critique of Robertson's views on the Jesuits see James Broderick, *The economic morals of the Jesuits,* 1934.

1145 Rogers, J. E. Thorold. *A history of agriculture and prices in England.* Oxford, 1866–1900, 7 vols. Cf. (1100) and (1296).

1146 —— *Six centuries of work and wages.* Oxford, 1884.

1147 Roover, Raymond de. *Gresham on foreign exchange: an essay on early English mercantilism with the text of Sir Thomas Gresham's memorandum for the understanding of the exchange.* Cambridge, Mass., 1949. The author's discussion of international exchange in the sixteenth century is of great value. His ascribing the 'Memorandum' to Gresham is questionable. Cf. Lehmberg (246), p. 60 n., and Dewar (1192).

1148 Rowland, Albert L. *England and Turkey: the rise of diplomatic and commercial relations,* in *Studies in English commerce and exploration in the reign of Elizabeth.* Philadelphia, 1924.

1149 Ruddock, Alwyn A. *Italian merchants and shipping in Southampton, 1270–1600.* Southampton, 1951. Good on the decline of the Italian trade and of Southampton. Denies the latter was entirely a result of the former.

1150 Schanz, Georg von. *Englische Handelspolitik gegen Ende des Mittelalters ...* Leipzig, 1881. 2 vols. Vol. II is important for documents; vol. I is still the best general account of early Tudor trade with all parts of Europe. Cf. (1243).

1151 Schubert, H. R. *History of the British iron and steel industry from c. 450 B.C. to A.D. 1775.* 1957.

1152 Scott, William R. *The constitution and finance of English, Scottish, and Irish joint stock companies.* Cambridge, 1910–12, 3 vols. Not easy reading but indispensable.

1153 Simon, André L. *The history of the wine trade in England.* 1906–9, 3 vols. Vol. II covers the fifteenth and sixteenth centuries.

1154 Sweezy, Paul M. *Monopoly and competition in the English coal trade, 1550–1850* (Harvard Economic Studies, LXIII). Cambridge, Mass., 1938.

1155 Tawney, Richard H. *Religion and the rise of capitalism.* 1926. One of the great masterpieces of historical writing, dealing largely with England. Of great value, though the thesis, a modification of Max Weber's, is now more than questionable. Cf. Kurt Samuelsson, *Religion and economic action,* trans. E. Geoffrey French and ed. Donald C. Coleman, 1961.

1156 Unwin, George. *Industrial organization in the sixteenth and seventeenth centuries,* Oxford, 1904. A detailed study of crafts and companies, late sixteenth and early seventeenth century, with emphasis on England.

1157 —— *The gilds and companies of London.* 1908. The standard work on the subject.

1158 Vaughn, Earnest V. *English trading expeditions into Asia under the authority of the Muscovy Company (1557–1581),* in *Studies in the history of English commerce in the Tudor period.* New York, 1912, pp. 127–214.

1159 Volckmann, Erwin. *Der Grundstein britischer Weltmacht.* Würzburg, 1923. Anglo-Prussian economic relations, mainly the Eastland Company.

1160 Wee, Herman van der. *The growth of the Antwerp market and the European economy (fourteenth–sixteenth centuries)*. The Hague, 1963, 3 vols. Contains much that is relevant to England.

1161 Willan, Thomas S. *Studies in Elizabethan foreign trade*. Manchester, 1959. Mainly on English trade with Morocco. Also valuable on interlopers and the outports.

1162 —— *The early history of the Russia Company*. Manchester, 1956.

1163 —— *The Muscovy merchants of 1555*. Manchester, 1953.

1164 Williamson, James A. *Maritime enterprise, 1485–1558*. Oxford, 1913. Considers English commerce in a little-studied period.

1165 Wood, Alfred C. *A history of the Levant Company*. Oxford, 1935.

1166 Wright, Louis B. *Religion and empire: the alliance between piety and commerce in English expansion, 1558–1625*. Chapel Hill, 1943.

1167 Yamey, Basil S., Harold C. Edey and Hugh W. Thomson. *Accounting in England and Scotland, 1543–1800*. 1963. Extracts from books in English on accounting, essays on them, and an extensive bibliography.

4 Biographies

1168 Burgon, John W. *The life and times of Sir Thomas Gresham*. 1839, 2 vols.

1169 Stone, Lawrence. *An Elizabethan: Sir Horatio Palavicino*. 1956. Useful for politics as well as financial history.

1170 Tersen, André C. *John Hales, économiste Anglais du milieu de XVIᵉ siècle*. Avallon, 1907. Primarily an appraisal of Hales as an economist. Reprints (1078).

1171 Webb, John G. *Great Tooley of Ipswich: portrait of an early Tudor merchant*. Ipswich, 1963.

5 Articles

1172 Aston, Robert. 'Usury and high finance in the age of Shakespeare and Jonson', *Renaissance and Modern Studies*, **4** (1960), 14–43.

1173 Bindoff, Stanley T. 'Clement Armstrong and his treatises of the commonweal', *EcHR*, **14** (no. 1, 1944), 64–73.

1174 —— 'The greatness of Antwerp', *NCMH*, **II**, 50–69. C. 1499–1560. A most valuable little survey.

1175 Boissonade, Prosper. 'Le mouvement commercial entre la France et les Iles Britanniques au XVIᵉ siècle', *Rev. hist.*, **134** (May–Aug. 1920), 193–228; **135** (Sept.–Dec. 1920), 1–27.

1176 Bowden, Peter J. 'Movements in wool prices, 1490–1610', *Yorkshire Bulletin of Economic and Social Research*, **4** (Sept. 1952), 109–24.

1177 —— 'Wool supply and the woollen industry', *EcHR*, 2nd ser., **9** (Aug. 1956), 44–58. Changes in English wool supply, mainly sixteenth century, and their consequences for the woollen industry.

1178 Brenner, Y. S. 'The inflation of prices in early sixteenth-century England', *EcHR*, 2nd ser., **14** (no. 2, 1961), 225–39. This and (1179) emphasize the importance of population growth in the price rise. Cf. (1203).

1179 —— 'The inflation of prices in England, 1551–1650', *EcHR*, 2nd ser., **15** (no. 2, 1962), 266–84.

1180 —— 'The price revolution reconsidered: a reply', *EcHR*, 2nd ser., **18** (no. 2, 1965), 392–6. Reply to (1202).

1181 Brown, E. H. Phelps and Sheila V. Hopkins. 'Seven centuries of building wages', *Economica*, new ser., **22** (Aug. 1955), 195–206.

1182 —— 'Wage-rates and prices: evidence for population pressure in the sixteenth century', *Economica*, new ser., **24** (Nov. 1957), 289–306.

1183 Buckley, H. 'Sir Thomas Gresham and the foreign exchanges', *EcJ*, **34** (Dec. 1924), 589–601.

1184 Caillé, Jacques. 'Le commerce anglais avec le Maroc pendant la seconde moitié du XVIᵉ siècle', *Revue africaine*, **84** (1940), 186–219.

1185 Carus-Wilson, Eleanora M. 'The origins and early development of the Merchant Adventurers' organization in London as shown in their own mediaeval records', *EcHR*, **4** (Apr. 1932), 147–76. Good for development under Henry VII.

1186 Casimir, Nicholas, Baron de Bogoushevsky. 'The English in Muscovy during the sixteenth century', *TRHS*, **7** (1878), 58–129. A detailed account with many documents.

1187 Clarkson, L. A. 'English economic policy in the sixteenth and seventeenth centuries: the case of the leather industry', *BIHR*, **38** (Nov. 1965), 149–62. The roles of pressure groups and the government with regard to the leather act of 1563 and its enforcement.

1188 —— 'The organization of the English leather industry in the late sixteenth and seventeenth centuries', *EcHR*, 2nd ser., **13** (Dec. 1960), 245–56.

1189 Connell-Smith, Gordon. 'English merchants trading to the New World in the early sixteenth century', *BIHR*, **23** (May 1950), 53–67.

1190 Coomber, R. R. 'Hugh Oldcastle and John Mellis', in Ananias C. Littleton and Basil S. Yamey (eds.), *Studies in the history of accounting*. Homewood, Ill., 1956, pp. 206–14. Oldcastle wrote the first English book-keeping text (1543); Mellis reprinted it in 1588.

1191 Davis, Ralph. 'England and the Mediterranean, 1570–1670', in *Ec. & Soc. Hist.*, pp. 117–37. The expansion of England's Levant trade and the reversal of commercial position between England and Italy.

1192 Dewar, Mary. 'The memorandum "For the understanding of the exchange": its authorship and dating', *EcHR*, 2nd ser., **17** (no. 3, 1965), 476–87. Maintains Sir Thomas Smith wrote it in 1554. Cf. (1147).

1193 Dickin, E. P. 'Notes on the coast shipping and seaborne trade of Essex, 1565–77', *Essex Archaeological Society Transactions*, new ser., **17** (1926), 153–64.

1194 Edler, Florence. 'Winchcombe kerseys in Antwerp, 1538–44', *EcHR*, **7** (Nov. 1936), 57–62. Shipment of kerseys to Antwerp and thence to Italy and the Levant. An interesting example of the ways of early Tudor trade.

1195 Elton, Geoffrey R. 'State planning in early-Tudor England', *EcHR*, 2nd ser., **13** (Apr. 1961), 433–9. Points out difficulties involved in research on this matter.

1196 Fisher, F. J. 'Commercial trends and policy in sixteenth-century England', *EcHR*, **10** (Nov. 1940), 95–117. An important study of the ups and downs of the cloth trade and government policy toward the same, veering from *laissez-faire* during prosperity to control during depression.

1197 —— 'Influenza and inflation in Tudor England', *EcHR*, 2nd ser., **18** (Aug. 1965), 120–9. Speculates on the effects of the major influenza epidemics of the 1550s on prices, wages, and population.

1198 —— 'The development of London as a centre of conspicuous consumption in the sixteenth and seventeenth centuries', *TRHS*, 4th ser., **30** (1948), 37–50.

1199 —— 'The sixteenth and seventeenth centuries: the dark ages in English economic history?', *Economica*, new ser., **24** (Feb. 1957), 2–18.

1200 Gay, Margaret R. 'Aspects of Elizabethan apprenticeship', in *Facts and factors in economic history*. Cambridge, Mass., 1932, pp. 134–63.

1201 Gould, J. D. 'The crisis in the export trade, 1586–1587', *EHR*, **71** (Apr. 1956), 212–22. An interesting analysis with larger implications.

1202 —— 'The price revolution reconsidered', *EcHR*, 2nd ser., **17** (no. 2, 1964), 249–66. Calls for a more tentative use of the concept of a price revolution. Cf. (1180).

1203 —— 'Y. S. Brenner on prices: a comment', *EcHR*, 2nd ser., **16** (no. 2, 1963), 351–60. A comment on (1178) and (1179).

1204 Grampp, William D. 'The liberal elements in English mercantilism', *QJEc*, **66** (Nov. 1952), 456–501.

1205 Hamilton, Earl J. 'American treasure and the rise of capitalism (1500–1700)', *Economica*, **9** (Nov. 1929), 338–57.

1206 Hammersley, G. 'The crown woods and their exploitation in the sixteenth and seventeenth centuries', *BIHR*, **30** (Nov. 1957), 136–61.

1207   Heaton, Herbert. 'Heckscher on mercantilism', *Journal of Political Economy*, **45** (June 1937), 370–93.
1208   Heckscher, Eli F. 'Revisions in economic history, v, Mercantilism', *EcHR*, **7** (Nov. 1936), 44–54.
1209   Hewart, Beatrice. 'The cloth trade in the north of England in the sixteenth and seventeenth centuries', *EcJ*, **10** (Mar. 1900), 20–31.
1210   Hewins, William A. S. 'The regulation of wages by the justices of the peace', *EcJ*, **8** (Sept. 1898), 340–6.
1211   Hill, Christopher. 'Protestantism and the rise of capitalism', in *Ec. & Soc. Hist.*, pp. 15–39. Still maintains Tawney's thesis.
1212   Horniker, Arthur L. 'Anglo-French rivalry in the Levant from 1583 to 1612', *JMH*, **18** (Dec. 1946), 289–305.
1213   —— 'William Harborne and the beginning of Anglo-Turkish diplomatic and commercial relations', *JMH*, **14** (Sept. 1942), 289–316.
1214   Hoskins, William G. 'The rebuilding of rural England, 1570–1640', *PP*, no. 4 (Nov. 1953), 44–59. Deals with the 'housing revolution', its financing and its connection with the rise in population.
1215   Hughes, Edward. 'The authorship of the Discourse of the Common Weal', *BJRL*, **21** (Apr. 1937), 167–75. Says it was Sir Thomas Smith. Cf. (1078).
1216   —— 'The English monopoly of salt in the years 1563–71', *EHR*, **40** (July 1925), 334–50.
1217   Hutchins, Elizabeth L. 'The regulation of wages by gilds and town authorities', *EcJ*, **10** (Sept. 1900), 404–11.
1218   Jones, John R. 'Some aspects of London mercantile activity during the reign of Queen Elizabeth', in Norton Downs (ed.), *Essays in honor of Conyers Read*, Chicago, 1953, pp. 186–99.
1219   Kerridge, Eric. 'The movement of rent, 1540–1640', *EcHR*, 2nd ser., **6** (Aug. 1953), 16–34. Questions the view that rents lagged behind prices.
1220   Knoop, Douglas and Gwilym P. Jones. 'Overtime in the age of Henry VIII', *EcJ*, Economic History Supplement, **3** (Feb. 1938), 13–20.
1221   Lingelbach, William E. 'The internal organization of the Merchant Adventurers of England', *TRHS*, 2nd ser., **16** (1902), 19–67.
1222   Loomie, Albert J. 'Religion and Elizabethan commerce with Spain', *Catholic Historical Review*, **50** (Apr. 1964), 27–51.
1223   Lubimenko, Inna. 'Les marchands anglais en Russie au XVIᵉ siècle', *Rev. hist.*, **109** (Jan.–Feb. 1912), 1–26.
1224   Lutz, Harley L. 'Inaccuracies in Rogers' history of prices', *QJEc*, **23** (Feb. 1909), 350–8.
1225   McArthur, Ellen A. 'The regulation of wages in the sixteenth century', *EHR*, **15** (July 1900), 445–55. Entirely Elizabethan.
1226   Mallett, M. E. 'Anglo-Florentine commercial relations, 1465–1491', *EcHR*, 2nd ser., **15** (Dec. 1962), 250–65.
1227   Malowist, Marian. 'Poland, Russia and western trade in the 15th and 16th centuries', *PP*, no. 13 (Apr. 1958), 26–41. Points out the importance of trade with eastern Europe in the colonial, industrial, and trading expansion of Holland and England.
1228   Marshall, T. H. 'Capitalism and the decline of English gilds', *Camb. Hist. J.*, **3** (no. 1, 1929), 23–33.
1229   Mathew, David and Gervase. 'Iron furnaces in south-eastern England and English ports and landing-places, 1578', *EHR*, **48** (Jan. 1933), 91–9. Sheds light on the condition of the iron trade.
1230   Miller, Lewis R. 'New evidence on the shipping and imports of London, 1601–1602', *QJEc*, **41** (Aug. 1927), 740–60.
1231   Nef, John U. 'A comparison of industrial growth in France and England from 1540 to 1640', *Journal of Political Economy*, **44** (June–Oct. 1936), 289–317, 505–33, 643–66.
1232   —— 'English and French industrial history after 1540 in relation to the constitution', in Conyers Read (ed.), *The constitution reconsidered*. New York, 1938, pp. 79–103.
1233   —— 'Industrial Europe at the time of the Reformation', *Journal of Political Economy*, **49** (Feb.–Apr. 1941), 1–40, 183–224.

1234 Nef, John U. 'Note on the progress of iron production in England, 1540–1640', *Journal of Political Economy*, **44** (June 1936), 398–403.

1235 —— 'Prices and industrial capitalism in France and England, 1540–1640', *EcHR*, **7** (May 1937), 155–85. Questions the view that the price revolution was *the* significant cause of the rise of industrialism.

1236 —— 'War and economic progress, 1540–1640', *EcHR*, **12** (no. 1, 1942), 13–48. Sees peace as contributing more than war to the development of large-scale enterprise during the period.

1237 Nicholas, Frieda J. 'The assize of bread in London during the sixteenth century', *EcJ*, Economic History Supplement, **2** (Jan. 1932), 323–47.

1238 Nicholls, Laura M. 'The lay subsidy of 1523: the reliability of subsidy rolls as illustrated by Totnes and Dartmouth', *University of Birmingham Historical Journal*, **9** (no. 2, 1964), 113–29.

1239 Pelham, R. A. 'The establishment of the Willoughby iron works in north Warwickshire in the sixteenth century', *University of Birmingham Historical Journal*, **4** (no. 1, 1953), 18–29.

1240 Rabb, Theodore K. 'Investment in English overseas enterprise, 1575–1630', *EcHR*, 2nd ser., **19** (Apr. 1966), 70–81.

1241 Ramsay, George D. 'The distribution of the cloth industry in 1561–2', *EHR*, **57** (July 1942), 361–9. Distribution illustrated by lists of fines for defective cloth.

1242 —— 'The smugglers' trade: a neglected aspect of English commercial development', *TRHS*, 5th ser., **2** (1952), 131–57.

1243 Ramsey, Peter. 'Overseas trade in the reign of Henry VII: the evidence of customs accounts', *EcHR*, 2nd ser., **6** (Dec. 1953), 173–82. Corrects some of the figures given in Schanz (1150).

1244 —— 'Some Tudor merchants' accounts', in Ananias C. Littleton and Basil S. Yamey (eds.), *Studies in the history of accounting*. Homewood, Ill., 1956, pp. 185–201.

1245 Rawlinson, H. G. 'Embassy of William Harborne to Constantinople, 1583–8', *TRHS*, 4th ser., **5** (1922), 1–27. Harborne and the founding of the Turkey Company.

1246 Read, Conyers. 'Mercantilism: the old English pattern of a controlled economy', in *The constitution reconsidered*. New York, 1938, pp. 63–77.

1247 —— 'Tudor economic policy', in Robert L. Schuyler and Herman Ausubel (eds.), *The making of English history*. New York, 1952, pp. 195–201.

1248 Reddaway, T. F. 'The London Goldsmiths *circa* 1500', *TRHS*, 5th ser., **12** (1962), 49–62.

1249 Rees, James F. 'Mercantilism', *History*, new ser., **24** (Sept. 1939), 129–35. An examination of Heckscher's views (1124).

1250 Reynolds, Beatrice. 'Elizabethan traders in Normandy', *JMH*, **9** (Sept. 1937), 289–303.

1251 Richards, Richard D. 'The pioneers of banking in England', *EcJ*, Economic History Supplement, **1** (Jan. 1929), 485–502.

1252 Richards, Richard D. and Henry R. Hatfield. 'Early history of the term capital', *QJEc*, **40** (Feb.–May 1926), 329–38, 547–8.

1253 Riemersa, Jelle C. 'Government influence on company organization in Holland and England (1550–1650)', *Journal of Economic History*, Supplement, **10** (1950), 31–9. An interesting comparison stressing the stronger position of Dutch merchants in relation to government as compared to the weaker position of English merchants.

1254 Robertson, Hector M. 'Sir Bevis Bulmer, a large-scale speculator of Elizabethan and Jacobean times', *Journal of Economic and Business History*, **4** (Nov. 1931), 99–120.

1255 Roover, Raymond de. 'Early accounting problems of foreign exchange', *Accounting Review*, **19** (Oct. 1944), 381–407.

1256 —— 'Scholastic economics: survival and lasting influence from the sixteenth century to Adam Smith', *QJEc*, **69** (May 1955), 161–90.

1257 —— 'What is dry exchange? A contribution to the study of English mercantilism', *Journal of Political Economy*, **52** (Sept. 1944), 250–66.

1258 Rowse, A[lfred] L[eslie]. 'The dispute concerning the Plymouth pilchard fishery, 1584–91', *EcJ*, Economic History Supplement, **2** (Jan. 1932), 461–72.

1259 Ruddock, Alwyn A. 'London capitalists and the decline of Southampton in the early Tudor period', *EcHR*, 2nd ser., **2** (no. 2, 1949), 137–51.

1260 —— 'The Trinity House at Deptford in the sixteenth century', *EHR*, **45** (Oct. 1950), 458–76. The pilots' guild at Deptford Strand and its role in commercial development.

1261 Scammell, G. V. 'Shipowning in England *circa* 1450–1550', *TRHS*, 5th ser., **12** (1962), 105–22.

1262 Schubert, H. R. 'Shrewsbury Letters: a contribution to the history of ironmaking', *Journal of the Iron and Steel Institute*, **155** (Apr. 1947), 521–5.

1263 —— 'The first cast-iron cannon made in England', *Journal of the Iron and Steel Institute*, **146** (Autumn 1942), 131–40.

1264 —— 'The economic aspect of Sir Henry Sidney's steel works at Roberts-bridge, in Sussex, and Boxhurst, in Kent', *Journal of the Iron and Steel Institute*, **164** (Mar. 1950), 278–80.

1265 Sée, Henri. 'L'Evolution du capitalisme en Angleterre du XVI⁰ siècle au commencement du XIX⁰,' *Revue de synthèse historique*, **40** (Dec. 1925), 31–49.

1266 Stone, Lawrence. 'An Elizabethan coal mine', *EcHR*, 2nd ser., **3** (no. 1, 1950), 97–106.

1267 —— 'Elizabethan overseas trade', *EcHR*, 2nd ser., **2** (no. 1, 1949), 30–58.

1268 —— 'State control in sixteenth-century England', *EcHR*, **17** (no. 2, 1947), 103–20. Argues that security rather than prosperity was the main objective of Tudor economic policy.

1269 Tawney, Richard H. 'The assessment of wages in England by the justices of the peace', *Vierteljahrschrift für Sozial- und Wirtschaftsgeschichte*, **11** (1913), 307–37, 533–64. Important. See (1130).

1270 Thirsk, Joan. 'Industries in the countryside', in *Ec. & Soc. Hist.*, pp. 70–88. Seeks to explain why rural handicraft industries developed in particular localities.

1271 Unwin, George. 'Commerce and coinage in Shakespeare's England', in *Collected papers*, ed. Richard H. Tawney. 1958, pp. 302–35.

1272 —— 'The Merchant Adventurers' Company in the reign of Elizabeth', in *Collected papers*, ed. Richard H. Tawney. 1958, pp. 133–220. Lectures of 1913 which exploded common assumptions. Still important to an under-standing of Elizabethan economic history.

1273 Walker, P. C. Gordon. 'Capitalism and Reformation', *EcHR*, **8** (Nov. 1937), 1–19. Considers the Reformation as 'the result of needs created by capitalist advance'.

1274 Willan, Thomas S. 'Some aspects of English trade with the Levant in the sixteenth century', *EHR*, **70** (July 1955), 399–410.

1275 —— 'The Russia Company and Narva, 1558–81', *Slavonic Review*, **31** (June 1953), 405–19.

1276 Williams, N. J. 'Francis Shaxton and the Elizabethan port books', *EHR*, **66** (July 1951), 387–95.

1277 Wretts-Smith, Mildred. 'The English in Russia during the second half of the sixteenth century', *TRHS*, 4th ser., **3** (1920), 72–102.

1278 Wroth, Lawrence C. 'An Elizabethan merchant and man of letters', *HLQ*, **17** (Aug. 1954), 299–314. The merchant is John Frampton, a pioneer in writings encouraging overseas enterprise.

1279 Yakobson, S. 'Early Anglo-Russian relations (1553–1613)', *Slavonic Review*, **13** (Apr. 1935), 597–610. A very good survey mainly concerned with trade.

IX AGRICULTURAL HISTORY

1 Printed sources

1280 Chipendall, W. H. (ed.). *A sixteenth-century survey and year's account of the estates of Hornby Castle, Lancashire* (Chetham Society, new ser., CII). Manchester, 1939.

1281 Cowper, J. Meadows (ed.). *Certayne causes gathered together, wherein is shewed the decaye of England only by the great multitude of shepe . . .* (E.E.T.S., extra ser., XIII), 1871. Written in the early 1550s.

1282 Fitzherbert, Anthony. *The book of husbandry*, ed. Walter W. Skeat (English Dialect Society, XIII, no. 2). 1882. Reprinted from the ed. of 1534.

1283 Kirkus, Mary (ed.). *The records of the commissioners of sewers in the parts of Holland, 1547–1603* (Lincoln Record Society, LIV). Lincoln, 1959. Records dealing with the reclamation of marsh and fen.

1284 Leadam, Isaac S. (ed.). *The domesday of inclosures, 1517–18.* 1892, 2 vols. Returns to chancery for ten counties. Cf. (1324).

1285 Stratton, C. R. (ed.). *Survey of the lands of William, first earl of Pembroke.* 1909, 2 vols.

2 Surveys

1286 Ernle, Rowland E., Lord Prothero. *English farming past and present*, with introductions by George E. Fussell and O. R. McGregor. 1961. The introductions bring this old standard up to date.

1286a Thirsk, Joan (ed.). *The Agrarian history of England and Wales*, IV, *1500–1640.* Cambridge, 1967. An important, up-to-date, detailed, and authoritative survey. Considers farming regions, farming techniques, enclosures, landlords, farm labourers, marketing, agricultural prices, profits and rents, and rural housing.

1287 Trow-Smith, Robert. *English husbandry from the earliest times to the present day.* 1951.

3 Monographs

1288 Beresford, Maurice W. *The lost villages of England.* 1954. An attempt to restore the view that Yorkist and early Tudor enclosures produced widespread depopulation. Cf. (1325).

1289 Curtler, William H. R. *The enclosure and redistribution of our land.* Oxford, 1920. A good general account with four chapters on Tudor enclosures.

1290 Darby, Henry C. *The draining of the fens.* 1956.

1291 Davenport, Frances G. *The economic development of a Norfolk manor, 1086–1565.* Cambridge, 1906.

1292 Fussell, George E. *Farming systems from Elizabethan to Victorian days in the North and East Ridings of Yorkshire.* York, 1944. For a long list of articles by Fussell on farming systems in various parts of England see Read (24), pp. 221–2.

1293 —— *The farmer's tools, 1500–1900: the history of British farm implements, tools, and machinery before the tractor came.* 1952.

1294 —— *The old English farming books from Fitzherbert to Tull, 1523–1730.* 1947.

1295 Gonner, Edward C. K. *Common land and inclosure.* 1912.

1296 Gras, Norman S. B. *The evolution of the English corn market from the twelfth to the eighteenth century.* Cambridge, Mass., 1926. A standard survey that supplements Rogers (1145) on grain prices. The conclusions on Tudor policy are open to question. Cf. (1336).

1297 Gray, Howard L. *English field systems* (Harvard Historical Studies, XXII). Cambridge, Mass., 1915.

1298 Hoskins, William G. *Essays in Leicestershire history.* Liverpool, 1950. Valuable for the effects of enclosure.

1299 —— *The Midland peasant; the economic and social history of a Leicestershire village.* 1957. A detailed study of a village since the Norman Conquest.
1300 Hoskins, William G. and H. P. R. Finberg. *Devonshire studies.* 1952.
1301 Hoskins, William G. and L. Dudley Stamp. *The common lands of England and Wales.* 1963. A brief historical survey plus a full geographical survey of surviving common lands.
1302 Johnson, Arthur H. *The disappearance of the small landowner.* Oxford, 1909. Lecture III discusses Tudor enclosures.
1303 Orwin, Charles S. and Christabel S. *The open fields.* Oxford, 1954. Primarily a study of a Nottinghamshire manor. Little on the Tudor period but useful for the subject generally.
1304 Semeonov, V. F. *Enclosures and peasant revolts in England in the sixteenth century.* Moscow and Leningrad, 1949 (in Russian). 1485–1553. For a summary in English see Christopher Hill's review in *EcHR*, 2nd ser., **3** (no. 1, 1950), 138–9.
1305 Tawney, Richard H. *The agrarian problem in the sixteenth century.* 1912. Still indispensable though some of its conclusions are dated. Should be supplemented with (1298) and (1308).
1306 Thirsk, Joan. *English peasant farming; the agrarian history of Lincolnshire from Tudor to recent times.* 1957.
1307 —— *Fenland farming in the sixteenth century.* Leicester, 1953.
1308 —— *Tudor enclosures* (Historical Association Pamphlets, general series, no. 41). 1959. An up-to-date and judicious survey of a controversial subject.
1309 Trow-Smith, Robert. *A history of British livestock husbandry to 1700.* 1957. An excellent technical survey. Ignores economic issues.

4 Biographies

None.

5 Articles

1310 Allison, K. J. 'Flock management in the sixteenth and seventeenth centuries', *EcHR*, 2nd ser., **11** (Aug. 1958), 98–112.
1311 —— 'The sheep–corn husbandry of Norfolk in the sixteenth and seventeenth centuries', *AgHR*, **5** (pt. 1, 1957), 12–30.
1312 Ashley, William J. 'The character of villein tenure', *EHR*, **8** (Apr. 1893), 294–7. Critique of Leadam (1330).
1313 Beresford, Maurice W. 'Habitation versus improvement: the debate on enclosure by agreement', in *Ec. & Soc. Hist.*, pp. 40–69.
1314 —— 'Lot acres', *EcHR*, **13** (no. 1, 1943), 74–9.
1315 —— 'The poll tax and census of sheep, 1549', *AgHR*, **1** (1953), 9–15; **2** (1954), 15–29. Important to a consideration of the agrarian policies of the Protector Somerset and John Hales.
1316 Corbett, William J. 'Elizabethan village surveys', *TRHS*, 2nd ser., **11** (1897), 67–87. Discusses division of land, tenants, and enclosures.
1317 Du Boulay, F. R. H. 'Who were farming the English demesnes at the end of the middle ages?', *EcHR*, 2nd ser., **17** (no. 3, 1965), 443–55. A study of leases on the manorial demesnes of the see of Canterbury under Archbishop Warham.
1318 Ellis, Martha J. 'A study in the manorial history of Halifax parish in the sixteenth and early seventeenth centuries', *Yorks. Arch. J.*, **40** (pts. 2–3, 1960–1), 250–64, 420–42. A detailed study of a manor in the West Riding.
1319 Fisher, F. J. 'The development of the London food market, 1540–1640', *EcHR*, **5** (Apr. 1935), 46–64.
1320 Fussell, George E. 'Crop nutrition in Tudor and early Stuart England', *AgHR*, **3** (pt. 2, 1955), 95–106.
1321 —— 'Low Countries' influence on English farming', *EHR*, **74** (Oct. 1959), 611–22.
1322 —— 'The Elizabethan farmer', *History Today*, **3** (Nov. 1953), 762–70.

1323 Gay, Edwin F. 'Inclosures in England in the sixteenth century', *QJEc*, **17** (Aug. 1903), 576–97. A pioneer study. Now seriously out of date.

1324 —— 'The inquisitions of depopulation in 1517 and the domesday of inclosures', *TRHS*, 2nd ser., **14** (1900), 100, 231–67, 286–303. A critique of (1284) and (1330).

1325 Gould, J. D. 'Mr Beresford and the lost villages', *AgHR*, **3** (pt. 2, 1955), 107–13. Critical of Beresford's (1288) explanations of village mortality in the period 1450–1520 and of its decline after that.

1326 Habakkuk, H. John. 'La disparition du paysan anglais', *Annales: Economies Sociétés Civilisations*, **20** (July–Aug. 1965), 649–63. An up-to-date general discussion.

1327 Hoskins, William G. 'The reclamation of the waste in Devon, 1550–1800', *EcHR*, **13** (no. 1, 1943), 80–92.

1328 Kerridge, Eric. 'The returns of the inquisition of depopulation', *EHR*, **70** (Apr. 1955), 212–28. An important article questioning the returns.

1329 Kneisel, Ernst. 'The evolution of the English corn market', *Journal of Economic History*, **14** (Winter 1954), 46–52.

1330 Leadam, Isaac S. 'The inquisition of 1517: inclosures and evictions', *TRHS*, 2nd ser., **6** (1892), 167–314; **7** (1893), 127–292; **8** (1894), 251–331; **14** (1900), 267–86. Maintains copyholders were amply protected and secure, 1450–1550. Cf. (1312), (1324), and (1328).

1331 —— 'The last days of bondage in England', *LQR*, **9** (Oct. 1893), 348–65.

1332 —— 'The security of copyholders in the fifteenth and sixteenth centuries', *EHR*, **8** (Oct. 1893), 348–65. An answer to Ashley's critique (1312).

1333 Lennard, Reginald. 'Custom and change in sixteenth century England', *EHR*, **28** (Oct. 1913), 745–48. Considers the problem of fixity of tenure.

1334 Malden, Henry E. 'Bondmen in Surrey under the Tudors', *TRHS*, 2nd ser., **19** (1905), 305–7.

1335 Peyton, S. A. 'The village population in the Tudor lay subsidy rolls', *EHR*, **30** (Apr. 1915), 234–50. A study of rolls in Nottinghamshire. Suggests mobility of rural population, 1558–1641.

1336 Ponko, Vincent, Jr. 'N. S. B. Gras and Elizabethan corn policy: a reexamination of the problem', *EcHR*, 2nd ser., **17** (Aug. 1964), 24–42. Critical of the conclusions of Gras (1296) that London imposed corn policy on the government.

1337 Purvis, John S. 'A note on XVI century farming in Yorkshire', *Yorks. Arch. J.*, **36** (pt. 3, 1946), 435–54. Useful information on Yorkshire farming gleaned from ecclesiastical records.

1338 Savine, Alexander. 'Bondmen under the Tudors', *TRHS*, 2nd ser., **17** (1903), 235–89.

1339 —— 'English customary tenure in the Tudor period', *QJEc*, **19** (Nov. 1904–5), 33–80. A penetrating and scholarly analysis, still of importance.

1340 Simpson, Alan. 'The East Anglian foldcourse: some queries', *AgHR*, **6** (pt. 2, 1958), 87–96. Asks questions raised by Allison's article (1311).

1341 Stratton, C. R. 'An English manor in the time of Elizabeth', *Wiltshire Archaeological and Natural History Magazine*, **32** (1902), 288–310. Manors in the Seignory of Wilton.

1342 Taylor, Eva G. R. 'The surveyor', *EcHR*, **17** (no. 2, 1947), 121–33.

1343 Thirsk, Joan. 'Farming in Kesteven, 1540–1640', *Lincolnshire Architectural and Archaeological Society Reports and Papers*, new ser., **6** (1955–6), 37–53.

X SCIENCE AND TECHNOLOGY

1 Printed Sources

1344 Bourne, William. *A regiment for the sea*, ed. Eva G. R. Taylor. Cambridge, 1963. Three technical manuals on navigation by an Elizabethan.

1345 Debus, Allen G. (ed.). 'An Elizabethan history of medical chemistry', *Annals of Science*, **18** (Mar. 1962), 1–29. By R. Bostocke, Esq., this is one of the earliest histories of science in the English language.

1346 Evans, Arthur H. (trans. and ed.). *Turner on birds.* Cambridge, 1903. A translation of William Turner's *Avium praecipuarum.*

1347 Gilbert, William. *De magnete*, trans. P. Fleury Mottelay. New York, 1958. The main contribution of the Tudor period in physics.

1348 Halliwell, James D. (ed.). *The private diary of Dr John Dee, and the catalogue of his library of manuscripts* (Camden Society, old ser., XIX). 1842. A diary, 1577–1601, and a catalogue made in 1573.

1349 Lowe, Peter. *A discourse of the whole art of chirurgery*, revised ed. 1612. Written in 1597, this is the first treatise in English on surgery.

1350 Turner, William. *The names of herbes*, ed. James Britten. 1881. By the 'father of English botany'.

1351 Vicary, Thomas. *Anatomie of the bodie of man, 1548*, ed. Frederick J. and Percy Furnivall (E.E.T.S., extra ser., LIII). 1888. Probably transcribed from a medieval manuscript.

2 Surveys

1352 Boas, Marie. *The scientific Renaissance, 1450–1630* (The Rise of Modern Science, II). 1962. Useful for facts but not as satisfactory for ideas as (1353) and (1355).

1353 Butterfield, Herbert. *The origins of modern science, 1300–1800.* 1957. A brilliant survey.

1354 Derry, Thomas K. and Trevor I. Williams. *A short history of technology.* Oxford, 1960. An excellent survey.

1355 Hall, Alfred R. *The scientific revolution, 1500–1800: the formation of the modern scientific attitude.* 2nd ed., Boston, 1956. Particularly good on the sixteenth century.

1356 Jenkins, Rhys. *Links in the history of engineering and technology from Tudor times.* Cambridge, 1936. A valuable collection of papers. Includes 'An Elizabethan human-power engine: John Payne and the history of the treadmill', 'Bevis Bulmer', 'Railways in the sixteenth century', 'Some old iron castings', 'The beginnings of ironfounding in England', 'Notes on the London Bridge waterworks', 'An early water closet, 1596', 'Paper-making in England, 1495–1788', and 'The alum trade in the fifteenth and sixteenth centuries, and the beginnings of the alum industry in England'.

1357 Osler, William. *The evolution of modern medicine.* New Haven, 1921.

1358 Singer, Charles, Eric J. Holmyard, Alfred R. Hall and Trevor I. Williams. *A history of technology*, III, *From the Renaissance to the industrial revolution.* Oxford, 1957.

1359 Taton, René (ed.). *Histoire générale des sciences*, II, *La science moderne (de 1450 à 1800).* Paris, 1959. An excellent survey by a team of French authorities.

1360 Wightman, William P. D. *Science and the Renaissance: an introduction to the study of the emergence of the sciences in the sixteenth century* (Aberdeen University Studies, CXLIII–CXLIV). Edinburgh and London, 1962. Vol. I is the best general introduction; vol. II is a useful annotated bibliography of sixteenth-century scientific books in the Library of the University of Aberdeen.

3 Monographs

1361 Cipolla, Carlo M. *Guns, sails, & empire: technological innovation and the early phases of European expansion, 1400–1700.* New York, 1963.

1362 Creighton, Charles. *A history of epidemics in Britain*, I. Cambridge, 1891. This old standard is very detailed on the Tudor period. It should be supplemented with Mullett (1371).

1363 Copeman, William S. C. *Doctors and disease in Tudor times.* 1960. A good broad study in layman's language.

1364 Donald, Maxwell B. *Elizabethan copper: the history of the Company of Mines Royal, 1568–1605.* 1955. Illustrates German influence on English mining technology.

1365 Donald, Maxwell B. *Elizabethan monopolies: the history of the Company of Mineral and Battery Works from 1565 to 1604.* Edinburgh and London, 1961. A legal and technical survey.

1366 Hall, Alfred R. and C. Donald O'Malley. *Scientific literature in sixteenth & seventeenth century England.* Los Angeles, 1961.

1367 Handover, Phyllis M. *Printing in London from 1476 to modern times.* 1960. Good for economic and technological developments in the printing trade.

1368 Johnson, Francis R. *Astronomical thought in Renaissance England.* Baltimore, 1937. An important study indicating the 'Baconian' spirit of Elizabethan science before Bacon.

1369 Kocher, Paul H. *Science and religion in Elizabethan England.* San Marino, 1953. A careful and thoughtful study.

1370 Mullett, Charles F. *Public baths and health in England, 16th–18th century* (Bulletin of the History of Medicine Supplements, no. 5). Baltimore, 1946.

1371 —— *The bubonic plague in England.* Lexington, 1956. Excellent on the Tudor period. A contribution to social as well as medical history.

1372 Singer, Charles. *The earliest chemical industry: an essay in the historical relations of economics and technology, illustrated from the alum trade.* 1948.

1373 Taylor, Eva G. R. *The mathematical practitioners of Tudor and Stuart England.* Cambridge, 1954. Brief on the Tudor period but the best account.

1374 Waters, David W. *The art of navigation in England in Elizabethan and early Stuart times.* 1958. A major work by an experienced navigator. In large part an account of the development of navigation from an art to a science.

1375 Wilson, Frank P. *The plague in Shakespeare's London.* Oxford, 1927.

4 Biographies

1376 Anderson, Fulton H. *Francis Bacon: his career and thought.* Los Angeles, 1962.

1377 Crowther, James G. *Francis Bacon, the first statesman of science.* 1960.

1378 Farrington, Benjamin. *Francis Bacon, philosopher of industrial science.* New York, 1949. Good on the development of Bacon's scientific ideas in Elizabeth's reign.

1379 Johnson, John N. *The life of Thomas Linacre.* 1835.

1380 Osler, William. *Thomas Linacre.* Cambridge, 1908.

1381 Smith, C. F. *John Dee, 1527–1608.* 1909.

1382 Thompson, Silvanus P. *Gilbert of Colchester.* 1891.

5 Articles

1383 Albion, Gordon. 'Caius of Cambridge', *Clergy Review*, new ser., **16** (Feb. 1939), 115–24.

1384 Bayon, H. P. 'William Gilbert, 1544–1603, Robert Fludd, 1574–1637, and William Harvey, 1578–1657, as medical exponents of Baconian doctrines', *Royal Society of Medicine Proceedings for 1938–9*, History of Medicine Section, **32** (pt. 1, 1939), 31–42.

1385 Benham, W. Gurney. 'Dr William Gilberd of Tymperlys, Colchester', *Essex Review*, **48** (Jan. 1939), 36–9.

1386 Challinor, John. 'The early progress of British geology: 1, From Leland to Woodward, 1538–1728', *Annals of Science*, **9** (June 1953), 124–53.

1387 Debus, Allen G. 'The Paracelsian compromise in Elizabethan England', *Ambix*, **8** (June 1960), 71–97. The reception of the new medicine of Paracelsus in England.

1388 Donald, Maxwell B. 'Burchard Kranich (*c.* 1515–78), miner and queen's physician, Cornish mining stamps, antimony, and Frobisher's gold', *Annals of Science*, **6** (Mar. 1950), 308–22.

1389 Easton, Joy B. 'A Tudor Euclid', *Scripta mathematica*, **27** (Mar. 1966), 339–55. On Robert Recorde's *Pathway to knowledg*, an elementary manual on geometry of 1552.

1390 Edgar, Irving I. 'Elizabethan conceptions of the physiology of the circulation', *Annals of Medical History*, new ser., **8** (July–Sept. 1936), 359–70, 456–65.

1391 Forbes, Thomas R. 'The regulation of English midwives in the sixteenth and seventeenth centuries', *Medical History*, **8** (July 1964), 235–44.

1392 Fussell, George E. 'William Turner, the father of English botany', *Estate Magazine*, **37** (May 1937), 367–70.

1393 Hall, Alfred R. 'Science', *NCMH*, II, 386–414. A good introduction to sixteenth-century science by a leading authority.

1394 Jacquot, Jean. 'Humanisme et science dans l'Angleterre élisabéthaine: l'œuvre de Thomas Blundeville', *Revue d'histoire des sciences et de leurs applications*, **6** (July–Sept. 1953), 189–202.

1395 Johnson, Francis R. 'The influence of Thomas Digges on the progress of modern astronomy in sixteenth century England', *Osiris*, **1** (Jan. 1936), 390–410.

1396 —— 'Thomas Hill: an Elizabethan Huxley', *HLQ*, **7** (Aug. 1944), 329–51.

1397 Johnson, Francis R. and Sanford V. Larkey. 'Robert Recorde's mathematical teaching and the anti-Aristotelian movement', *Huntington Library Bulletin*, **7** (Apr. 1935), 59–87.

1398 —— 'Thomas Digges, the Copernican system and the idea of the universe in 1575', *Huntington Library Bulletin*, **5** (Apr. 1934), 69–117.

1399 Kocher, Paul G. 'The idea of God in Elizabethan medicine', *JHI*, **11** (Jan. 1950), 3–29.

1400 —— 'The old cosmos: a study of Elizabethan science and religion', *HLQ*, **15** (Feb. 1952), 101–21.

1401 —— 'The physician as atheist in Elizabethan England', *HLQ*, **10** (May 1947), 229–49.

1402 Larkey, Sanford V. 'Public health in Tudor England', *American Journal of Public Health*, **24** (Nov. 1934), 1099–1102. Indicates increasing government concern and activity in the field of public health.

1403 —— 'The Hippocratic oath in Elizabethan England', *Bulletin of the Institute of the History of Medicine*, **4** (Mar. 1936), 201–19.

1404 Lilley, Samuel. 'Robert Recorde and the idea of progress: a hypothesis and a verification', *Renaissance and Modern Studies*, **2** (1958), 3–37.

1405 McCulloch, Samuel C. 'John Dee: Elizabethan doctor of science and magic', *South Atlantic Quarterly*, **1** (Jan. 1951), 72–85.

1406 MacNalty, Arthur S. 'Medicine in the time of Queen Elizabeth the First', *British Medical Journal*, **1** (30 May 1953), 1179–85.

1407 Mason, Stephen F. 'The scientific revolution and the Protestant Reformation', *Annals of Science*, **9** (Mar.–June 1953), 64–87, 154–75.

1408 Matthews, Leslie G. 'Royal apothecaries of the Tudor period', *Medical History*, **8** (Apr. 1964), 170–80.

1409 Mitchell, Rosamond J. 'Thomas Linacre', *EHR*, **50** (Oct. 1935), 696–8.

1410 Mitchell, William S. 'William Bullein, Elizabethan physician and author', *Medical History*, **3** (July 1959), 188–200.

1411 Morant, Valerie. 'The settlement of Protestant refugees in Maidstone during the sixteenth century', *EcHR*, 2nd ser., **4** (no. 2, 1951), 210–24. The introduction of the 'new draperies' and threadmaking by Dutch refugees.

1412 Mullett, Charles F. 'Some neglected aspects of plague medicine in sixteenth century England', *Scientific Monthly*, **44** (Apr. 1937), 325–37.

1413 —— 'The plague of 1603 in England', *Annals of Medical History*, new ser., **9** (May 1937), 230–47.

1414 Nef, John U. 'The genesis of industrialism and of modern science (1560–1640)', in Norton Downs (ed.), *Essays in honor of Conyers Read*, Chicago, 1953, pp. 200–69.

1415 —— 'The progress of technology and the growth of large-scale industry in Great Britain, 1540–1640', *EcHR*, **5** (Oct. 1934), 3–24. Sees the progress of technology and the growth of large-scale industry during the period as 'scarcely less striking' than that in the later 'Industrial Revolution'. Interesting but debatable. See (1423).

1416 O'Neil, B. H. St John. 'Stepan von Haschenberg, an engineer to King Henry VIII, and his work', *Arch.*, **91** (1945), 137–55.

1417 Roberts, R. S. 'The personnel and practice of medicine in Tudor and Stuart England', *Medical History*, 6 (Oct. 1962), 363–82; 8 (July 1964), 217–34.

1418 Sharpe, William D. 'Thomas Linacre, 1460–1524: an English physician scholar of the Renaissance', *Bulletin of the History of Medicine*, 34 (May–June 1960), 233–56.

1419 Simpson, John. 'A note on the Elizabethan sanitary code', *Medical History*, 6 (July 1962), 275–80.

1420 Smith, Goldwin. 'The practice of medicine in Tudor England', *Scientific Monthly*, 50 (Jan. 1940), 65–72. Sees Tudor medicine as not equalling the great advances made in Tudor art, literature, science, etc.

1421 Stearns, Raymond P. 'The scientific spirit in England in early modern times', *Isis*, 34 (pt. 4, 1943), 293–300. Brief but interesting on the development of the 'scientific spirit' in Tudor England.

1422 Taube, Edward. 'German craftsmen in Tudor England', *EcJ*, Economic History Supplement, 3 (Feb. 1939), 167–78. Stresses the role of German immigrants in introducing industrial techniques to Tudor England.

1423 Williams, Lionel. 'Alien immigrants in relation to industry and society in Tudor England', *Hug. Soc. Proc.*, 19 (no. 4, 1956), 146–69. Accepts Nef's theory of an early industrial revolution (1415), but not on the basis of coal-mining alone. Emphasizes the textile industry which had been revolutionized by alien immigrants.

1424 Zeman, Frederic D. 'The amazing career of Doctor Rodrigo Lopez (?–1594)', *Bulletin of the History of Medicine*, 39 (July–Aug. 1965), 295–308.

XI MILITARY AND NAVAL HISTORY

1 Printed sources

1425 Ascham, Roger. *Toxophilus*, in *English works*, ed. W. Aldis Wright, Cambridge, 1904, pp. 3–119. A famous work on archery, first published in 1545.

1426 Churchyard, Thomas. *Share in, and eye witness account of the siege of Guisnes, 11th–22nd January, 1558, A.D.*, in *Tud. Tr.*, pp. 321–30.

1427 Coningsby, Thomas. *Journal of the siege of Rouen, 1591*, ed. John G. Nichols (Camden Miscellany, I, old ser., XXXIX). 1847.

1428 Corbett, Julian S. (ed.). *Papers relating to the navy during the Spanish war, 1585–1587* (Navy Records Society, XI). 1898. Documents of the period before the war was 'official'. Contains an appendix, pp. 315–36, on 'Guns and gunnery in the Tudor navy'.

1429 Fernández Duro, Cesáreo (ed.). *La Armada Invencible*. Madrid, 1884–5, 2 vols. The best collection of Spanish sources, with an introduction presenting the Spanish side of the story.

1430 Ferrers, George. *The winning of Calais by the French, January 1558 A.D.*, in *Tud. Tr.*, pp. 289–320. The narrative appeared in 1569. Useful documents and letters are appended by the editor.

1431 Grey of Wilton, Arthur, Lord. *A commentary of the services and charges of William Lord Grey of Wilton, K.G.*, ed. Philip de M. G. Egerton (Camden Society, old ser., XL). 1847. Mainly the siege of Guisnes, 1558.

1432 Laughton, John K. (ed.). *State papers relating to the defeat of the Spanish Armada, anno 1588* (Navy Records Society, I–II). 1894. The best collection of English sources.

1433 Leng, Robert. *Sir Francis Drake's memorable service done against the Spaniards in 1587*, ed. Clarence Hopper (Camden Miscellany, V, old ser., LXXXVII). 1864. Leng was a gentleman serving with Drake. This ed. also contains extracts from state papers on the expedition of 1587.

1434 Loomie, Albert J. (ed.). 'An Armada pilot's survey of the English coastline, October 1587', *Mariner's Mirror*, 49 (Nov. 1963), 288–300. An interesting survey suggestive of Spanish strategy.

1435 Mackie, John D. (ed.). *The English army at Flodden* (Scottish History Society Miscellany, VIII, 3rd ser., XLIII). Edinburgh, 1951, pp. 35–85. Documents plus an introduction discussing the tactics and organization of the English army.

1436 Monson, William. *Naval tracts*, ed. Michael Oppenheim (Navy Records Society, XXII, XXIII, XLIII, XLV, XLVII). 1902–14. Tracts on naval actions under Elizabeth and on naval administration. Important introductions by Oppenheim.

1437 Naish, George P. B. (ed.). *Documents illustrating the history of the Spanish Armada*, in *The Naval Miscellany*, IV (Navy Records Society, XCII). 1952, pp. 1–84.

1438 Patten, William. *The expedition into Scotland of . . . Edward, duke of Somerset*, in *Tud. Tr.*, pp. 53–157. This account of the expedition of 1547 is one of the earliest and fullest of Tudor military tracts.

1439 Raleigh, Walter. *The last fight of the Revenge*, ed. Henry N. Bolt. 1908.

1440 Smythe, John. *Certain discourses military*, ed. John R. Hale. Ithaca, N.Y. 1964. A tract of 1590 advocating the use of the long bow in preference to the gun. Hale's preface contains a good discussion of the bow-*versus*-gun controversy.

1441 Spont, Alfred (ed.). *Letters and papers relating to the war with France, 1512–1513* (Navy Records Society, X). 1897.

1442 *The late expedition in Scotland*, in *Tud. Tr.*, pp. 37–51. A contemporary account of Hertford's expedition of 1544.

1443 Williams, Roger. *The actions of the Low Countries*, ed. David W. Davies. Ithaca, N.Y. 1964.

2 Surveys

1444 Clowes, William L. *et al. The royal navy: a history*, I–II, 1897–8.

1445 Fortescue, John W. *A history of the British army*, I, 1899. A standard history but brief on the Tudor period.

1446 Lewis, Michael. *The history of the British navy*. 1959.

1447 Marcus, Geoffrey J. *A naval history of England:* I. *The formative centuries* (Naval History of England Series, no. 1). 1961.

3 Monographs

1448 Abrue, Pedro de. *Historia del saqueo de Cadiz por los Ingleses en 1596*. Cadiz, 1866.

1449 Andrews, Kenneth R. *Elizabethan privateering: English privateering during the Spanish war, 1585–1603*. Cambridge, 1964. An important study of a little-explored subject. Particularly valuable on privateering prizes and profits.

1450 Corbett, Julian S. *The successors of Drake*. 1900. Naval warfare, 1596–1603.

1451 Cruickshank, Charles G. *Elizabeth's army*, 2nd ed. Oxford, 1966. Considerably expanded over the 1st ed. of 1946, which it replaces as the standard study.

1452 Falls, Cyril. *Elizabeth's Irish wars*. 1950. Excellent and full.

1453 Ffoulkes, Charles J. *Armour and weapons*. Oxford, 1909.

1454 —— *Gun founders of England*. Cambridge, 1937.

1455 —— *The armourer and his craft from the eleventh to the sixteenth century*. 1912.

1456 Ffoulkes, Charles J. and E. C. Hopkinson. *Sword, lance and bayonet: a record of the arms of the British army and navy*. Cambridge, 1938.

1457 Fowler, Elaine W. *English sea power in the early Tudor period, 1485–1558*. Ithaca, N.Y. 1965.

1458 Froude, James A. *English seamen in the sixteenth century*. New York, 1896.

1459 —— *The Spanish story of the Armada*. 1882.

1460 Gardner, J. Starkie. *Armour in England from the earliest times to the seventeenth century*. 1898. Well illustrated.

1461 Green, Emanuel. *The preparations in Somerset against the Spanish Armada, A.D. 1558–88.* 1888.

1462 Hale, John R. *The art of war and Renaissance England.* Washington, 1961.

1463 Lewis, Michael. *Armada guns.* 1961. Shows the English had no great superiority over the Spaniards in gunpower. Sees their victory in terms of better ships and men.

1464 —— *The Spanish Armada.* 1960. Excellent on ships and guns; inferior to Mattingly (833) in narration.

1465 Mackenzie, William M. *The secret of Flodden.* With 'The rout of the Scots'. Edinburgh, 1931. 'The rout of the Scots' is a translation of a contemporary Italian poem.

1466 Noble, William M. *Huntingdonshire and the Spanish Armada.* 1896.

1467 Oman, Charles W. C. *A history of the art of war in the sixteenth century.* 1937. A standard work by a great military historian.

1468 O'Neil, B. H. St John. *Castles and cannon: a study of early artillery fortifications in England.* Oxford, 1960. The influence of cannon on the construction of castles and fortifications in the sixteenth and seventeenth centuries.

1469 Oppenheim, Michael. *History of the administration of the royal navy.* 1896. Remains the standard work.

1470 Richmond, Herbert. *The navy as an instrument of policy, 1558–1727,* ed. E. A. Hughes. Cambridge, 1953.

1471 Rowse, A[lfred] L[eslie]. *The expansion of Elizabethan England.* 1955. Besides being good on Elizabeth's wars, valuable for the Borderlands of Scotland, Cornwall, and Wales. Particularly worth while is chapter 9, 'War on land: military organisation'.

1472 Unwin, Rayner. *The defeat of John Hawkins.* 1960. A readable account of Hawkins' third voyage.

1473 Webb, Henry J. *Elizabethan military science: the books and the practice.* Madison, 1965. A significant study of Elizabethan military writings and their influence on the development of Elizabeth's army.

1474 Woodrooffe, Thomas. *The enterprise of England.* 1958. A pedestrian account of Anglo-Spanish naval rivalry through the defeat of the Armada.

4 Biographies

1475 Bradford, Ernle. *The wind commands me: a life of Sir Francis Drake.* New York, 1965. Published in England as *Drake.* Of little independent value but readable and generally sound.

1476 Coke, Dorothea. *The last Elizabethan: Sir John Coke, 1563–1644.* 1937. The early part deals with Coke's work in naval administration under Elizabeth.

1477 Corbett, Julian S. *Drake and the Tudor navy.* 1899, 2 vols. Full and important. Very favourable to Drake. Also see (1490).

1478 Cranfill, Thomas M. and Dorothy H. Bruce. *Barnaby Rich: a short biography.* Austin, Texas, 1953. An Elizabethan soldier and writer.

1479 Falls, Cyril. *Mountjoy: Elizabethan general.* 1955. A good and readable life of perhaps Elizabeth's best general.

1480 Jones, Frederick M. *Mountjoy, 1563–1606: the last Elizabethan deputy,* Dublin, 1958. More satisfactory than (1479) for Mountjoy's rule in Ireland.

1481 Laughton, John K. (ed.). *From Howard to Nelson.* 1899. Contains short biographies of Howard (by Laughton) and Drake (by Frederick G. D. Bedford).

1482 Markham, Clements R. 'The fighting Veres'. 1888. Mainly on Sir Francis Vere, Elizabeth's general in the Low Countries, called by Markham 'the first great English general in modern history'.

1483 Prouty, Charles T. *George Gascoigne, Elizabethan courtier, soldier and poet.* 1942. Contains a long chapter on the poet's involvement in the revolt of the Netherlands, 1572–4.

1484 Rowse, A[lfred] L[eslie]. *Sir Richard Grenville of the Revenge, an Elizabethan hero.* 1949.

1485 Southey, Robert. *English seamen,* ed. David Hannay. Chicago, 1895. Dated but fine portraits of Lord Howard of Effingham, the Earl of Cumberland, Hawkins and Drake, and Thomas Cavendish.

1486 Williamson, George C. *George, third earl of Cumberland, 1558–1605*. Cambridge, 1920.

1487 Williamson, James A. *Hawkins of Plymouth*. 1949. Not as full as (1489) but presents new information.

1488 —— *Sir Francis Drake*, 1953. An admirable brief life.

1489 —— *Sir John Hawkins, the times and the man*. Oxford, 1927. A first-rate scholarly biography.

1490 —— *The age of Drake*, 5th ed. 1965. Excellent. More objective about Drake than (1477).

5 Articles

1491 Abbott, Wilbur C. 'A true Elizabethan: Sir William Monson', in *Conflicts with Oblivion*. New Haven, 1924, pp. 71–102.

1492 Adair, Edward R. 'English galleys in the sixteenth century', *EHR*, **35** (Oct. 1920), 497–512.

1493 Anscombe, Alfred. 'Prégent de Bidoux's raid in Sussex in 1514', *TRHS*, 3rd ser., **8** (1914), 103–11.

1494 Armstrong, Edward. 'Venetian despatches on the Armada and its results', *EHR*, **12** (Oct. 1897), 659–78.

1495 Barrington, Michael. 'The most high-spirited man on earth: Sir Richard Grenville's last fight, Sept. 1591, new evidence', *Mariner's Mirror*, **36** (Oct. 1950), 350–3.

1496 Bovill, Edward W. 'Queen Elizabeth's gunpowder', *Mariner's Mirror*, **33** (July 1947), 179–86. Elizabethan trafficking in arms with the Moors of North Africa.

1497 Boynton, Lindsay. 'The Tudor provost-marshal', *EHR*, **77** (July 1962), 437–55. Deals with the provost-marshal in civilian as well as military police work.

1498 Burne, A. H. 'The siege of Ostend', *Royal Artillery Journal*, **65** (no. 2, 1938), 238–53. 1601.

1499 Busch, Wilhelm. 'Englands Kriege im Jahre 1513: Guingate und Flodden', *Historische Vierteljahrsschrift*, **13** (1910), 1–69.

1500 Callender, Geoffrey A. R. 'The evolution of sea power under the first two Tudors', *History*, new ser., **5** (Oct. 1920), 141–58.

1501 —— 'The naval campaign of 1587', *History*, new ser., **3** (July 1918), 82–91.

1502 Chadwick, Michael. 'Defence measures for the West Riding, 1586', *Yorks. Arch. J.*, **40** (pt. 2, 1960), 227–31.

1503 Christy, Miller. 'Queen Elizabeth's visit to Tilbury in 1588', *EHR*, **34** (Jan. 1919), 43–61.

1504 Clepham, Robert C. 'The military handgun of the 16th century', *Archaeological Journal*, **67**, new ser., **17** (1910), 109–50. A good discussion of different types of guns.

1505 Cruickshank, Charles G. 'Dead-pays in the Elizabethan army', *EHR*, **53** (Jan. 1938), 93–7. A futile experiment in military finance aimed at promoting efficiency and the welfare of the private soldier.

1506 —— 'Elizabethan pensioner reserve', *EHR*, **56** (Oct. 1941), 637–9.

1507 Davies, C. S. L. 'The administration of the royal navy under Henry VIII: The origins of the navy board', *EHR*, **80** (Apr. 1965), 268–86.

1508 Davis, Harold H. 'The military career of Thomas North', *HLQ*, **12** (May 1949), 315–21. A late Elizabethan soldier.

1509 Dyer, Florence E. 'Reprisals in the sixteenth century', *Mariner's Mirror*, **21** (Apr. 1935), 187–97. Anglo-French incidents during Elizabeth's reign.

1510 Esper, Thomas. 'The replacement of the longbow by firearms in the English army', *Technology and Culture*, **6** (Summer 1965), 382–93. Attributes the replacement of the longbow in the late sixteenth century, despite its superiority over firearms, to a decline in the practice of archery.

1511 Ewen, C. H. l'Estrange. 'Organized piracy round England in the sixteenth century', *Mariner's Mirror*, **35** (Jan. 1949), 29–42.

1512 Gairdner, James. 'The Battle of Bosworth', *Arch.*, **55** (1896), 159–78.
1513 Gibbs, J. 'Richard Cooper and the Spanish plate fleet of 1533', *University of Birmingham Historical Journal*, **7** (no. 1, 1959), 101–3.
1514 Glasgow, Tom, Jr. 'The shape of the ships that defeated the Spanish Armada', *Mariner's Mirror*, **50** (Aug. 1964), 177–88.
1515 Goldingham, Cecil S. 'Development of tactics in the Tudor navy', *United Service Magazine*, **177** (June 1918), 207–15.
1516 —— 'The expedition to Portugal, 1589', *Royal United Service Institution Journal*, **63** (Aug. 1918), 469–78.
1517 —— 'The navy under Henry VII', *EHR*, **33** (Oct. 1918), 472–88.
1518 —— 'The personnel of the Tudor navy and the internal economy of the ships', *United Service Magazine*, **177** (Mar. 1918), 427–51.
1519 —— 'The warships of Henry VIII', *United Service Magazine*, **179** (Mar. 1919), 453–62.
1520 Hale, John R. 'Armies, navies, and the art of war', *NCMH*, II, 481–509. An authoritative general article. 1519–1559.
1521 —— 'Gunpowder and the Renaissance: an essay in the history of ideas', in *Ren. to C.-Ref.*, pp. 113–44. Explodes many of the myths historians have made about the influence of gunpowder on civilization.
1522 —— 'War and public opinion in the fifteenth and sixteenth centuries', *PP*, no. 22 (July 1962), 18–33.
1523 Henry, L. W. 'The earl of Essex as strategist and military organizer, 1596–7', *EHR*, **68** (July 1953), 363–93.
1524 Hogg, O. F. G. 'The "Gunner" and some other early masters of ordnance', *Royal Artillery Journal*, **62** (Jan. 1936), 463–73.
1525 Hooker, James R. 'Notes on the organization and supply of the Tudor military under Henry VII', *HLQ*, **23** (Nov. 1959), 19–31. Emphasizes Henry's dependence on the support of local magnates to raise an army.
1526 James, J. B. 'Mountjoy: an Elizabethan man of principle', *History Today*, **16** (Jan. 1966), 29–37. Elizabeth's ablest soldier and governor in Ireland.
1527 Johns, A. W. 'The principal officers of the navy', *Mariner's Mirror*, **14** (Jan. 1928), 32–9. Mainly sixteenth century.
1528 Jorgensen, Paul A. 'Moral guidance and religious encouragement for the Elizabethan soldier', *HLQ*, **13** (May 1950), 241–59. On standards of conduct and courtesy expected of Elizabethan soldiers.
1529 —— 'Theoretical views of war in Elizabethan England', *JHI*, **13** (Oct. 1952), 469–79.
1530 Ker, William P. 'The Spanish story of the Armada', *SHR*, **17** (Apr. 1920), 165–76.
1531 Laughton, John K. 'The Elizabethan naval war with Spain', in *CMH*, III, 294–327.
1532 Laughton, Leonard G. C. 'Early Tudor ship-guns', *Mariner's Mirror*, **66** (Nov. 1960), 242–85. A good technical study.
1533 —— 'The burning of Brighton by the French', *TRHS*, 3rd ser., **10** (1916), 163–73.
1534 Lewis, Michael. 'The guns of the Jesus of Lübeck', *Mariner's Mirror*, **22** (July 1936), 324–45. Hawkins's flagship.
1535 Lloyd, Christopher. 'The title of Lord High Admiral', *Mariner's Mirror*, **60** (Aug. 1954), 236–67.
1536 Marsden, Reginald G. 'The vice-admiral of the coast', *EHR*, **22** (July 1907), 468–77; **23** (Oct. 1908), 736–57.
1537 Mathew, David. 'Cornish and Welsh pirates in the reign of Elizabeth', *EHR*, **39** (July 1924), 337–48.
1538 Mattingly, Garrett. 'No peace beyond what line?', *TRHS*, 5th ser., **13** (1963), 145–62. Fails to find the expression 'no peace beyond the line' relevant for sixteenth- and seventeenth-century England.
1539 Oman, Charles W. C. 'The battle of Pinkie, September 10, 1547', *Archaeological Journal*, **90** (pt. 1, 1934), 1–25.
1540 Oppenheim, Michael. 'The royal and merchant navy under Elizabeth', *EHR*, **6** (July 1891), 465–94. A good summary and statistical study. Cf. (1545).

1541 Owen, L. V. D. 'Sir Roger Williams and the Spanish power in the Netherlands', *Army Quarterly*, **34** (Oct. 1937), 53–66.

1542 Pearce, Brian. 'Elizabethan food policy and the armed forces', *EcHR*, **12** (no.
1, 1942), 39–46.

1543 Robinett, C. M. 'Ship technology and the defeat of the Armada', *U.S.
Naval Institute Proceedings*, **78** (Feb. 1952), 171–9.

1544 Rose, J. Holland. 'Was the failure of the Spanish Armada due to storms?',
PBA, **22** (1936), 207–44. Says no but gives out-of-date explanations of
Spain's failure.

1545 Round, John H. and Michael Oppenheim. 'The royal navy under Queen
Elizabeth', *EHR*, **9** (Oct. 1894), 709–15. Critique of Oppenheim (1540) by
Round and reply by Oppenheim.

1546 Waters, David W. 'Limes, lemons and scurvy in Elizabethan and early
Stuart times', *Mariner's Mirror*, **61** (May 1955), 167–9.

1547 —— 'The Elizabethan navy and the Armada campaign', *Mariner's Mirror*,
35 (Apr. 1949), 90–138.

1548 Webb, Henry J. 'Elizabethan field artillery', *Military Affairs*, **19** (Winter,
1955), 197–202.

1549 —— 'Elizabethan soldiers: a study in the ideal and the real', *Western
Humanities Review*, **4** (Winter-Spring, 1949–50), 19–33, 141–54.

1550 —— 'The science of gunnery in Elizabethan England', *Isis*, **45** (May 1954),
10–21.

1551 —— 'Thomas Digges, an Elizabethan combat historian', *Military Affairs*,
14 (no. 2, 1950), 53–6.

1552 Webb, John G. 'William Sabyn of Ipswich: an early Tudor sea-officer and
merchant', *Mariner's Mirror*, **61** (Aug. 1955), 209–21.

1553 Wernham, Richard B. 'Elizabethan war aims and strategy', in *Govt. & Soc.*,
pp. 340–68. A cautious defence of Elizabeth's management of the Anglo-
Spanish war. Also see (1554).

1554 —— 'Queen Elizabeth and the Portugal expedition of 1589', *EHR*, **66**
(Jan.–Apr. 1951), 1–26, 194–218.

1555 —— 'Queen Elizabeth and the siege of Rouen in 1591', *TRHS*, 4th ser.,
15 (1932), 163–79.

XII RELIGIOUS HISTORY

1 Printed sources

1556 Allen, Percy S. and Helen M. (eds.). *Letters of Richard Fox, 1486–1527.*
Oxford, 1928.

1557 Allen, Percy S. *et al. Opus epistolarum Des. Erasmi Roterodami.* Oxford,
1906–58, 12 vols. A monumental collection. English translations in (1637).

1558 Allen, William. *An admonition to the nobility and people of England and
Ireland . . . A.D. MDLXXXVIII*, ed. Eupater. 1842. A poisonous attack
on Elizabeth, calling on her subjects to abandon their allegiance. Though
written by others, signed and therefore approved by Cardinal Allen.

1559 —— *A true, sincere and modest defence of English Catholics . . .* 1914, 2 vols.
Tract of 1584 answering charges made by Burghley (1577).

1560 —— *Souls departed: being a defence and a declaration of the Catholic Church's
doctrine touching purgatory and prayers for the dead*, ed. Thomas E.
Bridgett. 1886.

1561 —— *Some correspondence of 1579–85, from the Jesuit archives*, ed. Patrick
Ryan (Catholic Record Society Miscellanea, VII). 1911, pp. 12–105.

1562 Arber, Edward (ed.). *A brief discourse of the troubles at Frankfort, 1554–1558
A.D.* 1908. Conflicts among the Marian exiles that presage later conflicts
between Anglican and Puritan. Commonly attributed to William Whittingham, but cf. (1928).

1563 —— *An introductory sketch to the Martin Marprelate controversy.* 1879. A
good collection of documents.

1564   Bale, John. *Select works*, ed. Henry Christmas (Parker Society, I). Cambridge, 1849. Includes Anne Askew's examinations.

1565   Bateson, Mary (ed.). *A collection of original letters from the bishops to the privy council, 1564, with returns of the justices of the peace and others within their respective dioceses, classified according to their religious convictions* (Camden Miscellany, IX, new ser., LIII). 1895. The returns are useful as indicators of the progress of the Reformation among the gentry in different parts of England.

1566   —— 'Archbishop Warham's visitation of monasteries, 1511', *EHR*, 6 (Jan. 1891), 18–35.

1567   Batten, Edmund C. (ed.). *The registers of Richard Fox, while bishop of Bath and Wells, 1492–4.* 1889. Contains a life of Fox.

1568   Beccatelli, Ludovico. *The life of Cardinal Pole.* trans. B. Pye, 1776. By Pole's secretary.

1569   Becon, Thomas. *Prayers and other pieces*, ed. John Ayre (Parker Society, IV). Cambridge, 1844.

1570   —— *The catechism ... with other pieces written ... in the reign of King Edward the Sixth*, ed. John Ayre (Parker Society, III). Cambridge, 1844.

1571   —— *The early works ..., being the treatises published ... in the reign of King Henry VIII*, ed. John Ayre (Parker Society, II). Cambridge, 1843.

1572   Bilson, Thomas. *The perpetual government of Christ's church*, ed. Robert Eden. Oxford, 1842. A defence of episcopacy, 1593.

1573   Bradford, John. *Writings*, ed. Aubrey Townshend (Parker Society, V–VI). Cambridge, 1848–53. Sermons, treatises, letters, examinations, etc., of a Marian martyr.

1574   Brett, John. 'A narration of the pursuit of English refugees in Germany under Queen Mary', ed. Isaac S. Leadam. *TRHS*, 2nd ser., II (1897), 113–31.

1575   Brinkelow, Henry. *The complaynt of Roderyck Mors*, ed. J. Meadows Cowper (E.E.T.S., extra ser., XXII). 1874. Written *c.* 1542. Complains of the results of the Henrician Reformation, particularly for the peasants.

1576   Brinkworth, E. R. C. (ed.) *The archdeacon's court: liber actorum, 1584* (Oxford-shire Record Society, XXIII–XXIV). Oxford, 1942–6. The 2nd vol. contains an essay on the types of cases handled.

1577   Burghley, William Cecil, Lord. *The execution of justice in England, 1583.* New York, 1936. Defends Elizabeth's treatment of Catholics. Cf. Allen (1559).

1578   Burrage, Champlin (ed.). *A 'New Years Gift': an hitherto lost treatise by Robert Browne, the father of congregationalism, in the form of a letter to his uncle Mr Flower.* 1904.

1579   —— *John Penry, the so-called martyr of congregationalism, as revealed in the original record of his trial and in documents relating thereto.* Oxford, 1913.

1580   Burton, Edwin H. and Thomas L. Williams (eds.). *The Douay College diaries, third, fourth, and fifth, 1598–1654, with the Rheims report, 1579–80* (Catholic Record Society, X–XI). 1911. For the first two diaries see (1630).

1581   Caley, John and Joseph Hunter (eds.). *Valor ecclesiasticus.* 1810–34, 6 vols. The great survey of all ecclesiastical benefices, 1535. For an analysis and appraisal see Knowles (1756), pp. 241–54.

1582   Cardwell, Edward (ed.). *A history of conferences and other proceedings connected with the book of common prayer from the year 1558 to the year 1690.* Oxford, 1849. This and (1586) comprise a documentary history of the prayer-book. The commentary is superseded by (1791).

1583   —— *Documentary annals of the reformed Church of England: being a collection of injunctions, declarations, orders, articles of inquiry, &c., from the year 1546 to the year 1716.* Oxford, 1844, 2 vols.

1584   —— *Synodalia: a collection of articles of religion, canons and proceedings of convocations in the province of Canterbury from the year 1547 to the year 1717.* Oxford, 1842, 2 vols.

1585   —— *The reformation of the ecclesiastical laws as attempted in the reigns of*

King Henry VIII, King Edward VI and Queen Elizabeth. Oxford, 1850. Originally *Reformatio legum ecclesiasticarum,* 1571. Still in Latin.

1586 —— *The two books of common prayer, set forth by authority of parliament in the reign of King Edward the Sixth, compared.* Oxford, 1841.

1587 Carlson, Leland H. (ed.). *The writings of Henry Barrow, 1587–1590* (Elizabethan Nonconformist Texts, III). 1962. This and (1588) are important collections of tracts and documents for the history of Elizabethan Separatism.

1588 —— *The writings of John Greenwood, 1587–1590* (Elizabethan Nonconformist Texts, IV). 1962.

1589 Chamier, Adrian C. (ed.). *Les actes des colloques des églises françaises et des synodes des églises étrangères réfugiées en Angleterre, 1581–1654* (Huguenot Society of London, II). 1890.

1590 Chaubard, A. H. (ed.). *Une œuvre inconnue de Théodore de Bèze: Response a la confession due feu Jean de Northumberlande, n'agueres decapité en Angleterre.* Lyons, 1959. Beza's answer to Northumberland's recantation of Protestantism at his execution.

1591 Clay, William K. (ed.). *Liturgies and occasional forms of prayer set forth in the reign of Queen Elizabeth* (Parker Society, XXX). Cambridge, 1847. Includes the prayer book of 1559.

1592 Cobb, Cyril S. (ed.). *The rationale of ceremonial, 1540–1543, with notes and appendices and an essay on the regulation of ceremonial during the reign of King Henry VIII* (Alcuin Club, XVIII). 1910. Includes the book of ceremonies of *c.* 1540 and excerpts from the Articles of Religion of 1536.

1593 Collinson, Patrick (ed.). *Letters of Thomas Wood, Puritan, 1566–1577* (*BIHR,* Special Supplement, no. 5). 1960. Contains letters between Wood and Leicester that shed some light on Leicester's 'puritanism'.

1594 Cook, George H. (ed.). *Letters to Cromwell and others on the suppression of the monasteries.* 1965.

1595 Cooper, Thomas. *An admonition to the people of England: against Martin Mar-Prelate.* 1847. An 'official' tract of 1589, by the bishop of Winchester, attacking Martin Marprelate and defending the bishops.

1596 Coverdale, Myles. *Remains,* ed. George Pearson (Parker Society, XIV). Cambridge, 1846.

1597 —— *Writings and translations,* ed. George Pearson (Parker Society, XIII). Cambridge, 1844.

1598 —— (ed.). *The letters of the martyrs,* ed. Edward Bickersteth. 1837. Letters of Protestant martyrs.

1599 Cranmer, Thomas. *Miscellaneous writings and letters,* ed. John E. Cox (Parker Society, XVI). Cambridge, 1846.

1600 —— *Writings and disputations . . . relative to the sacrament of the Lord's Supper,* ed. John E. Cox (Parker Society, XV). Cambridge, 1844.

1601 Dickens, Arthur G. (ed.). 'Archbishop Holgate's Apology', *EHR,* **54** (July 1941), 450–9.

1602 —— *Register or chronicle of Butley Priory, Suffolk, 1510–35.* Winchester, 1951.

1603 —— 'Robert Parkyn's narrative of the Reformation', *EHR,* **62** (Jan. 1947), 58–83. A Catholic account of 1532–55.

1604 —— *Tudor treatises* (Yorkshire Archaeological Society, Record Ser., CXXV). Wakefield, 1959. Sir Francis Bigod's *A treatise concerning impropriations of benefices,* five devotional treatises of Robert Parkyn, and Michael Sherbrook's *The fall of religious houses.*

1605 Duffield, Gervase (ed.). *The work of William Tyndale.* Appleford, Berkshire, 1964. Four treatises plus extracts from other works.

1606 Fish, Simon. *A supplicacyon for the beggers, written about the year 1529,* ed. Frederick J. Furnivall and J. Meadows Cowper (E.E.T.S., extra ser., XIII). 1871. With three other tracts, all attacks on the ignorance and worldliness of the clergy.

1607 Fisher, John. *English works,* ed. John E. B. Mayer (E.E.T.S., extra ser., XXVI). 1876.

1608 Foster, Charles W. (ed.). *The state of the church in the reigns of Elizabeth and*

James I as illustrated by documents relating to the diocese of Lincoln (Lincoln Record Society, XXIII). Horncastle, 1926.

1609 Frere, Walter H. and Charles E. Douglas (eds.). *Puritan manifestoes.* 1954. Important documents, including *An admonition to the Parliament.*

1610 Frere, Walter H. and William P. M. Kennedy (eds.). *Visitation articles and injunctions of the period of the Reformation* (Alcuin Club, XIV–XVI). 1908. 1536–75. Continued in (1626).

1611 Gairdner, James (ed.). 'Bishop Hooper's visitation of Gloucester', *EHR*, **19** (Jan. 1904), 98–121. Abstract, visitation of 1551.

1612 Gerard, John. *The autobiography of a hunted priest*, trans. Philip Caraman. New York, 1952. Published in England as *The autobiography of an Elizabethan.*

1613 Gibson, Edmund (ed.). *Codex juris ecclesiastici anglicani.* Oxford, 1761, 2 vols. When a document is in Latin there is an English abridgement.

1614 Grindal, Edmund. *Remains*, ed. William Nicholson (Parker Society, XIX). Cambridge, 1843.

1615 Hale, William H. (ed.). *A series of precedents and proceedings in criminal causes . . . 1475–1640; extracted from the act-books of ecclesiastical courts in the diocese of London, 1847.*

1616 [Hall, Richard.] *The life of Fisher*, ed. Ronald Bayne (E.E.T.S., extra ser. CXVII). 1921. An edition of a 1535 life of John Fisher.

1617 Henry VIII. *Assertio septem sacramentorum*, ed. Louis O'Donovan. New York, 1908. Latin original plus English translation.

1618 Hicks, Leo (ed.). *Letters and memorials of Father Robert Persons, S.J.*, I, *To 1588* (Catholic Record Society, XXXIX). 1942.

1619 Hinde, Gladys (ed.). *The registers of Cuthbert Tunstall, bishop of Durham, 1530–59, and James Pilkington, bishop of Durham, 1561–76* (Surtees Society, CLXI). Durham, 1952.

1620 Hodgett, G. A. J. (ed.). *The state of the ex-religious and former chantry priests in the diocese of Lincoln, 1547–1574* (Lincoln Record Society, LIII). Hereford, 1959. Lists of pensioners with a valuable introduction.

1621 Hooper, John. *Early writings*, ed. Samuel Carr (Parker Society, XX). Cambridge, 1843.

1622 —— *Later writings . . . together with . . . letters and other pieces*, ed. Charles Nevinson (Parker Society, XXI). Cambridge, 1852.

1623 Hutchinson, Roger. *Works*, ed. John Bruce (Parker Society, XXII). Cambridge, 1842.

1624 Jessop, August (ed.). *Visitations of the diocese of Norwich, A.D. 1492–1532* (Camden Society, new ser., XLIII). 1888.

1625 Jewel, John. *Works*, ed. John Ayre (Parker Society, XXIII–XXVI). Cambridge, 1840–50. The 3rd vol. contains Jewel's *Apology*, the first significant defence of the Elizabethan church.

1626 Kennedy, William P. M. (ed.). *Elizabethan episcopal administration* (Alcuin Club, XXV–XXVII). 1924. 1579–1603. A continuation of (1610).

1627 Kitchin, George W. (ed.). *Records of the northern convocation* (Surtees Society, CXIII). Durham, 1907. 1279–1714.

1628 Knox, John. *A narrative of the proceedings and troubles of the English congregation at Frankfort on the Main, 1554–5*, in David Laing (ed.), *Works of John Knox*, Edinburgh, 1846–64, 6 vols., IV, 41–9.

1629 Knox, Thomas F. (ed.). *Letters and memorials of William Allen* (Records of the English Catholics under the Penal Laws, II). 1882.

1630 —— *The first and second diaries of the English college, Douai, and an appendix of unpublished documents* (Records of the English Catholics under the Penal Laws, I). 1878. The third diary is in (1580).

1631 Latimer, Hugh. *Works*, ed. George E. Conie (Parker Society, XXVII–XXVIII). Cambridge, 1844–5. Mainly sermons.

1632 Law, Thomas G. (ed.). *The archpriest controversy: documents relating to the dissensions of the Roman Catholic clergy, 1597–1602* (Camden Society, new ser., LVI, LVIII). 1896–8.

1633 Lehmberg, Stanford E. (ed.). 'Archbishop Grindal and the prophesyings', *Historical Magazine of the Protestant Episcopal Church*, XXXIV (June 1965),

87–145. Letters, 1574–77, relating to the religious exercises called 'prophesyings', which led to Grindal's fall.

1634 Le Neve, John (ed.). *Fasti ecclesiae anglicanae.* Oxford, 1854, 3 vols.; revised ed., 1962–. A useful calendar of the principal ecclesiastical dignitaries in England and Wales.

1635 Lloyd, Charles (ed.). *Formularies of faith put forth by authority during the reign of Henry VIII.* Oxford, 1825. Contains the *Ten Articles* of 1536, the *Bishop's Book* of 1537, and the *King's Book* of 1543.

1636 Merrill, Thomas F. (ed.). *William Perkins, 1558–1602, English puritanist.* Nieuwkoop, 1966. Prints Perkins' *A discourse of conscience* and *The whole treatise of cases of conscience.*

1637 Nichols, Francis M. (trans.). *The epistles of Erasmus, from his earliest letters to his fifty-fifth year.* 1901–18, 3 vols. An English translation of most of the letters of Erasmus.

1638 Nichols, John G. (ed.). *Narratives of the days of the Reformation, chiefly from the manuscripts of John Foxe, the martyrologist; with two contemporary biographies of Archbishop Cranmer* (Camden Society, old ser., LXXVII). 1859.

1639 —— *Two sermons preached by the boy bishop at St Paul's, temp. Henry VIII, and at Gloucester, temp. Mary* (Camden Miscellany, VII, new ser., XIV). 1875.

1640 Parker, Matthew. *Correspondence,* ed. John Bruce and Thomas T. Perowne (Parker Society, XXXIII). Cambridge, 1853. Letters to and from Parker, 1535–75.

1641 Peckham, W. D. (ed.). *The acts of the dean and chapter of the cathedral church of Chichester, 1545–1642.* Lewes, 1959. Documents illustrative of the financial difficulties of a cathedral chapter in the century following the Reformation.

1642 Peel, Albert (ed.). *The Brownists in Norwich and Norfolk about 1580: some new facts together with 'A treatise of the church and the kingdome of Christ', by R. H. [Robert Harrison?].* Cambridge, 1920.

1643 —— *The notebook of John Penry, 1593* (Camden Society, 3rd ser., LXVII). 1944. Peel's introduction discusses the authorship of the Marprelate tracts but reaches no definite conclusion.

1644 —— *The seconde parte of a register, being a calendar of manuscripts under that title intended for publication by the Puritans about 1593 . . .* Cambridge, 1915, 2 vols.

1645 —— *Tracts ascribed to Richard Bancroft.* Cambridge, 1953. Anti-Puritan tracts.

1646 Peel, Albert and Leland H. Carlson (eds.). *Cartwrightiana* (Elizabethan Nonconformist Texts, I). 1951.

1647 Peel, Albert and Leland H. Carlson (eds.). *The writings of Robert Harrison and Robert Browne* (Elizabethan Nonconformist Texts, II). 1953. Includes Browne's important separatist tract, *A treatise of Reformation without tarying for anie,* pp. 150–70.

1648 Penry, John. *Three treatises concerning Wales,* ed. David Williams. Cardiff, 1960. Three tracts on religious conditions in Elizabethan Wales by a Puritan.

1649 Philpot, John. *Examinations and writings,* ed. Robert Eden (Parker Society, XXXIV). Cambridge, 1842. Philpot was martyred in 1555.

1650 Pierce, William (ed.). *The Marprelate tracts, 1588, 1589,* 1911.

1651 Pilkington, James. *Works,* ed. James Scholefield (Parker Society, XXXV). Cambridge, 1842.

1652 Pole, Reginald. *Epistolae . . . ,* ed. Angelo M. Quirini. Brescia, 1744–57, 5 vols.

1653 —— *Pole's defense of the unity of the Church,* trans. and ed. Joseph G. Dwyer. Westminster, Md., 1965. The *Pro ecclesiastica unitatis defensione,* written for Henry VIII and in defence of the papacy.

1654 Pollard, Alfred W. (ed.). *Records of the English Bible, the documents relating to the translation and publication of the Bible in English, 1525–1611.* Oxford, 1911.

1655 Pollen, John H. (ed.). *Unpublished documents relating to the English martyrs, 1584–1603* (Catholic Record Society, V, XXI). 1908–14.

1656 Purvis, John S. (ed.). *Select XVI century cases in tithe from the York diocesan registry* (Yorkshire Archaeological Society, Record Ser., CXIV). 1949.

1657 —— *Tudor parish documents of the diocese of York.* Cambridge, 1948.

1658 Raine, James (ed.). *The correspondence of Dr Matthew Hutton, archbishop of York* . . . (Surtees Society, XVII). 1843. 1565–1605.

1659 Renold, Penelope (ed.). *The Wisbech stirs (1595–1598)* (Catholic Record Society, LI). 1958. Documents on the quarrels among imprisoned priests at Wisbech.

1660 Ridley, Nicholas. *Works*, ed. Henry Christmas (Parker Society, XXXIX). Cambridge, 1841.

1661 Robinson, Hastings (trans. and ed.). *Original letters relative to the English Reformation, written during the reigns of King Henry VIII, King Edward VI, and Queen Mary: chiefly from the archives of Zurich* (Parker Society, LII–LIII). Cambridge, 1846–7. This and (1662) comprise an invaluable source.

1662 —— *The Zurich letters, comprising the correspondence of several English bishops and others during the early part of the reign of Queen Elizabeth* (Parker Society, L–LI). Cambridge, 1842–5.

1663 Rogers, Richard and Samuel Ward. *Two Elizabethan Puritan diaries*, ed. Marshall M. Knappen. Chicago, 1933.

1664 Sander, Nicholas. *Report to Cardinal Moroni on the change of religion in 1558–9*, ed. John H. Pollen, in *Catholic Record Society Miscellany*, I (1905), 1–46.

1665 —— *The rise and growth of the Anglican schism*, trans. and ed. David Lewis. 1877. An embittered Catholic work of more than doubtful veracity. Vicious toward Anne Boleyn and Elizabeth.

1666 Sandys, Edwin. *Sermons*, ed. John Ayre (Parker Society, XLI). Cambridge, 1841.

1667 Smith, Richard. *An Elizabethan recusant house: the life of the Lady Magdalen, Viscountess Montague*, ed. A. C. Southern. 1954.

1668 Southwell, Robert. *An humble supplication to Her Maiestie*, ed. Robert C. Bald. Cambridge, 1953. A Jesuit tract of 1591 anticipating the secular reconciliation of loyalty to church and state.

1669 Thompson, A. Hamilton (ed.). *Visitations in the diocese of Lincoln, 1517–1531* (Lincoln Record Society, XXXIII, XXXV, XXXVII). Hereford, 1940–7.

1670 Townshend, George and Stephen R. Cattley (eds.). *The acts and monuments of John Foxe*. 1837–41, 8 vols. Of great historical value despite Foxe's obvious prejudice. The best discussion of Foxe's veracity is in (1872). See also (2060).

1671 Tyndale, William. *An answer to Sir Thomas More's dialogue, the Supper of the Lord* . . . , ed. Henry Walter (Parker Society, XLIV). Cambridge, 1850.

1672 —— *Doctrinal treatises and introductions to different portions of the Holy Scriptures*, ed. Henry Walter (Parker Society, XLII). Cambridge, 1848.

1673 —— *Expositions and notes on sundry portions of the Holy Scripture, together with the practice of prelates*, ed. Henry Walter (Parker Society, XLIII). Cambridge, 1849.

1674 Udall, John. *A demonstration of the trueth of that discipline which Christe hath prescribed in his worde for the gouernment of his church* . . . , ed. Edward Arber. 1880. This and (1675) are extreme Puritan tracts of 1588.

1675 —— *The state of the Church of Englande laide open in a conference between Diotrephes a byshop, Tertullus a papist, Demetrius a vsurer, Pandocheus an inne-keeper and Paule a preacher of the words of God*, ed. Edward Arber. 1880.

1676 Usher, Roland G. (ed.). *The Presbyterian movement in the reign of Queen Elizabeth as illustrated by the minute book of the Dedham Classis, 1582–1589* (Camden Society, 3rd ser., VIII). 1905. Valuable material and discussion.

1677 Wainewright, John B. (ed.). *Some letters and papers of Nicholas Sander, 1562–80*, in *Catholic Record Society Miscellany*, 13 (1926), 1–57.

1678 Waldegrave, Robert (ed.). *A parte of a register* . . . [Middelburg, 1593.] 33 Puritan tracts. Very valuable.

1679 Weston, William. *An autobiography from the Jesuit underground*, trans. Philip Caraman. New York, 1955.

1680 Whatmore, Leonard E. (ed.). *Archdeacon Harpsfield's visitation, 1557* (Catholic Record Society, XLV–XLVI). 1950–1.

1681 —— 'The sermon against the Holy Maid of Kent, delivered at Paul's Cross, November 23, 1533 and at Canterbury, Dec. 7', *EHR*, **58** (Oct. 1943), 463–75.

1682 Whitgift, John. *Works*, ed. John Ayre (Parker Society, XLVI–XLVIII). Cambridge, 1851–3.

1683 Wilkins, David (ed.). *Concilia Magnae Britanniae et Hiberniae.* 1737, 4 vols. Extant records of convocations, 446–1718.

1684 Willis, Arthur J. (ed.). *Winchester consistory court depositions, 1561–1602.* Lyminge, 1960.

1685 Wright, Thomas (ed.). *Three chapters of letters relating to the suppression of the monasteries* (Camden Society, old ser., XXVI). 1843.

1686 Youings, Joyce A. (ed.). *Devon monastic lands: calendar of particulars for grants, 1536–1558* (Devon and Cornwall Record Society, new ser., 1). Torquay, 1955.

2 Surveys

1687 Burnet, Gilbert. *History of the Reformation of the Church of England*, ed. Nicholas Pocock. Oxford, 1865, 7 vols. Answers Sander (1665). Useful for documents.

1688 Constant, Gustave. *The Reformation in England*, I, *The English schism: Henry VIII (1509–1547)*, trans. R. E. Scantlebury, 1934; II, *Introduction of the Reformation into England: Edward VI (1547–1553)*, trans. E. I. Watkin, 1942. A serviceable survey based mainly on secondary works.

1689 Dickens, Arthur G. *The English Reformation.* 1964. Very much the best survey, but somewhat slight on the Elizabethan period.

1690 Dixon, Richard W. *History of the Church of England from the abolition of the Roman jurisdiction.* Oxford, 1872–1902, 6 vols. Covers 1529–70 from a High Anglican viewpoint. Detailed and useful for documentation.

1691 Dodd, Charles. *The church history of England from 1500 to the year 1688 . . .*, ed. Mark A. Tierney. 1839–43, 5 vols. Tierney's notes and documents make this Catholic account of real value.

1692 Frere, Walter H. *The English Church in the reigns of Elizabeth and James I.* 1904. This and Gairdner (1694) are vols. IV and V of *A history of the English Church.* Both are factually reliable; Frere is by far the more objective.

1693 Fuller, Thomas. *Church history of Britain from the birth of Jesus Christ until the year 1648*, ed. John S. Brewer. Oxford, 1845, 6 vols. A charming and entertaining survey worth reading despite its obvious Anglican bias.

1694 Gairdner, James. *The English Church in the sixteenth century from the accession of Henry VIII to the death of Mary.* 1902. See (1692).

1695 Hughes, Philip. *The Reformation in England.* 1951–4, 3 vols. A detailed and important Catholic account, the objectivity of which has been too hastily acclaimed.

1696 Hurstfield, Joel (ed.). *The Reformation crisis.* 1965. Stimulating essays by X leading scholars, some on England and all relevant to England.

1697 Maitland, Samuel R. *Essays on subjects connected with the Reformation in England.* 1849. Dated but still interesting.

1698 Parker, Thomas M. *The English Reformation to 1558.* Oxford, 1950. A good brief survey.

1699 Powicke, F[rederick] M[aurice]. *The Reformation in England.* 1941. Sees the Reformation as an act of state.

1700 Strype, John. *Ecclesiastical memorials relating chiefly to religion, and its reformation, under the reigns of King Henry VIII, King Edward VI, and Queen Mary . . .* 1816, 7 vols. This and (1701) comprise a lengthy survey that is still of use for documents.

1701 —— *Annals of the Reformation and establishment of religion, and other various occurrences in the Church of England, during Queen Elizabeth's happy reign.* Oxford, 1824, 4 vols.

3 Monographs

1702 Archbold, William A. J. *The Somerset religious houses.* Cambridge, 1892.

1703 Arrowsmith, Richard S. *The prelude to the Reformation: a study of English church life from the age of Wycliffe to the breach with Rome.* 1923.

1704 Aveling, Hugh. *Post-Reformation Catholicism in East Yorkshire, 1558–1790* (East Yorkshire Local History Society, no. 11). York, 1960.

1705 —— *The Catholic recusants of the West Riding of Yorkshire, 1558–1790.* Leeds, 1963.

1706 Baskerville, Geoffrey. *English monks and the suppression of the monasteries.* 1937. Contains valuable information on the ex-religious, but is overly hostile to the monks.

1707 Bertrand, Pierre. *Genève et la Grande-Bretagne de John Knox à Oliver Cromwell.* Geneva, 1948.

1708 Birt, Henry N. *The Elizabethan religious settlement.* 1907. A Catholic critique of Gee (1732), primarily over the number of clergy who refused to accept the new Church. For sensible conclusions on this number debate, see (1774) and (1787).

1709 Blench, J. W. *Preaching in England in the late fifteenth and sixteenth centuries: a study of English sermons, 1450–c. 1600.* New York, 1964.

1710 Bridgett, Thomas E. and Thomas F. Knox. *The true story of the Catholic hierarchy deposed by Queen Elizabeth.* 1889. A Catholic account.

1711 Brooks, Peter. *Thomas Cranmer's doctrine of the eucharist.* 1965. Attempts to show Cranmer's movement toward the 'spiritualism' of Geneva.

1712 Burrage, Champlin. *The early English dissenters in the light of recent research (1550–1641).* Cambridge, 1912, 2 vols. Vol. I deals with the history and literature of Separatism; vol. II is a collection of documents. Both are valuable.

1713 Butterworth, Charles C. *The English primers (1529–1545): their publication and connection with the English Bible and the Reformation in England.* Philadelphia, 1953.

1714 Churchill, Irene J. *Canterbury administration.* 1933, 2 vols. An important and detailed study of archiepiscopal administration, mainly before the break with Rome.

1715 Clebsch, William A. *England's earliest Protestants, 1520–1535* (Yale Publications in Religion, 11). New Haven, 1964. Barnes, Frith, Tyndale, etc.

1716 Coulton, George C. *Five centuries of religion, IV, The last days of medieval monachism.* Cambridge, 1950. The final vol. of a controversial study by a great historian.

1717 Cremeans, Charles D. *The reception of Calvinist thought in England* (Illinois Studies in the Social Sciences, XXXI, no. 1). Urbana, Ill., 1949.

1718 Davies, Ebenezer T. *Episcopacy and the royal supremacy in the Church of England in the XVI century.* Oxford, 1950. Makes a significant case for the royal supremacy. Very good on the official formularies.

1719 Davies, D. Horton. *The worship of the English Puritans.* Westminster, 1948. The most useful work on the subject.

1720 Devlin, Christopher. *Hamlet's divinity and other essays.* 1963. Includes several essays relevant to the history of Elizabethan Catholicism.

1721 Dickens, Arthur G. *Lollards and Protestants in the diocese of York, 1509–1558.* Oxford, 1959. A major contribution. Demonstrates, through a study of a Catholic diocese, the survival of Lollardy and its continuing influence on Protestantism.

1722 —— *The Marian reaction in the diocese of York* (St Anthony's Hall Publications, XI–XII). 1957. Pt. I deals with the clergy; pt. II, the laity.

1723 Doernberg, Erwin. *Henry VIII and Luther: an account of their personal relations.* Stanford, 1961. Ordinary on the Reformation but interesting on the personal encounter between Henry and Luther.

1724 Dugmore, Clifford W. *The mass and the English reformers.* 1958. Suggests that the English reformers derived their Eucharistic doctrine from the Fathers and early medieval writings rather than Zwingli or Calvin. See also Brink (1919).

1725 Foley, Henry. *Records of the English province of the Society of Jesus.* 1877–84, 7 vols. The documents are far more valuable than the text.

1726 Frere, Walter H. *The Marian reaction in its relation to the English clergy* (Church History Society, XVIII). 1896.

1727 Gairdner, James. *Lollardy and the Reformation in England.* 1908–13, 4 vols. Much more concerned with the Reformation than with Lollardy. Marred by a strong prejudice against 'heresy'.

1728 Garrett, Christina H. *The Marian exiles: a study in the origins of Elizabethan Puritanism.* Cambridge, 1938. The interpretations are most doubtful, but it contains valuable information on individual exiles.

1729 Gasquet, Francis A. *Henry VIII and the English monasteries.* 1888–89, 2 vols. A sentimental Catholic account that may safely be ignored. Definitely superseded by Knowles (1756).

1730 —— *The eve of the Reformation.* 1900. Smith (1802) is preferable.

1731 Gasquet, Francis A. and Edmund Bishop. *Edward VI and the Book of Common Prayer.* 1890. Useful for its appendix of documents. Cf. (1791).

1732 Gee, Henry. *The Elizabethan clergy, and the settlement of religion, 1558–64.* Oxford, 1898. An investigation of the treatment of the clergy. Cf. (1708).

1733 —— *The Elizabethan Prayer Book and ornaments, with an appendix of documents.* 1902.

1734 Gelder, H. A. Enno van. *The two Reformations of the sixteenth century,* trans. J. F. Finlay. The Hague, 1961. Maintains Christian humanism was the major Reformation and Protestantism the minor one. Not convincing and has Catholic bias on the English Reformation.

1735 George, Charles H. and Katherine. *The Protestant mind of the English Reformation, 1570–1640.* Princeton, 1961. A stimulating broad study of the 'Protestant ideology' in England. Excludes Separatism.

1736 Gillow, Joseph. *A literary and biographical history, or bibliographical dictionary, of the English Catholics from the breach with Rome, in 1534, to the present time.* 1885–1903, 5 vols.

1737 Greenslade, Stanley L. *The English reformers and the fathers of the Church.* Oxford, 1960.

1738 Guilday, Peter. *The English Catholic refugees on the continent.* New York, 1914. A strongly Catholic account of various religious communities.

1739 Haller, William. *Foxe's 'Book of Martyrs' and the elect nation.* 1963. Shows Foxe's contribution to the development of the notion of Elizabethan England as the 'elect nation'.

1740 —— *The rise of Puritanism: or, the way to the New Jerusalem as set forth in pulpit and press from Thomas Cartwright to John Lilburne and John Milton.* New York, 1938. Mainly early seventeenth century but excellent for what it has on the sixteenth.

1741 Hardwick, Charles. *A history of the Articles of Religion.* 3rd ed., Cambridge, 1859. Has an appendix of documents, 1536–1615.

1742 Hart, A. Tindal. *The country clergy in Elizabethan and Stuart times, 1558–1660.* 1958.

1743 Hill, Christopher. *Economic problems of the Church, from Archbishop Whitgift to the Long Parliament.* Oxford, 1956. An important study of the financial problems of the church and the economic and social status of the clergy.

1744 —— *Society and Puritanism in pre-revolutionary England.* 1964. Suggests non-theological reasons for supporting Puritanism or being a Puritan.

1745 Hinds, Allen B. *The making of the England of Elizabeth.* 1895. An account of the Marian exiles.

1746 Hodges, Joseph P. *The nature of the lion: Elizabeth I and our Anglican heritage.* 1962. Based entirely on secondary material. Sees Elizabeth as an Anglo-Catholic.

1747 Holden, William P. *Anti-Puritan satire, 1572–1642.* New Haven, 1954.

1748 Hughes, Philip. *Rome and the Counter-Reformation in England.* 1942.

1749 Jacobs, Henry E. *A study in comparative symbolics: the Lutheran movement in England during the reigns of Henry VIII and Edward VI, and its literary monuments.* Philadelphia, 1908.

1750 Janelle, Pierre. *L'Angleterre catholique à la veille du schisme*. Paris, 1935. Mainly on Stephen Gardiner.

1751 Jessop, Augustus. *One generation of a Norfolk house: a contribution to Elizabethan history*. 1879. On a Catholic family, the Walpoles, under persecution.

1752 Jordan, Wilbur K. *The development of religious toleration in England from the beginning of the English Reformation to the death of Queen Elizabeth*. Cambridge, Mass., 1932.

1753 Kennedy, William P. M. *Parish life under Queen Elizabeth*. 1914.

1754 Klein, Arthur J. *Intolerance in the reign of Elizabeth, Queen of England*. Boston, 1917.

1755 Knappen, Marshall M. *Tudor Puritanism*. Chicago, 1939. The best general account.

1756 Knowles, David. *The religious orders in England*, III, *The Tudor age*. Cambridge, 1959. A scholarly, judicious, and beautifully written account by a Benedictine. Definitely the best work on the subject.

1757 Law, Thomas G. *A historical sketch of the conflicts between Jesuits and seculars in the reign of Queen Elizabeth*. 1889. Includes Christopher Bagshaw's 'True relation of the faction begun at Wisbech' and other documents.

1758 Leatherbarrow, J. Stanley. *The Lancashire Elizabethan recusants* (Chetham Society, new ser., CX). Manchester, 1947. A study of Lancashire recusancy and the failure of the Elizabethan Church to make much headway against it.

1759 Lechat, Robert. *Les refugiés anglais dans les Pays-Bas espagnols durant le règne d'Elisabeth*. Louvain, 1914.

1760 Liljegren, Sten B. *The fall of the monasteries and the social changes leading up to the Great Revolution* (Lunds Universitets Arsskrift, N.F., 1923, Avd. 1, XIX Teologi). Lund, 1924. Stresses financial aspects.

1761 Lupton, Joseph H. *The influence of Dean Colet upon the Reformation of the English Church*. 1893.

1762 MacColl, Malcolm. *The Reformation Settlement*. 1899. Cf. Frederic W. Maitland, 'Canon MacColl's new convocation', in *Collected papers*, ed. Herbert A. L. Fisher. Cambridge, 1911, III, 119–36.

1763 McConica, James K. *English humanists and Reformation politics under Henry VIII and Edward VI*. Oxford, 1965. Stresses the continuing influence of the Erasmians on the English Reformation. Important but the case may be overstated.

1764 McGinn, Donald J. *The admonition controversy*. New Brunswick, N.J., 1949. A sound account of the first important literary controversy between Puritans and Anglicans, with abridgements of tracts of Cartwright and Whitgift.

1765 Maclure, Millar. *The Paul's Cross sermons, 1534–1642*. Toronto, 1958. Deals with social criticism as well as religious questions.

1766 Magee, Brian. *The English recusants: a study of the post-Reformation Catholic survival and the operation of the recusancy laws*. 1938.

1767 Makower, Felix. *The constitutional history and constitution of the Church of England*. New York, 1895. A translation of a valuable German work which, though dated in some respects, has not been replaced.

1768 Marchant, Ronald A. *The Puritans and the church courts in the diocese of York, 1560–1642*. 1960. Shows light treatment of Puritans by church courts.

1769 Marti, Oscar A. *Economic causes of the Reformation in England*. New York, 1929. Sees the roots of the Henrician Reformation as primarily economic. The case is certainly overstated.

1770 Martin, Charles. *Les protestants anglais refugiés à Genève au temps de Calvin, 1555–60*. Geneva, 1915.

1771 Mathew, David, *Catholicism in England, 1535–1935*. 2nd ed., 1948.

1772 Mathew, David and Gervase. *The Reformation and the contemplative life. a study of the conflict between the Carthusians and the state*. 1934.

1773 Messenger, Ernest C. *The Reformation, the mass and the priesthood: a documented history with special reference to the question of Anglican orders. 1936–7*, 2 vols.

1774 Meyer, Arnold O. *England and the Catholic Church under Queen Elizabeth*, trans. John R. McKee. 1916. The soundest work on the subject.

1775 Meyer, Carl S. *Elizabeth I and the religious settlement of 1559*. St Louis, 1960. An attempted reappraisal, emphasizing the theological side.

1776 Morgan, Edmund S. *Visible saints: the history of a Puritan idea*. New York, 1963. Mainly on New England but excellent on the English background.

1777 Morgan, Irvonwy. *The godly preachers of the Elizabethan Church*. 1965. A good and sympathetic picture of the Puritan preachers.

1778 Moorman, John R. H. *The Grey Friars in Cambridge, 1225–1538*. Cambridge, 1952.

1779 Mortimer, C. G. and S. C. Barber. *The English bishops and the Reformation, 1530–1560*. 1936. Deals mainly with the question of apostolic succession from a Roman Catholic point of view.

1780 New, John F. H. *Anglican and Puritan: the basis of their opposition, 1558–1640*. Stanford, 1964. Emphasizes the importance of religious and doctrinal differences as opposed to political and economic. A useful antidote to some recent views.

1781 Oxley, James E. *The Reformation in Essex to the death of Mary*. Manchester, 1965. A detailed study of the Reformation in one of the earliest shires to become strongly Protestant.

1782 Peel, Albert. *The first congregational churches: new light on separatist congregations in London, 1567–81*. Cambridge, 1920.

1783 Pennington, Edgar L. *The episcopal succession during the English Reformation*. 1952.

1784 Peters, Robert. *Oculus episcopi: administration in the archdeaconry of St Albans, 1580–1625*. Manchester, 1963. A valuable little study of ecclesiastical administration.

1785 Phillips, G. E. *The extinction of the ancient hierarchy*. 1905. A Catholic account of the Elizabethan 'persecution' of eleven Marian bishops.

1786 Pierce, William. *An historical introduction to the Marprelate tracts*. 1908. A worthwhile account of Elizabethan Puritanism. Favourable to the Puritans.

1787 Pollen, John H. *The English Catholics in the reign of Elizabeth*. 1920. Useful but not as objective as Meyer (1774).

1788 —— *The institution of the Arch-Priest Blackwell, 1595–1602*. 1916.

1789 Porter, Harry C. *Reformation and reaction in Tudor Cambridge*. Cambridge, 1958. An important study of the development of Puritanism and opposition to it at Cambridge. Particularly good on the theological controversies involved.

1790 Primus, John H. *The vestments controversy: an historical study of the earliest tensions within the Church of England in the reigns of Edward VI and Elizabeth*. Kampen, 1960. More satisfactory for Edward VI's reign than for Elizabeth's, but the first full study of the subject.

1791 Proctor, Francis, and Walter H. Frere. *A new history of the Book of Common Prayer* . . . 1914. The best history of the prayer-book.

1792 Ramsey, Michael *et al. The English Prayer Book, 1549–1662*. 1963. Esp. chapter 2, 'The first ten years, 1549–59' by Clifford W. Dugmore, and chapter 3, 'The problem of uniformity, 1559–1604' by Thomas M. Parker.

1793 Ratcliff, Edward C. *The Book of Common Prayer of the Church of England: its making and revisions, M.D.XLIX–M.D.CLXI*. 1949.

1794 Read, Conyers. *Social and political forces in the English Reformation*. Houston, 1953.

1795 Ritchie, Carson I. A. *The ecclesiastical courts of York*. Arbroath, Scotland, 1956. A study of the organization and procedure of courts Christian in York, mainly during Elizabeth's reign.

1796 Routley, Erik. *English religious dissent*. Cambridge, 1960. A good introduction to the subject.

1797 Rupp, E[rnest] G[ordon]. *Six makers of the English Reformation, 1500–1700*.

1957. Includes chapters on Tyndale and the Bible, Cranmer and the Prayer Book, and Foxe and his martyrology.

1798 Rupp, E[rnest] G[ordon]. *Studies in the making of the English Protestant tradition*. Cambridge, 1947. Essays on the Henrician Reformation stressing its religious side. Particularly good on the Lutheran influence.

1799 Savine, Alexander. *English monasteries on the eve of the dissolution* (Oxford Studies in Social and Legal History, I). Oxford, 1909. Important on the monastic economy.

1800 Smith, Lacey B. *Tudor prelates and politics, 1536–1558* (Princeton Studies in History, VIII). Princeton, 1953. Concerned mainly with the fears of conservative prelates that doctrinal change might lead to civil and social disorder.

1801 Smith, H. Maynard. *Henry VIII and the Reformation*. 1948.

1802 —— *Pre-Reformation England*. 1938. Good for the state of the Church.

1803 Southern, A. C. *Elizabethan recusant prose, 1559–1582*. 1950. A study of the books of English Catholic refugees with an excellent bibliography.

1804 Summers, William H. *The Lollards of the Chiltern Hills*. 1906.

1805 Sykes, Norman. *Old priest and new presbyter*. Cambridge, 1956. The first two chapters of this stimulating book are devoted to the Elizabethan period.

1806 —— *The Church of England and non-episcopal churches in the sixteenth and seventeenth centuries*. 1948.

1807 Taunton, Ethelred L. *The history of the Jesuits in England, 1580–1773*. Philadelphia, 1901. The appendix contains summaries of the main writings of Robert Parsons.

1808 Taylor, Henry O. *Thought and expression in the sixteenth century*. New York, 1920, 2 vols. Vol. II, book iv, 'England', deals mainly with religious thought.

1809 Thompson, B. M. H. *The consecration of Archbishop Parker*. 1934.

1810 Thompson, James V. P. *Supreme governor: a study of Elizabethan ecclesiastical policy and circumstance*. 1940.

1811 Thomson, John A. F. *The later Lollards, 1414–1520*. Oxford, 1965. A good study of the middle period of Lollardy.

1812 Thornton, Lionel S. *Richard Hooker: a study of his theology*. 1924.

1813 Tjernagel, Neelak S. *Henry VIII and the Lutherans: a study in Anglo-Lutheran relations from 1521 to 1547*. St Louis, 1965.

1814 Trimble, William R. *The Catholic laity in Elizabethan England, 1558–1603*. Cambridge, Mass., 1964. Much better on the political and religious side than on the social and economic.

1815 Usher, Roland G. *The reconstruction of the English Church*. New York, 1910, 2 vols. Vol. I is good on the late Elizabethan period.

1816 —— *The rise and fall of the high commission*. Oxford, 1913. The standard authority.

1817 Vetter, Theodor. *Literarische Beziehungen zwischen England und der Schweiz im Reformationszeitalter*. Zurich, 1901.

1818 Ware, Sedley L. *The Elizabethan parish in its ecclesiastical and financial aspects* (Johns Hopkins University Studies in Historical and Political Science, ser. XXVI, nos. 7–8). Baltimore, 1908.

1819 Watkin, Edward I. *Roman Catholicism in England from the Reformation to 1950*. Oxford, 1957. A readable and judicious survey.

1820 White, Helen C. *The Tudor books of private devotion*. Madison, Wis., 1951.

1821 —— *Tudor books of saints and martyrs*. Madison, Wis., 1963. Suggests links between medieval saint-worship and sixteenth-century martyr-worship. Has an interesting chapter on Foxe.

1822 Whitebrook, John C. *The consecration of Matthew Parker, archbishop of Canterbury*. 1945.

1823 Whitley, W. T. *The English Bible under the Tudor sovereigns*. 1937.

1824 Williams, George H. *The radical reformation*. 1962. A study of radical religious movements in Europe, including England, 1520–80.

1825 Williams, Glanmor. *The Welsh Church from conquest to Reformation*. Cardiff, 1962. Over half of this detailed study is devoted to the Tudor period, mainly up to 1536.

1826 Willoughby, Harold R. *The Coverdale Psalter and the quatrocentenary of the printed English Bible.* Chicago, 1935.
1827 —— *The first Authorized English Bible and the Cranmer preface.* Chicago, 1942.
1828 Woodhouse, H. F. *The doctrine of the Church in Anglican theology, 1574–1603.* 1954.

4 Biographies

1829 Babbage, Stuart S. *Puritanism and Richard Bancroft,* 1962. Contains a discussion of Bancroft's rise under Elizabeth.
1830 Bailey, Derrick S. *Thomas Becon and the Reformation of the Church in England.* Edinburgh, 1952.
1831 Biron, Reginald and Jean. *Reginald Pole,* Paris, 1923. A Catholic life.
1832 Booty, John E. *John Jewel as apologist of the Church of England,* 1963.
1833 Bridgett, Thomas E. *The life of Blessed John Fisher . . . ,* 5th ed. 1935.
1834 Bromiley, Geoffrey W. *Nicholas Ridley, 1500–1555, scholar, bishop, theologian, martyr.* 1953.
1835 —— *Thomas Cranmer: archbishop and martyr.* 1955.
1836 —— *Thomas Cranmer, theologian.* New York, 1956. Apologetic but sound on theology.
1837 Brook, Victor J. K. *A life of Archbishop Parker,* Oxford, 1962. Partial to Parker but the best life.
1838 —— *Whitgift and the English Church.* 1957. Sympathetic to Whitgift but sound.
1839 Brown, William J. *Life of Rowland Taylor.* 1959. A good life of a learned divine and Marian martyr.
1840 Burrage, Champlin. *The true story of Robert Browne (1550?–1633), father of congregationalism . . .* Oxford, 1906. A well-documented short study.
1841 Butterworth, Charles C. and Allan G. Chester. *George Joye, 1495?–1553.* Philadelphia, 1962. A minor biblical translator and Protestant pamphleteer.
1842 Camm, Bede. *Lives of the English martyrs.* 1904–5, 2 vols. Catholic martyrs, 1535–83.
1843 Campbell, William E. *Erasmus, Tyndale and More.* 1949. Strong on the religious side. Somewhat prejudiced against Tyndale.
1844 Chester, Allan G. *Hugh Latimer: apostle to the English.* Philadelphia, 1954. This and (1845) are both sound.
1845 Darby, Harold S. *Hugh Latimer.* 1953.
1846 Dawley, Powel M. *John Whitgift and the English Reformation.* New York, 1954.
1847 Demaus, Robert. *Hugh Latimer, a biography.* 1869. Still important for factual detail. For more up-to-date interpretations see (1844) and (1845).
1848 Devlin, Christopher. *The life of Robert Southwell, poet and martyr.* 1956.
1849 Dickens, Arthur G. *Robert Holgate, archbishop of York and president of the king's council in the north* (St Anthony's Hall Publications, VIII). 1955. A useful and penetrating little study.
1850 —— *Thomas Cromwell and the English Reformation.* 1959. Excellent on Cromwell and his religious policies.
1851 Eells, Hastings. *Martin Bucer.* New Haven, 1931.
1852 Gasquet, Francis A. *The last abbot of Glastonbury and his companions.* 1934. The abbot is Richard Whiting, who died in 1539.
1853 Gray, Charles M. *Hugh Latimer and the sixteenth century: an essay in interpretation.* Cambridge, Mass., 1950.
1854 Greenslade, Stanley L. *The work of William Tindale.* 1938. A short biography, an essay on Tyndale's thought, and selections from his works.
1855 Haile, Martin. *An Elizabethan cardinal, William Allen.* 1914. Quite partial but the only halfway satisfactory life.
1856 —— *Life of Reginald Pole.* 1910. A strongly biased Catholic life.
1857 Hopf, Constantin L. R. A. *Martin Bucer and the English Reformation.* Oxford, 1946.
1858 Hunt, Ernest W. *Dean Colet and his theology.* 1956.

1859 Hutchinson, Francis E. *Cranmer and the English Reformation.* 1951.
1860 Kennedy, William P. M. *Archbishop Parker.* 1908.
1861 Knox, Samuel J. *Walter Travers: paragon of Elizabethan puritanism.* 1962. Somewhat pro-Travers but generally sound.
1862 Lewis, John. *The life of Dr John Fisher.* 1855, 2 vols. Vol. II contains a useful collection of papers relating to Fisher's life.
1863 Loane, Marcus L. *Masters of the English Reformation.* 1954. Short biographies of Bilney, Tyndale, Latimer, Ridley, and Cranmer by an Anglican.
1864 —— *Pioneers of the Reformation in England.* 1964. Biographical sketches of John Frith, Robert Barnes, John Rogers, and John Bradford.
1865 Longden, Henry I. *Northampton and Rutland clergy,* A.D. *1500–1900.* Northampton, 1939–52, 16 vols. Biographies of many hundreds of clergy.
1866 Lupton, Joseph H. *A life of John Colet.* 1887. Still the best life.
1867 McGinn, Donald J. *John Penry and the Marprelate controversy.* New Brunswick, N.J., 1966. More objective than Pierce (1877) on Penry and the fullest study of the controversy. Presents the strongest case yet to identify Penry as Martin Marprelate.
1868 Marriot, John A. R. *The life of John Colet.* 1933.
1869 Marshall, John S. *Hooker and the Anglican tradition.* 1963. Useful but not always convincing on the *Ecclesiastical Polity.*
1870 Maynard, Theodore. *The life of Thomas Cranmer.* Chicago, 1956. A Catholic life.
1871 Mozley, James F. *Coverdale and his Bibles.* 1953.
1872 —— *John Foxe and his book.* 1940. A defence of Foxe.
1873 —— *William Tyndale.* 1937. Sound but uncritical.
1874 O'Connell, Marvin R. *Thomas Stapleton and the Counter-Reformation* (Yale Publications in Religion, no. 9). New Haven, 1964. An Elizabethan exile and important Catholic thinker and propagandist.
1875 Pearson, A. F. Scott. *Thomas Cartwright and Elizabethan Puritanism.* Cambridge, 1925. The best work on Elizabethan Presbyterianism.
1876 Perry, Edith W. *Under four Tudors, being the story of Matthew Parker, sometime archbishop of Canterbury.* 1964. Cf. Carter (1921).
1877 Pierce, William. *John Penry, his life, times and writings.* 1923. Strongly partial to Penry. Cf. McGinn (1867).
1878 Pollard, Albert F. *Thomas Cranmer and the English Reformation, 1489–1556.* 1926. Still important but cf. Ridley (1885).
1879 Pollen, John H. and Edwin H. Burton. *Lives of the English martyrs.* 1914. Catholic martyrs, 1583–1603.
1880 Powicke, Frederick J. *Henry Barrow, Separatist (1550?–1593), and the exiled church of Amsterdam (1593–1622).* 1900.
1881 —— *Robert Browne, pioneer of modern congregationalism.* 1910.
1882 Read, Evelyn. *My Lady Suffolk: a portrait of Catherine Willoughby, duchess of Suffolk.* New York, 1963. An admirable portrait and a painless introduction to Tudor Puritanism.
1883 Reynolds, Ernest E. *Saint John Fisher.* 1955.
1884 Ridley, Jasper. *Nicholas Ridley: a biography.* 1957.
1885 —— *Thomas Cranmer.* Oxford, 1962. Now the best biography. Better theologically than (1878).
1886 Schenk, Wilhelm. *Reginald Pole: cardinal of England.* 1950. A judicious treatment of a controversial man.
1887 Seebohm, Frederic. *The Oxford reformers.* 1938. Colet, Erasmus, and More.
1888 Shirley, Frederick J. J. *Elizabeth's first archbishop.* 1948. Second to Brook (1837).
1889 Shirley, Timothy F. *Thomas Thirlby, Tudor bishop.* 1964. A Marian bishop who tried to reconcile his loyalties to Rome and England under Elizabeth.
1890 Smyth, C. H. *Cranmer and the Reformation under Edward VI.* Cambridge, 1926.
1891 Southgate, Wyndham M. *John Jewel and the problem of doctrinal authority* (Harvard Historical Monographs, XLIX). Cambridge, Mass., 1962. Useful for Jewel's *Apology* but tends to overestimate his influence.

1892   Strype, John. *Historical collections of the life and acts of the Right Reverend Father in God, John Aylmer . . .* 1701. This and the following works by Strype are still of use for documents, though they are sometimes carelessly edited.

1893   —— *Memorials of the Most Reverend Father in God, Thomas Cranmer . . . ,* revised ed. 1853, 2 vols.

1894   —— *The history of the life and acts of the Most Reverend Father in God, Edmund Grindal . . .* 1710.

1895   —— *The life and acts of Matthew Parker . . .* 1711.

1896   —— *The life and acts of the Most Reverend Father in God, John Whitgift . . .* 1718.

1897   Sturge, Charles. *Cuthbert Tunstal.* 1938. Sound enough. At any rate, the only biography.

1898   Waugh, Evelyn. *Edmund Campion.* 1935.

1899   Zimmerman, Athanasius. *Kardinal Pole, sein Leben und seine Schriften, ein Beitrag zur Kirchengeschichte des 16. Jahrhunderts.* Regensburg, 1893. A Jesuit life and the best until Schenk (1886).

5 Articles

1900   Antheunis, Louis. 'Un Jésuite anglais aux Pays-Bas espagnols: Sir Edward Stanley (1564–1639),' *Rev. d'hist. ecc.,* **32** (Apr. 1936), 360–5.

1901   —— 'Un réfugié anglais, traducteur de Louis de Grenade: Richard Hopkins, 1546–94', *Rev. d'hist. ecc.,* **35** (Jan. 1939), 70–7.

1902   —— 'Un réfugié catholique aux Pays-Bas: Sir Roger Ashton (*d.* 1592)', *Rev. d'hist. ecc.,* **27** (July 1931), 589–91.

1903   Aston, Margaret. 'John Wycliffe's Reformation reputation', *PP,* no. 30 (Apr. 1965), 22–51.

1904   —— 'Lollardy and the Reformation: survival or Revival?', *History,* new ser., **49** (June 1964), 149–70. Emphasizes recovery, revival, and use of Lollard works by the early English Protestants.

1905   Arundale, R. L. 'Edmund Grindal and the northern province', *CQR,* **160** (Apr.–June 1959), 182–99. Stresses Grindal's role in the spread of Puritanism in the diocese of York.

1906   Aveling, Hugh. 'The marriage of Catholic recusants, 1559–1642', *JEH,* **14** (Apr. 1963), 68–83. Legal problems faced by Catholics who observed pre-Reformation canonical rules about impediments to marriage.

1907   Bailey, Sherwin. 'Robert Wisdom under persecution, 1541–43', *JEH,* **2** (Oct. 1951), 180–9. The persecution of a reformer during the latter part of Henry VIII's reign.

1908   Barnaud, Jean. 'Les causes économiques de la Réforme en Angleterre', *Etudes théologiques et religieuses,* **7** (1932), 27–49.

1909   Barry, J. C. 'The Convocation of 1563', *History Today,* **13** (July 1963), 490–501. The convocation that drew up the Thirty-Nine Articles.

1910   Baskerville, Geoffrey. 'Elections to convocation in the diocese of Gloucester under Bishop Hooper', *EHR,* **44** (Jan. 1929), 1–32.

1911   —— 'Married clergy and pensioned religious in Norwich diocese, 1555', *EHR,* **48** (Jan.–Apr. 1933), 43–64. 199–228.

1912   —— 'The dispossessed religious after the suppression of the monasteries', in Henry W. Carless Davis (ed.). *Essays in history presented to Reginald Lane Poole.* Oxford, 1927, pp. 436–65. This and (1913) are Baskerville's best studies of the ex-religious.

1913   —— 'The dispossessed religious in Surrey', in *Surrey Archaeological Collections,* XLVII Castle Arch, Guildford, 1941, pp. 12–28.

1914   —— 'The dispossessed religious of Gloucestershire', in H. P. R. Finberg (ed.), *Gloucestershire Studies,* Leicester, 1957, pp. 130–44.

1915   Bayne, Charles G. 'Visitation of the province of Canterbury, 1559', *EHR,* **28** (Oct. 1913). 636–77. Traces and documents the proceedings of the royal commissioners who carried out the visitation and thereby took the first step in the 'alteration of religion'.

1916 Bossy, John. 'Rome and the Elizabethan Catholics: a question of geography', *Hist. J.*, 7 (no. 1, 1964), 135–42. Problems of transportation and communication and their effects on Elizabethan Catholicism.

1917 —— 'The character of Elizabethan catholicism', *PP*, no. 21 (Apr. 1962), 39–59. The conflict between the gentry and the clerks resulting in the victory of the former and inertia.

1918 Bowker, Margaret. 'Non-residence in the Lincoln diocese in the early sixteenth century', *JEH*, 15 (Apr. 1964), 40–50.

1919 Brink, J. N. Bakhuizen van den. 'Ratramn's eucharistic doctrine and its influence in sixteenth-century England', in *Stud. Ch. Hist.*, 11, 54–77.

1920 Brinkworth, E. R. C. 'The study and use of Archdeacon's Court Records, illustrated from Oxford Records, 1566–1759', *TRHS*, 4th ser., 25 (1943), 93–119.

1921 Carter, C. Sydney. 'The real Matthew Parker', *CQR*, 137 (July–Sept. 1943), 205–20. Critique of Perry (1876).

1922 Chadwick, Owen. 'Richard Bancroft's submission', *JEH*, 3 (Apr. 1952), 58–73.

1923 Chester, Allan G. 'Robert Barnes and the burning of the books', *HLQ*, 14 (May 1951), 211–21.

1924 Clancy, Thomas H. 'Notes on Persons's "Memorial for the Reformation of England" (1596)', *Rec. Hist.*, 5 (Jan. 1959), 17–34. Discusses the *Memorial* as a statement of the aims of the Counter-Reformation.

1925 Cleary, Martin. 'The Catholic resistance in Wales, 1568–1678', *Blackfriars*, 38 (Mar. 1957), 111–25.

1926 Clebsch, William A. 'The earliest translations of Luther into English', *Harvard Theological Review*, 56 (Jan. 1963), 75–86.

1927 Collinson, Patrick. 'John Field and Elizabethan Puritanism', in *Govt. & Soc.*, pp. 127–62. Maintains the strength of Puritanism in the first half of Elizabeth's reign and attributes its failure to gain ground to the queen. Sees Field as the leader of the movement and a brilliant revolutionary.

1928 —— 'The authorship of *A brieff discours off the troubles begonne at Franckford*', *JEH*, 9 (Oct. 1958), 188–208. Suggests the author was Thomas Wood, not William Whittingham.

1929 —— 'The beginnings of English sabbatarianism', in *Stud. Ch. Hist.*, 1, 207–21.

1930 —— 'The "Nott Conformyte" of the young John Whitgift', *JEH*, 15 (Oct. 1964), 192–200.

1931 —— 'The role of women in the English Reformation illustrated by the life and friendships of Anne Locke', in *Stud. Ch. Hist.*, 11, 258–72.

1932 Constant, Gustave. 'Formularies of faith during the reign of Henry VIII', *Downside Review*, 54 (Autumn 1936), 428–55.

1933 —— 'La chute de Somerset et l'élévation de Warwick: leurs conséquences pour la réforme en Angleterre (Octobre 1549–Juillet 1553)', *Rev. hist.*, 172 (Nov.–Dec. 1933), 422–54.

1934 —— 'Le commencement de la restauration catholique en Angleterre par Marie Tudor (1553)', *Rev. hist.*, 112 (Jan.–Feb. 1913), 1–27.

1935 —— 'Les évêques Henriciens sous Henry VIII', *Revue des questions historiques*, 91 (1912), 384–425.

1936 —— 'Politique et dogme dans les confessions de foi d'Henri VIII, roi d'Angleterre', *Rev. hist.*, 155 (May–June 1927), 1–38.

1937 Couratin, A. H. 'The Holy Communion of 1549', *CQR*, 164 (Apr.–June 1963), 148–59.

1938 —— 'The Service of Communion', *CQR*, 163 (Oct.–Dec. 1962), 431–42.

1939 Cowell, Henry J. 'English Protestant refugees in Strasbourg, 1533–8', *Hug. Soc. Proc.*, 15 (pt. 1, 1934), 69–120.

1940 —— 'The sixteenth century English speaking refugee churches at Geneva and Frankfort', *Hug. Soc. Proc.*, 16 (no. 2, 1939), 209–30.

1941 —— 'The sixteenth century English speaking refugee churches at Strasbourg, Basle, Zurich, Aarau, Wesel and Emden', *Hug. Soc. Proc.*, 15 (no. 4, 1937), 612–65.

1942 Craig, Hardin, Jr. 'The Geneva Bible as a political document', *Pacific

Historical Review, **7** (Mar. 1938), 40–9. The use of the Geneva Bible against the Marian regime and then against the Elizabethan establishment.

1943 Crehan, J. H. 'The return to obedience: new judgement on Cardinal Pole', *Month*, new ser., **14** (Oct. 1955), 221–9. On Pole's reception of England back into the Roman Church and on the question of restoring church lands.

1944 Cross, M. Claire. 'An example of lay intervention in the Elizabethan Church', in *Stud. Ch. Hist.*, II, 273–82. Intervention by the puritanical Francis Hastings, brother of Henry, earl of Huntingdon.

1945 —— 'Noble patronage in the Elizabethan Church', *Hist. J.* **3** (no. 1, 1960), 1–16. The earl of Huntingdon and the spread of Protestantism.

1946 —— 'The third earl of Huntingdon and the trial of Catholics in the north, 1581–1595', *Rec. Hist.*, **8** (Oct. 1965), 136–46. Sees Huntingdon not as a Grand Inquisitor but as an agent of government policy.

1947 Cross, Wilford O. 'The doctrine of the church in Tudor and Caroline writings', *Historical Magazine of the Protestant Episcopal Church*, **12** (Mar. 1961), 12–24.

1948 Darlington, Ida. 'The Reformation in Southwark', *Hug. Soc. Proc.*, **14** (no. 3, 1955), 65–81. An interesting account of the Reformation in an untypical locality.

1949 Dawley, Powel M. 'Henry VIII and the church: an essay on some aspects of the Reformation in England', *Historical Magazine of the Protestant Episcopal Church*, **16** (Sept. 1947), 246–59. Shows the importance of the Henrician Reformation to later Anglicanism but overemphasizes Henry's role.

1950 Devlin, Christopher. 'Southwell and the Mar-prelates: the date of the *Epistle of Comfort*', *Month*, **185** (Feb. 1948), 88–95.

1951 —— 'The patriotism of Robert Southwell', *Month*, new ser., x (Dec. 1953), 345–54.

1952 Dickens, Arthur G. 'A new prayer of Sir Thomas More', *CQR*, **124** (July–Sept. 1937), 224–37.

1953 —— 'An Elizabethan defender of the monasteries', *CQR*, **130** (July–Sept. 1940), 236–62. A discussion of Michael Sherbrook's *Falle of religious howses*.

1954 —— 'Aspects of intellectual transition among the English parish clergy of the Reformation period: a regional example', *Archiv für Reformationsgeschichte*, **63** (no. 1, 1952), 51–69. The region is South Yorkshire.

1955 —— 'Heresy and the origins of English Protestantism', in John S. Bromley and Ernest H. Kossmann (eds.), *Britain and the Netherlands*, II, Groningen, 1964, pp. 47–66. Stresses the role of Lollardy.

1956 —— 'The first stages of Romanist Recusancy in Yorkshire, 1560–90', *Yorks. Arch.J.*, **35** (pt. 2, 1941), 157–82. Shows that recusancy came in slowly and at its peak included only two per cent of the population of one of the most Romanist shires.

1957 —— 'The marriage and character of Archbishop Holgate', *EHR*, **53** (July 1937), 428–42.

1958 —— 'The northern convocation and Henry VIII', *CQR*, **127** (Oct.–Dec. 1938), 84–102.

1959 —— 'Wilfrid Holme of Huntington: Yorkshire's first Protestant poet', *Yorks. Arch.J.*, **39** (pt. 153, 1956), 119–35. Examines Holme's *The fall and evill success of rebellion*, written in 1537. Interesting as an early manifestation of Protestant anticlericalism and Reformation Erastianism and as an anticipation of the Puritan outlook.

1960 Du Boulay, F. R. H. 'Archbishop Cranmer and the Canterbury temporalities', *EHR*, **67** (Jan. 1952), 19–36.

1961 Elton, Geoffrey R. 'The quondam of Rievaulx', *JEH*, **7** (Apr. 1956), 45–60. Studies the deposition of an abbot in 1533 and shows it was not due to opposition to the Henrician Reformation.

1962 —— 'The Reformation in England', *NCMH*, II, 226–50. A good short account to Elizabeth's accession.

1963 Fabre, Frédéric. 'The English College at Eu, 1582–1592', *Catholic Historical Review*, **37** (Oct. 1951), 257–80.

1964   Fines, John. 'Heresy trials in the diocese of Coventry and Lichfield, 1511–12', *JEH*, **14** (Oct. 1963), 160–74. The persecution of Coventry Lollards.

1965   Ganss, H. G. 'Sir Thomas More and the persecution of heretics', *American Catholic Quarterly*, **25** (July 1900), 531–48. Denies More was a persecutor. Cf. Miles (2009).

1966   Garrett, Christina M. 'John Ponet and the confession of the banished ministers', *CQR*, **137** (Oct.–Dec. 1943), 47–74; **137** (Jan.–Mar. 1944), 181–204.

1967   —— 'The legatine register of Cardinal Pole, 1554–57', *JMH*, **13** (June 1941), 189–94.

1968   Grieve, Hilda E. P. 'The deprived married clergy in Essex, 1553–61', *TRHS*, 4th ser., **22** (1940), 141–69. An important study of clerical marriage.

1969   Guppy, Henry. 'Miles Coverdale and the English Bible, 1488–1568', *BJRL*, **19** (July 1935), 300–28.

1970   —— 'The royal "injunctions" of 1538 and the "Great Bible", 1539–1541', *BJRL*, **22** (Apr. 1938), 31–71.

1971   Habakkuk, H. John. 'The market for monastic property, 1539–1603', *EcHR*, 2nd ser., **10** (Apr. 1958), 362–80. Presents evidence that Henry VIII did not squander the monastic lands.

1972   Hauben, Paul J. 'A Spanish Calvinist church in Elizabethan London, 1559–65', *Church History*, **34** (Mar. 1965), 50–6.

1973   Heriot, Duncan B. 'Anabaptism in England during the 16th and 17th centuries', *Congregational Historical Society Transactions*, **12** (Sept. 1935), 256–71; **12** (Aug. 1936), 312–20.

1974   Hicks, Leo. 'Cardinal Allen and the society', *Month*, **160** (Oct.–Dec. 1932), 342–53, 434–43, 528–36. Allen and the Jesuits.

1975   —— 'Elizabethan royal supremacy and contemporary writers', *Month*, **184** (Nov. 1948), 216–28.

1976   —— 'The Catholic exiles and the Elizabethan religious settlement', *Catholic Historical Review*, **22** (July 1936), 128–48. Discusses the writings of Catholic exiles on the Settlement.

1977   —— 'The ecclesiastical supremacy of Queen Elizabeth', *Month*, **183** (Mar. 1947), 170–7.

1978   Hill, Christopher. 'Puritans and "the dark corners of the land"', *TRHS*, 5th ser., **13** (1963), 77–102. The spread of Puritanism in the north and west, Elizabethan and early Stuart periods.

1979   —— 'Puritans and the poor', *PP*, no. 2 (Nov. 1952), 32–50. A study of the theology of William Perkins, an Elizabethan Puritan, and its outcome in social theory. See V. Kiernan's critique and Hill's reply in *ibid.*, no. 3 (Feb. 1953), 45–54.

1980   —— 'Social and economic consequences of the Henrician Reformation', in *Puritanism and revolution*, 1958, pp. 32–49. Something of an overstatement which practically ignores the religious side.

1981   Hodgett, G. A. J. 'The unpensioned ex-religious in Tudor England', *JEH*, **13** (Oct. 1962), 195–202.

1982   Hooper, Wilfred. 'The court of faculties', *EHR*, **25** (Oct. 1910), 670–86. The court that took over the pope's dispensing power after the break with Rome.

1983   Hurstfield, Joel. 'Church and state, 1558–1612: the task of the Cecils', in *Stud. Ch. Hist.*, II, 119–40. The religion and religious policies of William and Robert Cecil.

1984   Jacquot, Jean. 'Sébastien Castellion en l'Angleterre: quelques aspects de son influence', *Bibliothèque d'Humanisme et Renaissance*, **15** (1953), 15–44.

1985   Janelle, Pierre. 'Humanisme et unité chrétienne: John Fisher et Thomas More', *Etudes*, **223** (May 1935), 442–60.

1986   —— 'La controverse entre Etienne Gardiner et Martin Bucer sur la discipline ecclésiastique, 1541–1548', *Revue des sciences religieuses*, **7** (1927), 452–66.

1987   Jenkins, Claude. 'Cardinal Morton's register', in *Tud. Stud.*, pp. 26–74.

1988   Judd, Arnold. 'The office of subdean', *CQR*, **166** (Jan.–Mar. 1965), 36–46.

1989 Knowles, David. 'The case of St Albans Abbey in 1490', *JEH*, **3** (Oct. 1952), 144–58.

1990 —— 'The matter of Wilton', *BIHR*, **31** (May 1958), 92–6. Deals with the election of an abbess and Henry VIII's inconsistent policy which helped to ruin chances of reform.

1991 Krodel, Gottfried. 'Luther, Erasmus, and Henry VIII', *Archiv für Reformationsgeschichte*, **53** (no. 1, 1962), 60–78. Considers the claim that Erasmus wrote the *Assertio* for Henry.

1992 Lamont, William M. 'The rise and fall of Bishop Bilson', *JBS*, **5** (May 1966), 22–32. On the reputation of an Elizabethan 'Erastian' and 'clericalist'.

1993 Lang, August. 'Butzer in England', *Archiv für Reformationsgeschichte*, **28** (no. 2, 1941), 230–9.

1994 Lea, Kathleen M. 'Sir Anthony Standen and some Anglo-Italian letters', *EHR*, **68** (July 1932), 461–77.

1995 Lehmberg, Stanford E. 'Sir Thomas Elyot and the English Reformation', *Archiv für Reformationsgeschichte*, **68** (no. 1, 1957), 91–110.

1996 —— 'Supremacy and viceregency: a re-examination', *EHR*, **81** (Apr. 1966), 226–35. Argues that Cromwell's office of viceregent was intended to comprehend almost all spiritual jurisdiction and that, though a short-lived office, it effectively established the royal supremacy.

1997 Lillie, H. W. R. 'The English martyrs and English criminal law', *Clergy Review*, **12** (Oct. 1936), 294–309; **13** (Oct. 1937), 281–90.

1998 Loomie, Albert J. 'A Catholic petition to the earl of Essex', *Rec. Hist.*, **7** (Jan. 1963), 33–42. Proposes an oath to be taken by all Catholics and increased crown revenue from recusancy fines in exchange for toleration.

1999 McAleer, John. 'More and his detractors', *Month*, new ser., **26** (July 1961), 14–23. Mainly on the charge that More persecuted heretics. Cf. Miles (2009).

2000 McGee, Eugene K. 'Cranmer and nominalism', *Harvard Theological Review*, **57** (Apr. 1964), 189–206. Sees Cranmer's eucharistic theology as nominalist. See William J. Courtenay's critique in *ibid.*, **57** (Oct. 1964), 367–80, and McGee's reply in *ibid.*, **59** (Apr. 1966), 192–6.

2001 McGinn, Donald J. 'The real Martin Marprelate', *PMLA*, **58** (Mar. 1943), 84–107. Says he was John Penry. Cf. Neale (525), II, 220, who claims he was Job Throckmorton. See also McGinn (1867).

2002 Maitland, Frederic W. 'Elizabethan gleanings', in *Collected Papers*, ed. Herbert A. L. Fisher. Cambridge, 1911, III, 157–209. Includes 'Defender of the Faith, and so forth', 'Queen Elizabeth and Paul IV', 'Pius IV and the English Church Service', 'Thomas Sackville's message from Rome', and 'Supremacy and uniformity'. The last must be modified in light of (2013).

2003 —— 'The Anglican settlement and the Scottish Reformation', in *CMH*, II, 550–98. Still the best survey of 1558–68, though corrected in part by Neale (2013). See also Bell (171), pp. 128–9.

2004 Manning, Roger B. 'Richard Shelley of Warminghurst and the English Catholic petition for toleration of 1585', *Rec. Hist.*, **6** (Oct. 1962), 265–74.

2005 Marc'hadour, Germain. 'St Thomas More', *Month*, new ser., **29** (Feb. 1963), 69–84. On More's religious ideas.

2006 Merriman, Roger B. 'Some notes on the treatment of English Catholics in the reign of Queen Elizabeth', *AHR*, **13** (Apr. 1908), 480–500.

2007 Messenger, Ernest C. 'Bishop Bonner and Anglican orders', *Dublin Review*, **198** (Jan. 1936), 100–10.

2008 Meyer, Carl S. 'Henry VIII burns Luther's books, 12 May 1521', *JEH*, **9** (Oct. 1958), 173–87.

2009 Miles, Leland. 'Persecution and the *Dialogue of Comfort*: a fresh look at the charges against Thomas More', *JBS*, **5** (Nov. 1965), 19–30. Indicts More for 'persecuting' heretics by his own definition.

2010 Møller, Jens G. 'The beginnings of Puritan covenant theology', *JEH*, **14** (Apr. 1963), 46–67. Traces its development from Tyndale rather than Calvin.

2011 Muss-Arnolt, William. 'Puritan efforts and struggles, 1550–1603: a bio-bibliographical study', *American Journal of Theology*, **23** (July–Oct. 1919), 345–66, 471–99.

2012 Neale, John E. 'Parliament and the articles of religion, 1571', *EHR*, **67** (Oct. 1952), 510–21.

2013 —— 'The Elizabethan acts of supremacy and uniformity', *EHR*, **65** (July 1950), 304–32. Very important. Indicates Parliament went further and faster than Elizabeth liked.

2014 Norwood, Frederick A. 'The London Dutch refugees in search of a home, 1553–1554', *AHR*, **58** (Oct. 1952), 64–72.

2015 O'Connell, John R. 'Richard Topcliffe, priest-hunter and torturer', *Dublin Review*, **195** (Oct. 1934), 240–55. See also Devlin (1720), pp. 61–77.

2016 O'Dwyer, Michael. 'Recusant fines in Essex, 1583–1593', *Month*, new ser., **20** (July 1958), 28–37.

2017 Owen, H. Gareth. 'A nursery of Elizabethan nonconformity, 1567–72', *JEH*, **17** (Apr. 1966), 65–76. The Minories, a London parish with several Anabaptist congregations.

2018 —— 'Parochial curates in Elizabethan London', *JEH*, **10** (Apr. 1959), 66–73. Shows a rise in the number and quality of curates during the reign.

2019 —— 'The episcopal visitation: its limits and limitations in Elizabethan London', *JEH*, **11** (Oct. 1960), 179–85.

2020 Pantin, William A. 'English monks before the suppression of the monasteries', *Dublin Review*, **201** (Oct. 1937), 250–70. Mainly on the scholarly activities of the monks.

2021 Parris, J. R. 'Hooker's doctrine of the eucharist', *Scottish Journal of Theology*, **16** (June 1963), 151–64. Hooker's *via media* on the eucharist.

2022 Peck, George T. 'John Hales and the Puritans during the Marian exile', *Church History*, **10** (June 1941), 159–77.

2023 Peters, Robert. 'The administration of the archdeaconry of St Albans, 1580–1625', *JEH*, **13** (Apr. 1962), 61–75. An archdeaconry whose administration was reasonably effective.

2024 Petti, A. G. 'Richard Verstegan and Catholic martyrologies of the later Elizabethan period', *Rec. Hist.*, **5** (Apr. 1959), 64–90.

2025 Pineas, Rainer. 'John Bale's nondramatic works of religious controversy', *Studies in the Renaissance*, **9** (1962), 218–33.

2026 —— 'Thomas More's *Utopia* and Protestant polemics', *Renaissance News*, **17** (Aug. 1964), 197–201. Protestant use of *Utopia* as a weapon against More and the Catholic Church.

2027 Pocock, Nicholas. 'The conditions of morals and religious beliefs in the reign of Edward VI', *EHR*, **10** (July 1895), 417–44.

2028 Pollard, Albert F. 'The Reformation under Edward VI', in *CMH*, **II**, 474–511.

2029 Pollen, John H. 'The alleged papal sanction of the Anglican liturgy', *Month*, **100** (Sept. 1902), 274–80.

2030 Porter, Harry C. 'The Anglicanism of Archbishop Whitgift', *Historical Magazine of the Protestant Episcopal Church*, **31** (June 1962), 127–41. Whitgift and the theological disputes at Cambridge in 1595 which led to the 'Lambeth Articles'.

2031 —— 'The gloomy dean and the law: John Colet, 1466–1519', in Gareth V. Bennett and John D. Walsh (eds.), *Essays in modern English church history*, 1966, pp. 18–43.

2032 —— 'The nose of wax: Scripture and the spirit from Erasmus to Milton', *TRHS*, 5th ser., **14** (1964), 155–74. Brief but useful on Tudor attitudes toward the meaning of scripture.

2033 Price, F. Douglas. 'An Elizabethan church official—Thomas Powell, chancellor of Gloucester diocese', *CQR*, **128** (Apr.–June 1939), 94–112. This and the following articles by Price indicate the state of the church in a poorly run diocese.

2034 —— 'Elizabethan apparitors in the diocese of Gloucester', *CQR*, **134** (Apr.–June 1942), 37–55. Abuses and corruption in ecclesiastical administration. The apparitors served citations for courts Christian.

2035 —— 'Gloucester diocese under Bishop Hooper, 1551–3', *Transactions of the Bristol and Gloucestershire Archaeological Society*, **60** (1939), 51–151.

2036 —— 'The abuses of excommunication and the decline of ecclesiastical discipline under Queen Elizabeth', *EHR*, **57** (Jan. 1942), 106–15. In Gloucester diocese.

2037 —— 'The commission for ecclesiastical causes for the dioceses of Bristol and Gloucester, 1574', *Transactions of the Bristol and Gloucestershire Archaeological Society*, **59** (1938), 61–184.

2038 Purvis, John S. 'The registers of Archbishops Lee and Holgate', *JEH*, **13** (Oct. 1962), 186–94. 1531–53.

2039 Quinn, Edward. 'Bishop Tunstall's treatise on the Holy Eucharist, *Downside Review*, **51** (Autumn 1933), 674–89.

2040 Ratcliff, Edward C. 'The liturgical works of Archbishop Cranmer', *JEH*, **7** (Oct. 1956), 189–203.

2041 Ritchie, Carson I. A. 'Sir Richard Grenville and the Puritans', *EHR*, **77** (July 1962), 518–23.

2042 Rooke, G. R. 'Dom William Ingram and his account book, 1504–33', *JEH*, **7** (Apr. 1956), 30–44. Of interest for the conditions of a monastic cathedral on the eve of the Reformation.

2043 Rowse, A[lfred] L[eslie]. 'Nicholas Roscarrock and his lives of the saints', in J. H. Plumb (ed.), *Studies in Social History*, 1955, pp. 1–31.

2044 Russell, Henry G. 'Lollard opposition to oaths by creatures', *AHR*, **51** (July 1946), 668–84. The refusal of Lollards to swear by saints, relics, etc., and its continuance into the Reformation.

2045 Ryan, Lawrence V. 'The Haddon-Osorio Controversy (1563–1583)', *Church History*, **22** (June 1953), 142–54. A debate over the Elizabethan Reformation between two leading latinists.

2046 Sawada, P. A. 'Two anonymous Tudor treatises on the general council', *JEH*, **12** (Oct. 1961), 197–214. Discusses two treatises expressing the Henrician theory of a general council.

2047 Scarisbrick, J. J. 'Clerical taxation in England, 1485 to 1547', *JEH*, **11** (Apr. 1960), 41–54. Indicates the cost of liberation from Rome was high for the Church of England.

2048 Sisson, Rosemary A. 'William Perkins, apologist for the Elizabethan Church of England', *Modern Language Review*, **67** (Oct. 1952), 495–502. On Perkins also see (1789), (1979), and (2070).

2049 Smith, Dwight C. 'Robert Browne, Independent', *Church History*, **6** (Dec. 1937), 289–349.

2050 Smith, H. Maynard. 'A commentary on Trevisan', *CQR*, **121** (Oct. 1935), 71–96. On reports about English religion by a Venetian in 1497.

2051 —— 'The Reformation at home and abroad', *CQR*, **130** (July–Sept. 1940), 263–89.

2052 Smith, Lacey B. 'Henry VIII and the Protestant triumph', *AHR*, **71** (July 1966), 1237–64. Maintains convincingly that the Protestant triumph after Henry's death was not planned, envisioned, or desired by Henry.

2053 —— 'The Reformation and the decay of medieval ideals', *Church History*, **24** (Sept. 1955), 212–20. Sees the Reformation as an outcome of the decay of medieval spiritual ideals.

2054 Solt, Leo F. 'Revolutionary Calvinist parties in England under Elizabeth I and Charles I', *Church History*, **27** (Sept. 1958), 234–9.

2055 Southgate, Wyndham M. 'The Marian exiles and the influence of John Calvin', *History*, new ser., **27** (Sept. 1942), 148–52. Maintains that the Elizabethan churchmen who returned from the exile carried on the tradition of Cranmer rather than Calvin.

2056 Stone, Jean M. 'John Foxe's Book of Errors', *Month*, **95** (Apr. 1900), 352–69. Cf. Mozley (1872) and Thomson (2060).

2057 Stroud, Theodore A. 'Father Thomas Wright: a test case for toleration', *Biographical Studies*, **1** (no. 3, 1951), 189–219. A priest who advocated toleration and was an ally of the earl of Essex.

2058 Thompson, W. D. J. Cargill. 'Anthony Marten and the Elizabethan debate on episcopacy', in Gareth V. Bennett and John D. Walsh (eds.), *Essays in Modern English Church History*. 1966, pp. 44–75. Discusses Marten's *Reconciliation of all the pastors and clergy of the Church of England*, a defence of episcopacy of 1590.

2059 Thomson, G[ladys] S[cott]. 'The dissolution of Woburn Abbey', *TRHS*, 4th ser., **16** (1933), 129–60.

2060 Thomson, J. A. F. 'John Foxe and some sources for Lollard history: notes for a critical appraisal', in *Stud. Ch. Hist.*, II, 251–7. Finds Foxe emerges rather well as a historian, esp. when his sources were documentary.

2061 Thornley, Isabel D. 'The destruction of sanctuary', in *Tud. Stud.*, pp. 182–207.

2062 Trinterud, Leonard J. 'The origins of Puritanism', *Church History*, **20** (Mar. 1951), 37–57. Stresses non-Calvinist origins.

2063 Walker, R. B. 'Lincoln Cathedral in the reign of Queen Elizabeth I', *JEH*, **11** (Oct. 1960), 186–201. A study of the state and the problems of a cathedral.

2064 —— 'The growth of Puritanism in the county of Lincoln in the reign of Queen Elizabeth I', *Journal of Religious History*, **1** (June 1961), 148–59.

2065 Wall, James. 'William Whittingham of Chester (?1524–79)', *CQR*, **122** (Apr.–June 1936), 74–87. A Marian exile and Elizabethan dean of Durham.

2066 Whitley, W. T. 'Thomas Matthew's Bible', *CQR*, **135** (Oct.–Dec. 1937), 48–69. The Bible printed with the king's licence in 1537.

2067 Williams, Glanmor. 'The Elizabethan settlement of religion in Wales and the marches', *Journal of the Historical Society of the Church in Wales*, **2** (1950), 61–71. The visitation and the filling of vacant bishoprics.

2068 Woodward, George W. O. 'A speculation in monastic lands', *EHR*, **80** (Oct. 1964), 778–83.

2069 —— 'The exemption from suppression of certain Yorkshire priories', *EHR*, **76** (July 1961), 385–401.

2070 Wright, Louis B. 'William Perkins: Elizabethan apostle of practical divinity', *HLQ*, **3** (Jan. 1940), 171–96.

2071 Youings, Joyce A. 'The terms of disposal of the Devon monastic lands, 1536–58', *EHR*, **69** (Jan. 1954), 18–38.

2072 Yule, G. 'Theological developments in Elizabethan Puritanism', *Journal of Religious History*, **1** (June 1960), 16–25.

XIII HISTORY OF THE FINE ARTS

1 Printed sources

2073 Fuller-Maitland, John A. and William Barclay Squire (eds.). *The Fitzwilliam virginal book*. Leipzig, 1894–9, 2 vols. Commonly known as 'Queen Elizabeth's virginal book'. On it see Borren (2096) and Naylor (2132).

2074 Hilliard, Nicholas. *A treatise concerning the arte of limning*, in Philip Norman (ed.), *The first annual volume of the Walpole Society*. Oxford, 1912, pp. 1–50. The first great English treatise on painting.

2075 Morley, Thomas. *A plaine and easie introduction to practicall musicke*, ed. Edmund H. Fellowes (Shakespeare Association Facsimiles, no. 14). 1937. First published in 1597.

2076 *Musica britannica*. 1951–. A collection of British music, middle ages through eighteenth century. Includes much hitherto unpublished Tudor material.

2077 Osborn, James M. (ed.). *The autobiography of Thomas Whythorne*. Oxford, 1961. An interesting autobiography of a successful Tudor composer.

2078 Shute, John. *The first and chief grounds of architecture*, ed. Lawrence Weaver. 1912. The main Elizabethan work on architecture.

2 Surveys

2079 Grove, George. *Dictionary of music and musicians*. 5th ed. by Eric Blom, 1954, 9 vols. Indispensable.
2080 Harvey, John. *Tudor architecture*. New York, 1952.
2081 Hughes, Anselm and Gerald Abraham (eds.). *The New Oxford history of music*, III, *Ars nova and the Renaissance, 1300–1540*. Oxford, 1960. Vol. IV, *The age of humanism, 1540–1630*, of this expert survey is in progress.
2082 Mercer, Eric. *English art, 1553–1625* (Oxford History of English Art, VII). Oxford, 1962. Vol. VI, covering 1461–1553, in this fine series has not yet appeared.
2083 Milne, James Lees. *Tudor Renaissance*. 1951. Painting and architecture, mainly architecture.
2084 Nagel, Wilibald. *Geschichte der Musik in England*. Strassburg, 1894–7, 2 vols. Mainly Tudor and still regarded as authoritative.
2085 Reese, Gustave. *Music in the Renaissance*. New York, 1954. The standard account of Renaissance music with two chapters on England and an extensive bibliography.
2086 Summerson, John. *Architecture in Britain, 1530–1830*. Harmondsworth, 1953. This, (2088), and (2089) comprise the relevant vols. in the admirable *Pelican History of Art*.
2087 Walker, Ernest. *A history of music in England*, 3rd ed. revised by Jack A. Westrup. Oxford, 1952. The standard survey.
2088 Waterhouse, Ellis. *Painting in Britain, 1530–1790*. Harmondsworth, 1953.
2089 Whinney, Margaret. *Sculpture in Britain, 1530–1830*. Harmondsworth, 1964.

3 Monographs

2090 Auerbach, Erna. *Tudor artists*. 1954. Especially good for miniature painting and for its extensive bibliography.
2091 Baker, Charles H. C. and William G. Constable. *English painting of the sixteenth and seventeenth centuries*. New York, 1930. A scholarly study of lesser painters ignoring miniature painting. Good reproductions, many of little-known paintings.
2092 Barley, Maurice W. *The English farmhouse and cottage*. 1961. Good for rural homes in the sixteenth and seventeenth centuries and useful for social and economic history.
2093 Blomfield, Reginald. *History of Renaissance architecture in England, 1500–1800*. 1897, 2 vols. An old standard.
2094 —— *The formal garden in England*. 1901. Mainly Tudor.
2095 Bontoux, Germaine. *La chanson en Angleterre au temps d'Elisabeth*. Oxford, 1936.
2096 Borren, Charles van den. *The sources of keyboard music in England*, trans. James E. Matthew. New York, 1914. A detailed study of virginalists and virginal music.
2097 Boyd, Morrison C. *Elizabethan music and musical criticism*. 2nd ed., Philadelphia, 1962. An excellent broad study with a useful bibliography.
2098 Buck, Percy C. *et al.* (eds.). *Tudor church music*. 1923–30, 10 vols. A monumental collection, introductions and scores.
2099 Buxton, John. *Elizabethan taste*. 1963. About half on taste in architecture, painting, and sculpture.
2100 Castle, Sidney E. *Domestic Gothic of the Tudor period*. Jamestown, N.Y., 1927. Considers smaller and larger houses, Tudor details, and Tudor windows. Well illustrated.
2101 Chamberlain, Samuel. *Tudor homes of England*. New York, 1929.
2102 Chappell, William. *Old English popular music*, ed. Harry E. Woolridge. 1893, 2 vols. Essential for folk music.
2103 Clifton-Taylor, Alec. *The pattern of English building*. 1962.
2104 Colding, Torben H. *Aspects of miniature painting, its origins and development*. Copenhagen, 1953.

2105 Colvin, Sidney. *Early engraving and engravers in England, 1545–1695.* 1905.
2106 Crossley, Frederick H. *Timber building in England from early times to the end of the XVIIth century.* 1951.
2107 Davies, David W. *Dutch influences on English culture, 1558–1725.* Ithaca, N.Y., 1964. Of use for trade, religion, etc., but strongest for the fine arts.
2108 Esdaile, Katharine A. *English church monuments, 1510–1840.* 1946.
2109 Fellowes, Edmund H. *English cathedral music from Edward VI to Edward VII.* 1941.
2110 —— *The English madrigal.* 1925. A brief introduction by an authority.
2111 —— *The English madrigal composers.* 2nd ed., Oxford, 1948. Gives a complete list of the madrigals and other works of each composer.
2112 Foskett, Daphne. *British portrait miniatures.* 1963. A beautifully illustrated history.
2113 Fox, Cyril and Lord Raglan. *Monmouthshire houses.* Cardiff, 1951–4, 3 vols. A good local survey of country houses, fifteenth century to 1714.
2114 Galpin, Francis W. *Old English instruments of music, their history and character.* 4th ed. revised by Thurston Dart, 1965. The classic work on the subject.
2115 Ganz, Paul. *The paintings of Hans Holbein.* 1956. Includes reproductions of all of Holbein's extant paintings.
2116 Garner, Thomas and Arthur Stratton. *The domestic architecture of England during the Tudor period.* 2nd ed., 1929, 2 vols. The standard work.
2117 Glyn, Margaret H. *About Elizabethan virginal music and its composers.* 1934.
2118 Gotch, J. Alfred. *Early Renaissance architecture in England.* 1901. An old standard covering 1500–1625.
2119 Greenberg, Noah, Wystan H. Auden and Chester Kallman (eds.). *An Elizabethan song book.* 1954. An excellent selection of Tudor songs.
2120 Hayes, Gerald R. *Musical instruments and their music, 1500–1700.* 1928–30, 2 vols.
2121 Hind, Arthur M. *Engraving in England in the sixteenth and seventeenth centuries,* pt. I, *The Tudor period.* Cambridge, 1952. The standard work. Well illustrated.
2122 Hodnett, Edward. *English woodcuts, 1480–1535.* Oxford, 1935.
2123 Hulton, Paul and David B. Quinn (eds.). *The American drawings of John White, 1577–1590, with drawings of European and Oriental subjects.* 1964, 2 vols. Vol. I catalogues and appraises White's work; vol. II reproduces much of it. Sound both as history and art history.
2124 Jenkins, Frank. *Architect and patron: a survey of professional relations and practice in England from the sixteenth century to the present day.* 1961.
2125 Jourdain, Margaret. *English decoration and furniture of the early Renaissance (1500–1650), an account of its development and characteristic forms.* 1924.
2126 —— *English decorative plasterwork of the Renaissance.* 1927.
2127 —— *English interior decoration, 1500–1830.* 1950.
2128 Lindsay, David A. E., earl of Crawford and Balcarres (ed.). *Historical monuments of Great Britain.* 1955– . A survey of all extant buildings of archaeological or historical significance. Good illustrations.
2129 Mackerness, Eric D. *A social history of English music.* Toronto, 1964. A study of the changing musical tastes of Englishmen in their social setting from the middle ages to the present.
2130 Meyer, Ernst H. *English chamber music.* 1946.
2131 Milner-White, Eric. *Sixteenth century glass in York Minster and in the Church of St Michael-le-Belfrey* (St Anthony's Hall Publications, XVII). York, 1960.
2132 Naylor, Edward W. *An Elizabethan virginal book.* 1905. A study of *The Fitzwilliam virginal book* (2073).
2133 Papworth, Wyat. *The Renaissance and Italian styles of architecture in Great Britain.* 1883.
2134 Parker, Karl T. *The drawings of Hans Holbein ... at Windsor Castle.* 1945. Includes reproductions of drawings valuable for Tudor history.
2135 Pevsner, Nikolaus. *The planning of the Elizabethan country house.* 1961.
2136 Pope-Hennessy, John. *A lecture on Nicholas Hilliard.* 1949.

2137 Reynolds, Graham. *English portrait miniatures.* 1952.
2138 —— *Nicholas Hilliard and Isaac Oliver.* 1947.
2139 Rosenberg, Louis C. *Cottages, farmhouses, and other minor buildings in England of the sixteenth, seventeenth, and eighteenth centuries.* New York, 1923.
2140 Salzman, Louis F. *Building in England down to 1540.* Oxford, 1952.
2141 Stevens, Denis W. *Tudor church music.* New York, 1955.
2142 Stevens, John. *Music and poetry in the early Tudor court.* 1961. An excellent and well-documented study of the early Tudor musical scene.
2143 Stratton, Arthur. *Introductory handbook to the styles of English architecture,* pt. II, *Tudor and Renaissance.* 3rd ed., 1938, 2 vols.
2144 Thompson, A. Hamilton. *The English house* (Historical Association Pamphlets, no. 105). 1936. A good brief survey of English domestic architecture.
2145 Tipping, Henry A. (ed.). *English homes, period II, early Tudor, 1485–1558.* 1924.
2146 —— *English homes, period III, late Tudor and early Stuart, 1558–1649.* 1922–7, 2 vols.
2147 Vallance, Aymer. *Art in England during the Elizabethan and Stuart periods.* 1908.
2148 Warlock, Peter. *The English ayre.* 1926. For words and music of ayres see Peter Warlock and Philip Wilson (eds.), *English ayres, Elizabethan and Jacobean,* 1927–31, 6 vols.
2149 Whiffen, Marcus. *An introduction to Elizabethan and Jacobean architecture.* 1952.
2150 Whinney, Margaret. *Renaissance architecture in England.* 1952.
2151 Winter, Carl. *Elizabethan miniatures.* Harmondsworth, 1943. Includes beautiful colour plates illustrating an exquisite art.
2152 Woodfill, Walter L. *Musicians in English society from Elizabeth to Charles I* (Princeton Studies in History, IX). Princeton, 1953. A sound study with an extensive bibliography.
2153 Woodward, John. *Tudor and Stuart drawings.* 1951.
2154 Wüsten, Ernst. *Die Architektur des Manierismus in England.* Leipzig, 1951. A study of mannerist architecture and of particular houses.

4 Biographies

2155 Auerbach, Erna. *Nicholas Hilliard.* 1961. A very detailed biography that is also excellent for Hilliard's contemporaries, followers, and pupils.
2156 Chamberlain, Arthur B. *Hans Holbein the Younger.* 1913, 2 vols.
2157 Fellowes, Edmund H. *Orlando Gibbons and his family: the last of the Tudor school of musicians.* 1951.
2158 —— *William Byrd.* 1936. The premier Tudor composer.
2159 Flood, W[illiam] H[enry] G[rattan]. *Early Tudor composers.* 1925. Short lives of thirty-two musicians and composers.
2160 Harvey, John and Arthur Oswald (eds.). *English medieval architects: a biographical dictionary down to 1550.* 1954.
2161 Wornum, Ralph N. *Some account of the life and works of Hans Holbein, painter of Augsburg.* 1867. Still quite useful.

5 Articles

2162 Adams-Acton, Murray. 'Structural ceilings of the early Tudor house', *Connoisseur,* **123** (June 1949), 75–82.
2163 Barley, Maurice W. 'Farmhouses and cottages, 1550–1725', *EcHR,* 2nd ser., **7** (Apr. 1955), 291–306.
2164 Brett, Philip. 'Edward Paston (1550–1630): a Norfolk gentleman and his music collection', *Transactions of the Cambridge Bibliographical Society,* **4** (pt. I, 1964), 51–69. One of the earliest British collectors.
2165 Carden, R. W. 'Italian artists in England during the sixteenth century', *Proceedings of the Society of Antiquaries,* 2nd ser., **24** (1911–12), 171–205.

2166 Cudworth, C. L. 'Dutch influence in East Anglian architecture', *Proceedings of the Cambridge Antiquarian Society*, **37** (1937), 24–42.

2167 Cust, Lionel H. 'Notes on foreign artists of the reformed religion working in England from about 1560 to 1660', *Hug. Soc. Proc.*, **7** (1903), 45–82. Dutch and Huguenot artists.

2168 Dow, Helen J. 'John Hudde and the English Renaissance', *Renaissance News*, **18** (Winter, 1965), 289–94. The introduction of Renaissance ornament to Tudor sculpture during the early Tudor period.

2169 Esdaile, Katharine A. 'The inter-action of English and Low Country sculpture in the sixteenth century', *Journal of the Warburg and Courtauld Institutes*, **6** (1943), 80–8.

2170 Finney, Gretchen L. 'Music: a book of knowledge in Renaissance England', *Studies in the Renaissance*, **6** (1959), 36–63. An interesting study of the Renaissance notion that music might be a source of knowledge.

2171 Ganz, Paul. 'Holbein and Henry VIII', *Burlington Magazine*, **83** (Nov. 1943), 269–75.

2172 Hughes, Andrew. 'Continuity, tradition and change in English music up to 1600', *Music and Letters*, **46** (Oct. 1965), 306–15.

2173 Mercer, Eric. 'The houses of the gentry', *PP*, no. 5 (May 1954), 11–32. The house plan of the gentry as distinct from that of the courtiers, sixteenth and seventeenth centuries.

2174 Pope-Hennessy, John. 'Nicholas Hilliard and mannerist art theory', *Journal of the Warburg and Courtauld Institutes*, **6** (1943), 89–100. Derived mainly from *The art of limning* (2074).

2175 Purvis, John S. 'The use of continental woodcuts and prints by the "Ripon School" of woodcarvers in the early sixteenth century', *Arch.*, **85** (1935), 107–28.

2176 Strong, Roy C. 'Elizabethan painting: an approach through inscriptions—I: Robert Peake the Elder; II: Hieronimo Custodis; III: Marcus Gheeraerts the Younger', *Burlington Magazine*, **105** (Feb.–Apr. 1963), 53–7, 103–8, 149–57.

2177 Summerson, John. 'Three Elizabethan architects', *BJRL*, **40** (Sept. 1957), 202–28. Robert Adams, John Symonds, and Robert Stickells.

2178 Winter, Carl. 'Hilliard and Elizabethan miniatures', *Burlington Magazine*, **89** (July 1947), 175–83.

2179 —— 'Holbein's Miniatures', *Burlington Magazine*, **83** (Nov. 1943), 266–9.

2180 —— 'The British school of miniature portrait painters', *PBA*, **34** (1948), 119–37.

2181 Woodfill, Walter L. 'Education of professional musicians in Elizabethan England', *Medievalia et Humanistica*, **6** (Jan. 1950), 101–8.

XIV INTELLECTUAL HISTORY

1 Printed sources

2182 Ascham, Roger. *The scholemaster*, in *English works*, ed. W. Aldis Wright. Cambridge, 1904, pp. 171–302. A famous Tudor treatise on education, first published in 1570.

2183 Camden, William. 'Discourse concerning the prerogative of the crown', ed. Frank S. Fussner, *Proceedings of the American Philosophical Society*, **101** (Apr. 1957), 204–15. Written over a decade after Elizabeth's death.

2184 Craig, Thomas. *Concerning the right of succession to the kingdom of England*, ed. James Gatherer. 1703, 2 vols. A work of 1603. Appears to advocate the divine right of kings, but cf. Allen (2214), pp. 256–62.

2185 Doleman, Robert. *A conference about the next succession to the crown of England*, 'Imprinted at N. with License,' 1594. Probably written by Robert Parsons. See (687). Supports the claim of the Spanish Infanta.

2186 Dudley, Edmund. *The tree of commonwealth*, ed. Dorothy M. Brodie.

Cambridge, 1948. Written in the first year of Henry VIII's reign. Identifies royal power with the well-being of society.

2187 Elyot, Thomas. *The Boke named the Governour*, ed. Henry H. S. Croft. 1883, 2 vols. A work of 1531 concerned primarily with the education of the aristocracy.

2188 Gardiner, Stephen. *Obedience in church and state*, ed. Pierre Janelle. Cambridge, 1930. Prints in Latin and English *De vera obedientia* and other writings of Gardiner. Janelle's introduction discusses the political thought involved.

2189 Goodman, Christopher. *How superior powers ought to be obeyd*. New York, 1931. The 1558 ed. of a revolutionary tract by a Marian exile.

2190 Hales, John. *A declaration of the succession of the crowne imperiall of Ingland*, in Francis Hargrave [alias George Harbin], *The hereditary right of the crown of England asserted* . . . 1713, pp. xx–xliii. The main tract favouring the Suffolk claim. Though written in 1563, this tract, despite statements to the contrary, was not printed until 1713.

2191 Harington, John. *A tract on the succession to the crown, A.D. 1602* . . . , ed. Clements R. Markham. 1880. Supports James VI's claim.

2192 Hayward, John. *An answer to the first part of a certaine conference, concerning the succession, published not long since under the name of R. Dolman*. 1603. Supports James VI's claim and appears to advocate the divine right of kings. Cf. Allen (2214), pp. 256–62.

2193 Hooker, Richard. *Of the laws of ecclesiastical polity*. 1907, 2 vols. Written to defend the Elizabethan Church against Presbyterian attacks, this is the main Elizabethan contribution to political thought.

2194 Leslie, John. *A defence of the honour of . . . Marie, queene of Scotland, with a declaration as well of her right, title, and interest to the succession of the crowne of Englande, as that the regimente of women is conformable to the lawe of God and nature*. 1569.

2195 Levine, Mortimer (ed.). 'A "Letter" on the Elizabethan succession question, 1566', *HLQ*, **19** (Nov. 1955), 13–38. An anonymous tract favourable to the Suffolk claim.

2196 McIlwain, Charles H. (ed.). *The political works of James I*. Cambridge, Mass., 1918. The introduction is excellent on the Tudor background. Contains the *Trew law of free monarchies* of 1598 and the *Basilicon doron* of 1599.

2197 More, Thomas. *Utopia*, ed. Edward L. Surtz and Jack H. Hexter (The Complete Works of St Thomas More, IV). New Haven, 1965. The best ed. of a great work. Hexter's '*Utopia* and its historical milieu', pp. xxiii–cxxiv, is very important.

2198 [Morison, Richard.] *A remedy for sedition*, ed. E. M. Cox. 1933. On Morison's authorship see Baskerville (2295).

2199 Nugent, Elizabeth M. (ed.). *The thought and culture of the English Renaissance: an anthology of Tudor prose, 1481–1555*. Cambridge, 1956. An excellent selection with good introductions to the sections by noted scholars.

2200 Pepper, Robert D. (ed.). *Four Tudor books on education*. Gainesville, Fla., 1966. Thomas Elyot, *The education or bringing up of children*; Francis Clement, *The petie schols with an English orthographie*; Dudley Fenner, *The artes of logicke and rethorike*; William Kempe, *The education of children in learning*.

2201 Plummer, Charles (ed.). *Elizabethan Oxford* (Oxford Historical Society, VIII). Oxford, 1887. A collection of tracts, the largest part of which deal with Elizabeth's visits to Oxford in 1566 and 1592.

2202 Ponet, John. *A shorte treatise of politicke power*. Strasbourg, 1556. An important treatise advocating a limited monarchy by a Marian exile. There is a facsimile in Hudson (2276).

2203 Porter, Harry C. (ed.). *Erasmus and Cambridge: the Cambridge letters of Erasmus*, trans. Douglas F. S. Thomson. Toronto, 1963.

2204 St German, Christopher. *The dialogve in English, betweene a doctor of diuinitie, and a student in the lawes of England*. 1623. Cf. Vinogradoff (395) and Baumer (2296) on this important treatise.

2205 Scott, Edward J. L. (ed.). *Letter-book of Gabriel Harvey, A.D. 1573–1580* (Camden Society, new ser., XXXIII). 1884. Pp. 1–54 and 159–84 contain letters to and from Harvey during his residence at Pembroke Hall, Cambridge.

2206 Starkey, Thomas. *England in the reign of Henry VIII*, pt. 1, *Starkey's life and letters*, ed. Sidney J. Herrtage (E.E.T.S., extra ser., XXXII). 1878.

2207 —— *A dialogue between Reginald Pole & Thomas Lupset*, ed. Kathleen M. Burton. 1948. An invaluable reflection of the political and social thought of the 1530s.

2208 Tyndale, William. *The obedience of a Christian man*. Marburg, 1528. Stresses the powers of a Christian prince and the duty of obedience on the part of a subject. Reprinted in (1672).

2209 Watson, Foster (ed.). *Tudor school-boy life: the Dialogues 'Linguae latinae exercitatio' of Juan Luis Vives*. 1908.

2210 —— *Vives and the Renascence education of women*. 1912. Includes the *Instruction of a Christian woman* and four shorter works by Vives and works by Richard Hyrde and Thomas Elyot on the education of women.

2211 —— *Vives: On education: a translation of the 'De tradensis disciplinis' of Juan Luis Vives*. Cambridge, 1913. The best Renaissance work on education. Published in 1531 after Vives left England.

2212 Wentworth, Peter. *A pithie exhortation to her majesty for establishing her successor to the crowne*. Edinburgh, 1598. An answer to Doleman (2185). Advocates James VI's claim.

2213 Winny, James (ed.). *The frame of order: an outline of Elizabethan belief*. 1957. Extracts from late sixteenth-century treatises.

2 Surveys

2214 Allen, John W. *A history of political thought in the sixteenth century*. 1928. The standard account. Pp. 116–270 deal with English thought.

2215 Einstein, Lewis D. *Tudor ideals*. New York, 1921. A broad and interesting survey that deserves more attention than it has been given.

2216 Lewis, Clive S. *English literature in the sixteenth century excluding drama* (Oxford History of English Literature, III). Oxford, 1954. Brilliant, if sometimes controversial, on Tudor humanist and reformation writings. Has an extensive bibliography that is of much value but contains some serious errors.

2217 Morris, Christopher. *Political thought in England, Tyndale to Hooker*. 1953. Concise, interesting, and suggestive. Has a good bibliography.

2218 Ward, Adolphus W. and Alfred R. Waller (eds.), *The Cambridge History of English Literature*, III, *Renascence and Reformation*. New York and Cambridge, 1911. Contains still valuable chapters on the classical Renaissance, Reformation writings and thought, social literature, Hooker, and education.

3 Monographs

2219 Adams, Robert P. *The better part of valor: More, Erasmus, Colet and Vives on humanism, war and peace, 1496–1535*. Seattle, 1962.

2220 Baumer, Franklin L. V. *The early Tudor theory of kingship*. New Haven, 1940. Full and sound.

2221 Beales, A. C. F. *Education under penalty*. 1963. The education of English Catholics, the Reformation to 1688.

2222 Bennett, Henry S. *English books and readers*. Cambridge, 1952 & 1965, 2 vols. A history of the English book trade, 1475–1603, which contains a wealth of information on many related matters.

2223 Buckley, George T. *Atheism in the English Renaissance*. Chicago, 1932. Interesting but to be read with some caution.

2224 Bush, Douglas. *The Renaissance and English humanism*. Toronto, 1939. Stimulating lectures, but weak on the historical background.

2225 Campbell, William E. *More's Utopia & his social thinking*. 1930.

2226 Caspari, Fritz. *Humanism and the social order in Tudor England.* Chicago, 1954. Essays on the educational ideas of leading Tudor humanists.

2227 Charlton, Kenneth. *Education in Renaissance England.* Toronto, 1965. A useful survey with weak arguments.

2228 Clancy, Thomas H. *Papist pamphleteers.* Chicago, 1964. An interesting and sound study of the political thought of the Allen-Parsons party, 1572–1615.

2229 Clarke, Martin L. *Classical education in Britain, 1500–1900.* Cambridge, 1959.

2230 Curtis, Mark H. *Oxford and Cambridge in transition, 1558–1642.* Oxford, 1959. Maintains the vitality of the universities during a period when they are commonly supposed to have contributed little.

2231 Davies, Ebenezer T. *The political ideas of Richard Hooker.* 1946.

2232 Donner, Henry W. *Introduction to Utopia.* 1945. The best statement of the Catholic view, and that of Chambers (553), of *Utopia* as 'a picture of the state of society to which man can attain without revelation'.

2233 Einstein, Lewis D. *The Italian Renaissance in England.* 1902.

2234 Elliott-Binns, Leonard E. *England and the new learning.* 1937.

2235 Ferguson, Arthur B. *The articulate citizen and the English Renaissance.* Durham, N.C., 1965. An important study of the development of early Tudor thought stressing the concept of the commonweal.

2236 Figgis, John N. *The divine right of kings,* ed. Geoffrey R. Elton. New York, 1965. This pioneer work is dated but not replaced. Contains much that is relevant to Tudor England. Elton's introduction makes the 1965 ed. the best one.

2237 Fox, Levi (ed.). *English historical scholarship in the sixteenth and seventeenth centuries.* 1956. A useful collection of papers by leading scholars.

2238 Fussner, Frank S. *The historical revolution: English historical writing and thought, 1580–1640.* 1962. Valuable detail though the thesis may be over-stated.

2239 Greenleaf, W. H. *Order, empiricism and politics: two traditions of English political thought, 1500–1700.* 1964. Rather slight on the sixteenth century.

2240 Hale, John R. *England and the Italian Renaissance.* 1954.

2241 Hexter, Jack H. *More's Utopia: the biography of an idea.* Princeton, 1952. A judicious analysis of *Utopia* based on a sound historical reconstruction of its writing.

2242 Hoopes, Robert. *Right reason in the English Renaissance.* Cambridge, Mass., 1962. Esp. chapter 7, which deals mainly with Hooker's rehabilitation of the classical-Christian concept of right reason.

2243 Irwin, Raymond. *The heritage of the English library.* New York, 1964. Esp. chapter 11, 'Evidences of literacy'.

2244 Jayne, Sears. *John Colet and Marsilio Ficino.* Oxford, 1963.

2245 Kantorowicz, Ernst H. *The king's two bodies: a study in mediaeval political theology.* Princeton, 1957. A study of the medieval development of a Tudor concept. Heavy reading.

2246 Leach, Arthur F. *English schools at the Reformation, 1546–8.* 1896. Attempts to show the Reformation, esp. under Edward VI, as a great disaster for grammar schools and elementary education. Leach's views have been convincingly refuted by Simon (2343–2344).

2247 Lee, Sidney. *The French Renaissance in England.* Oxford, 1910. A subject that requires more study.

2248 Lutz, Heinrich. *Ragione di stato und christliche Staatsethik im 16. Jahrhundert.* Münster, 1961. Contains a discussion of Reginald Pole's political ideas.

2249 Mallet, Charles E. *A history of the university of Oxford,* II, *The sixteenth and seventeenth centuries.* New York, 1924. The standard history.

2250 Mason, Harold A. *Humanism and poetry in the early Tudor period.* 1959. Deals at length and interestingly with More. Stresses the importance of Vives as a humanist.

2251 Morison, Samuel E. *The founding of Harvard College.* Cambridge, Mass., 1935. Excellent on Tudor universities, esp. Cambridge.

2252 Mosse, George L. *The struggle for sovereignty in England: from the reign of Queen Elizabeth to the Petition of Right.* East Lansing, Mich. 1950. Contains an interesting but debatable discussion of late Tudor constitutional ideas.

2253　Mullinger, James B. *The university of Cambridge.* Cambridge, 1873–1919, 3 vols. The standard history. Vol. I goes from the earliest times to 1535; vol. II covers 1535–1625. Particularly detailed and strong on the Tudor period.

2254　Nef, John U. *Cultural foundations of industrial civilization.* Cambridge, 1958. Stresses the role of sixteenth-and seventeenth-century ideas in producing modern civilization. Challenging but debatable.

2255　Passerin d'Entrèves, Alessandro. *The medieval contribution to political thought: Thomas Aquinas, Marsilius of Padua, Richard Hooker.* 1939. Essential on Hooker.

2256　Pearson, A. F. Scott. *Church and state: political aspects of sixteenth-century Puritanism.* Cambridge, 1928. Mainly a study of Thomas Cartwright's political ideas.

2257　Raab, Felix. *The English face of Machiavelli: a changing interpretation, 1500–1700.* Toronto, 1964. An important study of Machiavelli's influence on English political thought.

2258　Salmon, John H. M. *The French religious wars in English political thought.* Oxford, 1959. Chapter II, 'The Elizabethan reception', is significant.

2259　Siebert, Frederick S. *Freedom of the press in England, 1476–1776: the rise and decline of government controls.* Urbana, Ill., 1952.

2260　Simon, Joan. *Education and society in Tudor England.* Cambridge, 1966. Likely to remain the last word on the subject for some time. Stresses Renaissance and Reformation advances in education. Has an extensive and valuable bibliography.

2261　Stowe, A. R. Monroe. *English grammar schools in the reign of Queen Elizabeth.* New York, 1908.

2262　Surtz, Edward L. *The praise of pleasure: philosophy, education, and communism in More's Utopia.* Cambridge, Mass., 1957.

2263　—— *The praise of wisdom: a commentary on the religious and moral problems and backgrounds of St Thomas More's* Utopia. Chicago, 1957. Stresses the Christian humanist side of More.

2264　Tillyard, Eustace M. W. *The Elizabethan world picture.* 1943. A stimulating essay on the Elizabethan view of the universe and of man's place in it.

2265　Watson, Foster. *The English grammar schools to 1660: their curriculum and practice.* Cambridge, 1908. Sound and full.

2266　Weston, Corinne C. *English constitutional theory and the House of Lords, 1556–1832.* 1965. Begins with a discussion of the development of the English theory of mixed government during the Tudor period.

2267　Wilson, Frank P. *Elizabethan and Jacobean.* Oxford, 1945. An enlightening analysis of the age.

2268　Wood, Norman. *The Reformation and English education: a study of the influence of religious uniformity on English education in the sixteenth century.* 1931.

2269　Woodward, William H. *Desiderius Erasmus concerning the aim and method of education.* Cambridge, 1904. The first part examines the ideas of Erasmus on education; the second contains translations of *De ratione studii, De pueris instituendis,* and passages from other works.

2270　—— *Studies in education during the age of the Renaissance, 1400–1600.* Cambridge, 1906. Esp. chapter XIII, 'The Renaissance and education in England'.

2271　Wormald, Francis and Cyril E. Wright (eds.). *The English library before 1700.* 1958. Valuable essays on the preservation of learning.

4 Biographies

2272　Ames, Russell. *Citizen Thomas More and his Utopia.* Princeton, 1949. Considers *Utopia* republican, bourgeois, and democratic.

2273　Buxton, John. *Sir Philip Sidney and the English Renaissance.* 1954.

2274　Gee, John A. *The life and works of Thomas Lupset.* 1928.

2275　Hay, Denys. *Polydore Vergil, Renaissance historian and man of letters.* Oxford, 1952. A valuable study of the father of Tudor historiography.

2276 Hudson, Winthrop S. *John Ponet (1516?–1556), advocate of limited monarchy*. Chicago, 1942.
2277 Kautsky, Karl. *Thomas More and his* Utopia, trans. Henry J. Stenning. New York, 1959. Considers More a modern socialist. This ed. contains an interesting foreword by Russell Ames.
2278 Lehmberg, Stanford E. *Sir Thomas Elyot, Tudor humanist*. Austin, Texas, 1960. A judicious study of a Tudor popularizer of humanism.
2279 Michaelis, Gottfried. *Richard Hooker als politischer Denker*. Berlin, 1933.
2280 Miles, Leland. *John Colet and the Platonic tradition*. La Salle, Ill., 1961.
2281 Munz, Peter. *The place of Hooker in the history of thought*. 1952. Sees Hooker's thought as essentially medieval.
2282 Passerin d'Entrèves, Alessandro. *Riccardo Hooker, contributo alla teoria e alla storia del diritto naturale*. Turin, 1932.
2283 Rosenberg, Eleanor. *Leicester, patron of letters*. New York, 1955. Good on a great nobleman as a patron.
2284 Ryan, Lawrence V. *Roger Ascham*. Stanford, 1963. Somewhat dull but solid.
2285 Shirley, Frederick J. J. *Richard Hooker and contemporary political ideas*. 1949. Judicious and sound.
2286 Sisson, Charles J. *The judicious marriage of Mr Hooker and the birth of the Laws of Ecclesiastical Polity*. Cambridge, 1940. Good on Hooker's life with many documents.
2287 Strathmann, Ernest A. *Sir Walter Ralegh: a study in Elizabethan skepticism*. New York, 1951. An interesting study of an elusive mind.
2288 Van Dorsten, J. A. *Poets, patrons and professors: Sir Philip Sidney, Daniel Rogers and the Leiden humanists*. Leiden, 1962. This and (2289) deal with Anglo-Dutch cultural and intellectual relations and the place of Leiden University in those relations.
2289 —— *Thomas Basson, 1555–1613: English printer at Leiden*. Leiden, 1961.
2290 Watson, Foster. *Les relaciones de Joan Lluís Vives amb els Anglesos i amb l'Anglaterra*. Barcelona, 1918. An interesting account of a Spanish humanist in England. In Catalan, which can be read by those who can read Spanish.

5 Articles

2291 Adair, Edward R. 'William Thomas: A forgotten clerk of the privy council', in *Tud. Stud.*, pp. 133–60. An account of an unimportant clerk who was a pioneer in England of Italian culture and Italian political thought.
2292 Adamson, J. W. 'The extent of literacy in England in the fifteenth and sixteenth centuries', *Library*, 4th ser., **10** (1930), 163–93.
2293 Allen, Peter R. '*Utopia* and European humanism: the function of the prefatory letters and verses', *Studies in the Renaissance*, **10** (1963), 91–107.
2294 Bainton, Roland H. 'Changing ideas and ideals in the sixteenth century', *JMH*, **8** (Dec. 1936), 417–43.
2295 Baskerville, Charles R. ' Sir Richard Morison as the author of two anonymous tracts on sedition', *Library*, 4th ser., **17** (1936), 83–7.
2296 Baumer, Franklin L. V. 'Christopher St German: the political philosophy of a Tudor lawyer', *AHR*, **42** (July 1937), 631–51. Describes St German as 'one of the first theorists of parliamentary sovereignty'.
2297 —— 'Thomas Starkey and Marsilius of Padua', *Politica*, **2** (Nov. 1936), 188–205. Maintains Marsilius of Padua was the main source of Starkey's advanced political ideas that anticipate the seventeenth century.
2298 Beales, A. C. F. 'Education under Mary Tudor', *Month*, new ser., **13** (June 1955), 342–51. Indicates Mary had an educational policy but her reign was too short to permit much to be achieved.
2299 Bush, Douglas. 'Tudor humanism and Henry VIII', *University of Toronto Quarterly*, **7** (1938), 162–77.
2300 Campbell, William E. 'Erasmus in England', *Dublin Review*, **211** (July 1942), 36–49.
2301 Charlton, Kenneth. 'Holbein's "Ambassadors" and sixteenth century education', *JHI*, **21** (Jan.–Mar. 1960), 99–109.

2302 Clancy, Thomas H. 'English Catholics and the papal deposing power, 1570–1640, part 1', *Rec. Hist.*, **6** (Oct. 1961), 114–40. This part covers the political thought of English Catholics, 1570–1603.

2303 Coles, Paul. 'The interpretation of More's "Utopia"', *Hibbert Journal*, **56** (July 1958), 365–70. Maintains *Utopia* is primarily a serious work of political thought.

2304 Dickens, Arthur G. 'The writers of Tudor Yorkshire', *TRHS*, 5th ser., **13** (1963), 49–76.

2305 Elton, Geoffrey R. 'The political creed of Thomas Cromwell', *TRHS*, 5th ser., **6** (1956), 69–92. Sees Cromwell as a moderate, influenced by Marsilius of Padua rather than Machiavelli, whose ideas derived mainly from his training in the common law and in parliament.

2306 Faulkner, Robert K. 'Reason and revelation in Hooker's ethics', *American Political Science Review*, **59** (Sept. 1965), 680–90. Studies Hooker's ethics for the basis of his political ideas.

2307 Ferguson, Arthur B. 'Renaissance realism in the "Commonwealth" literature of early Tudor England', *JHI*, **16** (June 1955), 287–305. Most of this and (2308) have been incorporated into (2235).

2308 —— 'The Tudor commonweal and the sense of change', *JBS*, **3** (Nov. 1963), 11–35.

2309 Figgis, John N. 'On some political theories of the early Jesuits', *TRHS*, 2nd ser., **11** (1897), 89–112.

2310 —— 'Political thought in the sixteenth century', in *CMH*, III, 736–69. Though somewhat out of date, still a masterly and valuable survey.

2311 Freund, Michael. 'Zur Deutung der Utopia des Thomas Morus: ein Beitrag zur Geschichte der Staatsräson in England', *Historische Zeitschrift*, **142** (no. 2, 1930), 154–78.

2312 Hanley, Thomas O. 'A note on Cardinal Allen's political thought', *Catholic Historical Review*, **45** (Oct. 1959), 327–34. Maintains Allen's political thought was not so different from that of Catholics in England as is generally supposed.

2313 Hay, Denys. 'Pietro Griffo, an Italian in England, 1506–1512', *Italian Studies*, **2** (Feb. 1939), 118–28.

2314 —— 'Schools and universities', *NCMH*, II, 414–37. An illuminating survey.

2315 —— 'The early Renaissance in England', in *Ren. to C.-Ref.*, pp. 95–112. Stimulating and suggestive, esp. with regard to lay education and the gentry.

2316 Hexter, Jack H. 'The education of the aristocracy in the Renaissance', in *Reappraisals*, pp. 45–70. Suggests a revision of the concept of a degenerate aristocracy.

2317 —— 'Thomas More: on the margins of modernity', *JBS*, **1** (Nov. 1961), 20–37. Sees More's *Utopia* as Utopian communism and More as a modern radical.

2318 Hill, Christopher. 'The many-headed monster in late Tudor and early Stuart thinking', in *Ren. to C.-Ref.*, pp. 296–324. The many-headed monster is the masses.

2319 Hinton, Raymond W. K. 'English constitutional theories from Sir John Fortescue to Sir John Eliot', *EHR*, **75** (July 1960), 410–25. Traces the switch from the medieval theory of mixed government to the theory of absolute government under the rule of law.

2320 Hoffman, C. Fenno, Jr. 'Catherine Parr as a woman of letters', *HLQ*, **23** (Aug. 1960), 349–67.

2321 Hogrefe, Pearl. 'Sir Thomas Elyot's intention in the opening chapters of the *Governour*', *Studies in Philology*, **60** (Apr. 1963), 133–40. A critique of Lehmberg's view (2278) that Elyot's opening chapters support the unlimited powers of the king.

2322 Hyma, Albert. 'The continental origins of English humanism', *HLQ*, **4** (Oct. 1944), 1–25.

2323 Kearney, Hugh F. 'Richard Hooker: a reconstruction', *Cambridge Journal*, **5** (Feb. 1952), 300–11. Stresses Hooker's emphasis on authority.

2324 Kingdon, Robert M. 'William Allen's use of Protestant political argument', in *Ren. to C.-Ref.*, pp. 164–78. Not surprising but interesting.

2325 Lehmberg, Stanford E. 'English humanists, the Reformation, and the problem of counsel', *Archiv für Reformationsgeschichte*, **52** (no. 1, 1961), 74–90. Views of More, Elyot, and Starkey on the scholar's obligation to serve his state by assisting in its administration.

2326 Lucchesi, Valerio. 'L'umanesimo e un terremoto nell'Inghilterra Elisabettiana', *Nuova Rivista Storica*, **43** (May–Aug. 1959), 242–53. Reconsiders the influence of Italian humanism in England.

2327 McGrade, Arthur S. 'The coherence of Hooker's polity: the books on power', *JHI*, **24** (Apr.–June 1963), 163–82.

2328 Milne, James Lees. 'Tudor travellers in Italy', *Month*, new ser., **5** (Jan. 1951), 15–23.

2329 Mosse, George L. 'Change and continuity in the Tudor constitution', *Speculum*, **22** (Jan. 1947), 18–28. Shows much continuity and little change in constitutional thinking during the Tudor period through a comparison of Sir John Fortescue and Sir Thomas Smith.

2330 —— 'The assimilation of Machiavelli in English thought: the casuistry of William Perkins and William Ames', *HLQ*, **17** (Aug. 1954), 315–26.

2331 Murray, John J. 'The cultural impact of the Flemish Low Countries on sixteenth- and seventeenth-century England', *AHR*, **62** (July 1957), 837–54. Sees the Flemings as the carriers of European culture to Tudor and Stuart England.

2332 Oakley, Francis. 'On the road from Constance to 1688: the political thought of John Major and George Buchanan', *JBS*, **1** (May 1962), 1–31. Sees Major and Buchanan as links between the conciliar theory and seventeenth-century doctrines of resistance.

2333 Parker, Thomas M. 'Sir Thomas More's *Utopia*', in Gareth V. Bennett and John D. Walsh (eds.), *Essays in modern English church history*. 1966, pp. 1–17. Reaffirms the views of Chambers (553) on the meaning of *Utopia*.

2334 Phillimore, J. S. 'Blessed Thomas More and the arrest of humanism in England', *Dublin Review*, **153** (July–Oct. 1913), 1–26. Sees English humanism as typified in More and his death as paralysing it.

2335 Pineas, Rainer. 'William Tyndale: controversialist', *Studies in Philology*, **60** (Apr. 1963), 117–32.

2336 Pratt, S. M. 'Antwerp and the Elizabethan mind', *Modern Language Quarterly*, **24** (Mar. 1963), 53–60.

2337 Praz, Mario. 'Machiavelli and the Elizabethans', *PBA*, **12** (1928), 49–97.

2338 Rope, H. E. G. 'The "Italianate" Englishman', *Month*, new ser., **11** (Feb. 1954), 93–103. On Roger Ascham.

2339 Schenk, Wilhelm. 'The student days of Cardinal Pole', *History*, new ser., **33** (Oct. 1948), 211–25.

2340 Schmidt, Albert J. 'Thomas Wilson and the Tudor commonwealth: an essay in civic humanism', *HLQ*, **23** (Nov. 1959), 49–60.

2341 Schoeck, Richard J. 'Sir Thomas More, humanist and lawyer', *University of Toronto Quarterly*, **34** (Oct. 1964), 1–14. Challenges the view that More hated the legal profession and argues that he must be viewed as both a humanist and a lawyer.

2342 Siegel, Paul N. 'English humanism and the new Tudor aristocracy', *JHI*, **13** (Oct. 1952), 450–68.

2343 Simon, Joan. 'A. F. Leach on the Reformation', *British Journal of Educational Studies*, **3** (May 1955), 128–43; **4** (Nov. 1955), 32–48.

2344 —— 'The Reformation and English education', *PP*, no. 11 (Apr. 1957), 48–65. Discusses the development of education at the expense of the church. Rejects the view of Leach (2246) on the destructive consequences of the Chantries Act. Also see (2343).

2345 Stone, Lawrence. 'The Educational Revolution in England, 1560–1640', *PP*, no. 28 (July 1964), 41–80. Shows an extraordinary growth of lay education among all classes except the very poor.

2346 Stone, Lawrence. 'The political programme of Thomas Cromwell', *BIHR*, **24** (May 1951), 1–18. Sees Cromwell's programme as endangering the common law and parliament. Answered by Elton in (289). Also cf. Elton (2305).

2347 Strathmann, Ernest A. 'The idea of progress: some Elizabethan considerations', *Renaissance News*, **2** (Spring 1949), 23–5. Sees Elizabethan philosophy as dominantly pessimistic, but some idea of progress involved in Elizabethan practice.

2348 Surtz, Edward L. 'Interpretations of *Utopia*', *Catholic Historical Review*, **38** (July 1952), 156–74. Surveys interpretations and concludes that *Utopia* is a 'pre-Reformation humanistic document' aimed at reforming Christendom.

2349 Sypher, G. Wylie. 'Similarities between the scientific and the historical revolutions at the end of the Renaissance', *JHI*, **26** (July–Sept. 1965), 353–68. An interesting attempt to relate Fussner's historical revolution (2238) to the scientific revolution of the seventeenth century through a study of the thought of the historian La Popelinière and Francis Bacon.

2350 Teall, John L. 'Witchcraft and Calvinism in Elizabethan England: divine power and human agency', *JHI*, **23** (Jan.–Mar. 1962), 21–36.

2351 Tilley, Arthur. 'Greek studies in England in the early sixteenth century', *EHR*, **53** (Apr.–July 1938), 221–9, 438–56.

2352 Trimble, William R. 'Early Tudor historiography, 1485–1548', *JHI*, **11** (Jan. 1950), 30–41.

2353 Walzer, Michael. 'Revolutionary ideology: the case of the Marian exiles', *American Political Science Review*, **57** (Sept. 1963), 643–54. Maintains the political thought of the Marian exiles was revolutionary as compared to the constitutional ideology of the Huguenots.

2354 Weiss, Roberto. 'Learning and education in Western Europe from 1470 to 1520', *NCMH*, I, 95–126. A conventional but sound survey.

2355 Weissberger, L. A. 'Machiavelli and Tudor England', *Political Science Quarterly*, **42** (Feb. 1927), 589–607. Concludes that Machiavelli had very little influence on the thought or policy of Tudor England.

2356 Whitney, Edward A. 'Erastianism and divine right', *HLQ*, **2** (July 1939), 373–98. Differentiates between the 'true' Erastianism of the reigns of Henry VIII and Edward VI and later Erastianism.

2357 Wright, Louis B. 'The Elizabethan middle-class taste for history', *JMH*, **3** (June 1931), 175–97.

2358 —— 'The significance of religious writings in the English Renaissance', *JHI*, I (Jan. 1940), 59–68. Emphasizes the importance of religious as opposed to secular thought in the English Renaissance.

2359 Zeeveld, W. Gordon. 'Richard Morison, official apologist for Henry VIII', *PMLA*, **55** (June 1940), 406–25. A study of Morison's writings in defence of the Cromwellian regime, seeing through him the influence of Machiavelli in Tudor England. Cf. (2355).

2360 —— 'Thomas Starkey and the Cromwellian polity', *JMH*, **15** (Sept. 1943), 177–91. Views similar to Elton's (2305), but probably overestimates Starkey's influence.

INDEX OF AUTHORS, EDITORS, AND TRANSLATORS

[Numbers are entry numbers except when otherwise specified]